Music in Perspective

Music in

Edith Borroff

STATE UNIVERSITY OF NEW YORK AT BINGHAMTON

Marjory Irvin

LAWRENCE UNIVERSITY

Perspective

HARCOURT BRACE JOVANOVICH, INC.

New York / Chicago / San Francisco / Atlanta

To the memory of
Milwaukee-Downer College
Lucia R. Briggs
and
John B. Johnson, Jr.

MUSIC IN PERSPECTIVE
Edith Borroff / Marjory Irvin

ISBN: 0-15-564883-7

Library of Congress Catalog Card Number: 75-39954
Printed in the United States of America

Cover: Composition by John Johnston, 1974. Oil on canvas, 20″ × 24″. Photo: Harbrace.

Color Plates: 1. The Museum of Primitive Art, New York. Photo by Lisa Little; 2. Reproduced by permission of The British Library Board; 3. Museum of Fine Arts, Boston. Photo by Francis G. Mayer © 1975/Photo Researchers; 4. Naples National Library, R. E. Kalmbach; 5. The National Palace Museum, Taipei, Taiwan. Photo by Louis Renault/Photo Researchers; 6. Photo by Burt Glinn/Magnum; 7. and 8. Bibliothèque Nationale; 9. The National Gallery, London; 10. The Metropolitan Museum of Art, Gift of Alexander Smith Cochran, 1913; 11. Smithsonian Institution, Washington, D.C. Photo by Lee Boltin; 12. The Louvre. Photo by Hubert Josse, Paris; 13. Musée des Beaux-Arts, Lyons, France. Photo by Agence TOP, Paris; 14. Photo by Gordon Gahan, 1974/Photo Researchers; 15. Photo by E. Fred Sher; 16. Photo by Jerry Cooke.

Chapter-opening Illustrations: p. 2. Seated man with harp, Cycladic sculpture, 11½″ high, c. 250 B.C. The Metropolitan Museum of Art, Rogers Fund; 18. Musicians, from the Palace of Assurbanipal, Kuyunjik. Assyrian casts. The Metropolitan Museum of Art, Crosby Brown Collection of Musical Instruments, 1889; 40. African cult object from Dahomey, Staatische Musikinstrumentensammlung. Photo by Claus Hansmann; 50. German oak carving of the Tree of Jesse, 15th century. Colby College Museum of Art; 74. Detail of a cittern, by Girolamo de Virchis, 1574. Kunsthistorisches Museum, Vienna; 98. Musicians, glazed ceramic figures, Chinese Sui dynasty, 581–618 A.D. The Royal Ontario Museum.

Illustration credits continue on page 304, which is regarded as part of the copyright page.

Preface

Music in Perspective is a basic introductory text that focuses on musical styles and structures. It is designed for college students who are taking music as an elective subject; it presupposes a lively curiosity but it does not assume prior study in music. Emphasis throughout the book is on aural perception. Musical concepts are explained in terms of what inexperienced listeners can hear fairly easily, and notation has been omitted as unnecessary to this approach.

The first three chapters present a basic vocabulary that makes possible the discussion of music in its own terms. Technical terminology has been restricted to the irreducible minimum necessary for understanding musical ideas and differentiating musical styles. Concepts are presented initially from a universal viewpoint, offering students the opportunity to compare and contrast non-Western music with music of the Western tradition. The musical examples chosen to illustrate these concepts range widely in time, place, and style, with the musical ideals of cultures other than our own accorded full respect.

To help students understand our own musical heritage, seven chapters are devoted to a chronology of Western music, presenting the fundamental style characteristics and essential forms of each historical period in context. Emphasis is on styles rather than forms, and four comparative style charts are included to help students distinguish the music of one period from that which immediately precedes and follows it. Similarly, the discussion of specific composers concentrates on their musical styles and whether those styles are typical of or at variance with the prevailing trend.

Interspersed in the chronology are four topical, cross-cultural chapters on musical instruments, musical performance, music in relation to the verbal and visual arts, and some of the social and business aspects of music. These chapters deal with music from a broad geographical base, emphasizing the contrasting roles music has played in different cultures and times.

To provide direct experience of the music itself, this book is accompanied by an album of six records containing the 79 complete works or movements specifically discussed in the text. Each work is discussed on its own terms, consistent with its own medium and style. The album encompasses the historical range of Western music and goes beyond those boundaries with the inclusion of a variety of non-Western selections. The book is not dependent on the records, however, and instructors can freely supplement or replace the album with selections of their own choice.

We have many people to thank. Stephen Haynes, Nicole Heuckeroth, Paul Hollinger, Martha Holmes, and Richard Rehl aided excellently in research, and the reference librarians of the Appleton Public Library were consistently and cheerfully helpful. Elizabeth Huggins, Michael Hunter, Michael Lofton, Lynne Marsh, James Ming, June C. Ottenberg, Charles Schwartz, and Paul O. Steg all read portions of the manuscript, which profited from their perceptive responses. The Harcourt Brace Jovanovich staff has provided a stimulating ambiance: Nina Gunzenhauser, enterprising and perspicacious, has been part of the book from the start; Natalie Bowen has been a spirited and discerning editor; Anna Kopczynski has provided a knowing hand in designing the book; and Yvonne Steiner has enriched it with her eye for illustration.

Contents

Music in Perspective

1. Dimensions of Sound

SENSITIVITY TO SOUND is a vital characteristic of virtually every zoological species, and it may possibly extend in some degree to the botanical world as well. Experiments in which plants seem to respond to music or tone of voice have proved fascinating but inconclusive, and they have not yet provided any justification for assumptions about the perception of and response to sound by members of the vegetable kingdom.

But within the animal kingdom the perception of sound is universal. It has contributed significantly to survival by providing warning of potential danger. Among the higher animals, an ability to classify and interpret aural stimuli leads to selective, appropriate responses that may even include enjoyment of the sound itself; and for human beings the world of sounds holds unique aesthetic potential.

Silence is rare in the human experience. Normally we are bombarded by concentric circles of competing sound signals, varying in intensity and reaching us from different directions with different messages. Unlike the eye, the ear cannot focus selectively, and the prodigious task of translating these multiple stimuli into some semblance of meaning is the province of the brain. Music, too, consists of multiple signals that the ear receives collectively and without discrimination; sorting out and understanding the total is the essence of perceptive listening.

CHARACTERISTICS OF A MUSICAL TONE

A single musical tone possesses several characteristics that contribute to its identification and significance: (1) pitch, (2) duration, (3) intensity, (4) tone color, and (5) the direction from which it comes. A musical tone is generated by a vibrating medium—a violin string, for example—that sets sound waves in motion, and *pitch* is the result of the frequency of vibration: the greater the number of vibrations per second, the higher the pitch. Although the frequency of vibration can be measured exactly and expressed in precise numerical terms, pitch is normally perceived relatively rather than absolutely. The tendency is to hear a tone as high, medium, or low, and to hear succeeding sounds as higher or lower in comparison simply with each other.

Duration, too, is usually perceived relatively. A sound may be regarded as long or short in an intuitive comparison with surrounding sounds.

Intensity is also a matter of degree. Measurement in decibels is of little concern to a listener, who perceives tones as loud, soft, louder, and softer—ranging from barely audible to a volume that reaches the threshold of pain.

Thus three important elements of sound are perceived relatively. In contrast to these, the element of *tone color,* or tone quality, is perceived absolutely, not as a type of effect (harsh, peaceful) but as a specific sound of known or unknown origin. The sound of an oboe is heard as the sound of an oboe, rather than as a more or less mellow sound than that of a trumpet or a violin. Recognition of tone color is dependent on conscious memory and on the unconscious perception of overtones, for it is the number and relative intensity of the overtones that enable a listener to distinguish one sound source from another. A "single" tone is actually a composite sound consisting of a fundamental (principal tone) and a series of overtones whose frequencies are multiples of that of the fundamental. For example, if the fundamental vibrates at a rate of 110 vibrations per second, its overtones will vibrate 220, 330, 440, 550, and so on, times per second, respectively. A bowed string, especially a large one on a cello or bass, offers visual evidence of the source of these overtones: the string can be seen to vibrate not only as a whole, but also in halves,

Side 1 Band 1

thirds, quarters, and other fractions. The recorded excerpt illustrating overtones presents a factory whistle, a soprano, and a piano, all sounding the same pitch. The overtones are then filtered out, and the residual tones can no longer be distinguished from one another by means of color; the factory whistle must be identi-

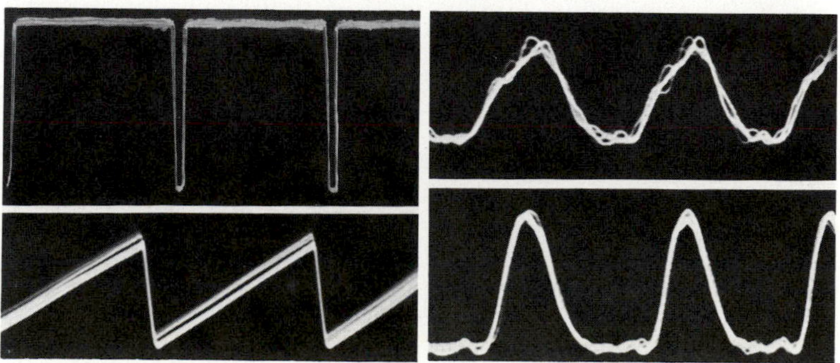

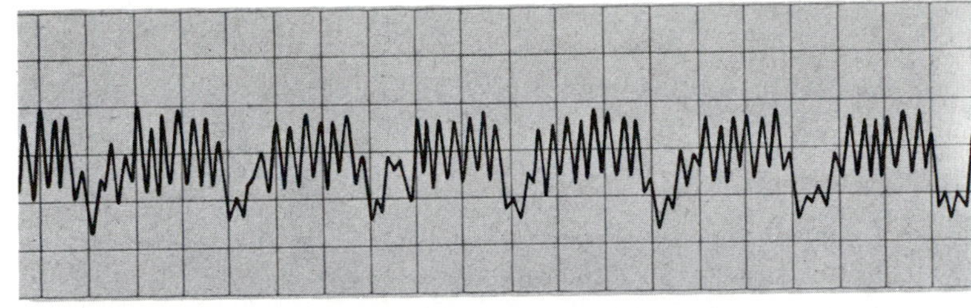

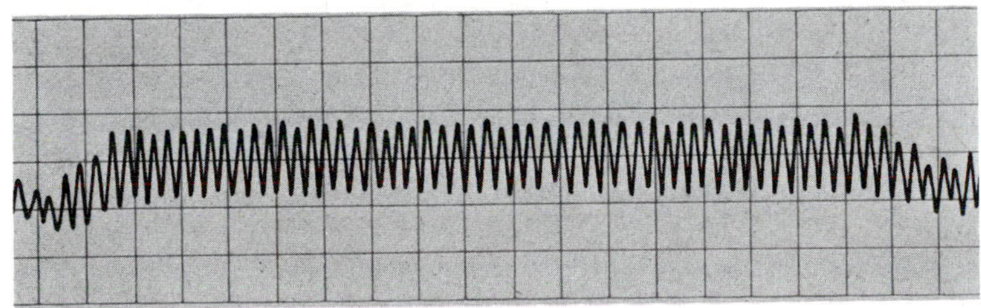

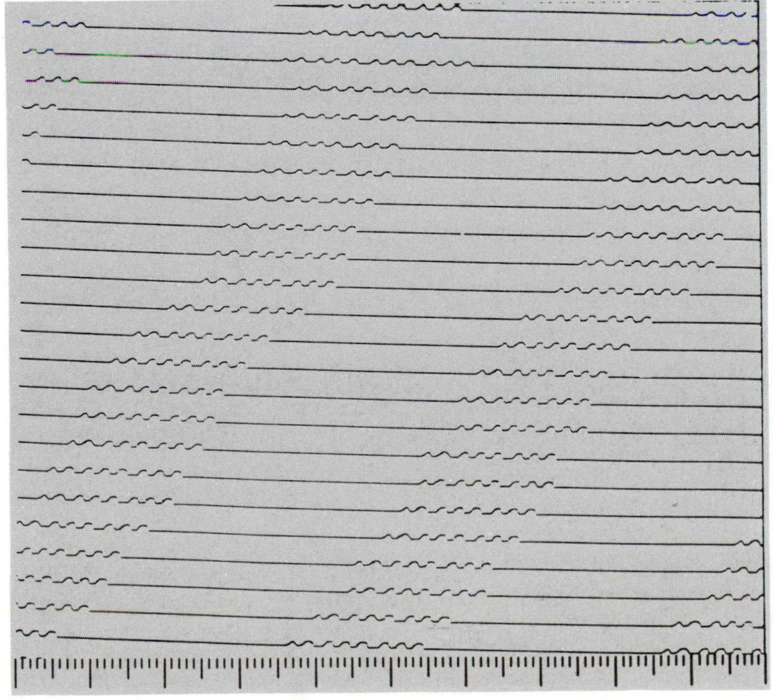

Every classification of sound has its characteristic shape (wave form), but even within each type individual sounds vary so that no two are exactly alike. Many wave forms are visually handsome in their own right. Shown here are the characteristic wave forms produced by a cello string bowed with varying degrees of force (opposite page), and (top to bottom) a chickadee, a katydid, and a cricket.

American marching bands often present a modern version of an ancient tradition: spatial representations—both stationary and moving—during musical performances.

fied by its unvarying intensity, the soprano by a characteristic "wobble," and the piano by the rapid decay of the tone.

Perception of the *direction* from which a sound comes is a factor sometimes crucial to survival—danger, for one thing, must either be faced head-on or escaped from in the opposite direction. This particular attribute of the ear was used to great aesthetic advantage by Medieval and Baroque composers writing for performance in palace courtyards and vaulted cathedrals. Such music was often performed with groups of singers and instrumentalists deployed in several locations, producing a stereophonic or even quadraphonic effect. During the performance, the musicians' progress from one place to another often constituted an eye-pleasing choreography, involving varying geometric designs. The rise of the concert hall, with its fixed stage, was inevitably accompanied by a corresponding decline in composers' use of space and directional subtleties. Except for American marching bands, space, direction, and choreography have played little part in nontheatrical music performance of recent centuries. In the second half of the twentieth century, however, composers are evincing renewed interest in this aspect of sound and are no longer restricting performers to the stage.

VERTICAL PITCH ORGANIZATION

A single tone, heard alone, has no musical significance. Meaning in music is communicated by the interaction of sounds occurring successively and simultaneously as the music moves forward in time. The successive, or horizontal, interaction of sounds involves melody and rhythm, and the simultaneous, or vertical, interaction involves harmony. Interest in horizontal relationships is universal, but extensive preoccupation with vertical relationships is a Western phenomenon:

> In the West, the musical system is based not only on a combination of melody and rhythm, but also on the highly developed elements that enrich the music—harmony (or the chordal, vertical structure of any given composition) and counterpoint (or the simultaneous sounding of two or more melodies). Indian music too is based on melody and rhythm, but has no comparable system of harmony and counterpoint. Rather, it is melody that has been developed and refined to a very high degree, with an infinite variety of subleties that are completely unknown in Western music.*

In the early Medieval era, Western cultures, too, were concerned largely with monophony (music based on a single melodic line), and it is only during the past thousand years that vertical considerations, harmonic and contrapuntal, have taken over to the extent of the virtual eclipse of monophony.

Intervals

The simplest vertical combination is one consisting of two tones; the distance between them is called an *interval.* When their two tones sound simultaneously some intervals create a sense of tension seeking resolution, and others evoke a sense of repose. The tension-producing combinations are referred to as *dissonant,* and the more passive ones as *consonant.* These two terms should not be equated with "ugly" and "attractive"; some of the most beautiful composite sounds are dissonances, and, conversely, a composition consisting solely of consonances would be deadly dull.

Intervals in our system are named numerically—seconds, thirds, fourths, fifths, sixths, sevenths, and *octaves* (rather than "eighths")—and are spelled correspondingly within the musical alphabet: A–B–C–D–E–F–G. The interval of a second involves consecutive letter names (A–B, B–C, and so on); a third skips one letter (A–C, B–D, and so on); and the two notes of an octave share

*Ravi Shankar, *My Music, My Life* (New York: Simon and Schuster, 1968), pp. 17–18.

the same letter name, since the musical alphabet has no eighth letter. (The piano is an ideal instrument for practice in constructing intervals because it reinforces aural concepts with visual perception.)

The organization of musical tones hinges on the relationship of the octave. The vibration ratio of the two tones of an octave is 1:2, which is the closest mathematical relationship possible between two different pitches. This relationship is readily apparent to the ear, which hears the two tones as "the same," despite their difference in pitch. The tendency to equate tones an octave apart goes far beyond Western culture—it is, in fact, one of the few musical concepts that has universality of application. But a major variable among different cultures is the manner in which they divide the octave to form smaller relationships.

There is a strong relationship to the physics of sound in our concept of consonance and dissonance. For the most part, intervals with low vibration ratios (1:2, 2:3, 4:5, 5:6) are perceived as consonant, whereas those with higher ratios (8:9, 11:12, and so on) are regarded as dissonant. Yet there is a gray area: the interval of a fourth (3:4) is sometimes regarded as dissonant, while some others with higher ratios are thought of as consonant. This would indicate that concepts of consonance and dissonance are as much a matter of cultural conditioning as of mathematical verity. Further, our reaction to a tonal combination is colored by the context in which it appears; a sound that produces tension in one setting might seem peaceful in another. Consonance and dissonance, like single pitches, tend to be perceived relatively rather than absolutely. This has enabled opinions of what is dissonant to vary in time and place, while the idea that music must balance the consonant with the dissonant remains a universal. Many cultures also add the concept of fixed and variable intervals. In the West, intervals of low ratio (up to 3:4) are considered fixed, whereas the others, whether consonant or dissonant, can vary.

Drone

Most cultures make some use of simultaneous sounds. In many cultures, a melody is enlivened by combining it with a *drone,* which is a constant, often insistent stationary pitch above which a melodic line proceeds independently. The two lines move forward

One man's choice of instruments for a one-man band: accordion, three horns, bells (on head and legs), and drums.

together in time, one stable and one varying. Such a structure is interesting vertically because of the ever-changing intervals that the melody creates moving against the drone. The most famous drone instrument is the bagpipes, which, although strongly associated with Scotland, has been widely used for centuries throughout much of Western and Central Europe. But music with a drone

Side 1 Band 2

is not limited to instrumental performance; it can also exist vocally (obviously requiring at least two performers). In the West, vocal drones occur chiefly in folk practice, often—as in the song of the Sardinian shepherds—in a remarkably long-lived tradition from early Medieval days. In this case, the drone consists of four levels of sound presenting a spectrum of low notes; the solo voice offers little of interest to compete with the amazing resonance of the vertical composite. The effect, however, is more commonly found in music combining vocal melody and instrumental drone as well as in purely instrumental combinations. In fact, the drone is something of a cross-cultural phenomenon; it seems to have neither historical nor geographical boundaries. Even the music of India, reputed to be purely melodic, sometimes uses the drone in the guise of a bowed stringed instrument, the tamboura, to accompany melody. Pitched drums are often used in other cultures.

Organum

Side 1 Band 3

Another type of intervallic vertical pitch organization can be found in *organum*. In a simple form, organum consists of two vocal lines, one of which creates a shadow of the other at the interval of a fourth, a fifth, or, with additional voices, combinations of fifth and octave. Here, again, one line creates horizontal interest, while the second one, by duplicating the first at another level, adds color and density (thickness). Because the lines remain the same distance apart, they are said to be *parallel* or to proceed in *parallel motion.* In the recorded example, sung by men only, every phrase begins and ends in unison, but for the most part the two voices proceed in parallel fourths.

Side 1 Band 4

Organum flourished during the early Middle Ages and was eventually superseded by a style that focused more strongly on linear (horizontal) progression than on vertical sonorities. Interest in the color potential and unifying effect of intervals did not resurge until the twentieth century, and although the sound of the new manifestation is far removed from that of organum, the principle of pitch organization is related. Béla Bartók, in the second movement of his *Concerto for Orchestra,* combined instrumental color with intervallic color, changing both in successive sections of the movement. Immediately after the drum introduction, two bassoons enter with a whimsical melody played in parallel sixths, followed by a pair of oboes playing in thirds. Then comes a pair of clarinets in sevenths, followed by flutes in fifths, and then two trumpets playing in seconds. This procession of twins is interrupted by a solemn, hymnlike contribution from the brass choir, following which the parade once more passes in review, with additional flourishes and embellishments.

Tertian Harmony

When more than two different pitches sound simultaneously as a unit, the result is called a *chord.* Composition based on chords is referred to as *harmonic.* The most widely used system is *tertian harmony,* in which chords are built up in thirds. Tertian harmony dominated Western music from the early eighteenth century until the second quarter of the twentieth, and to some extent the tertian sound has infiltrated the music of non-Western cultures as well. China and Japan, for example, have embraced some aspects of this harmony, although India continues to remain aloof from tertian or any other harmonic scheme. Blacks imported from Africa to North and South America achieved a musical union of two cultures by adding Western tertian harmony to melodies that were primarily African in character. Although contemporary composers have replaced tertian harmony with other sonorities, it continues to be the principal means of pitch organization in much of our popular music. Country-western and gospel are rooted in tertian harmony; some of rock is also tertially oriented, but rock tends to be more adventurous in experimenting with other means of organization and evades any pigeonhole.

Tonality

Most music that uses tertian harmony is *tonal.* Tonality is a system of pitch organization related to a seven-note scale in which the octave is divided into seconds of varying size. The seven tones are by no means equal in importance; one of them functions as "home base" *(tonic),* and the others tend to lead toward it. This tendency of a group of tones to center on one of their number is not inherent in the tones themselves, but involves expectations that their organization brings to the music. A tonal center serves as a musical security blanket. The confident expectation of eventual resolution to a predictable point of repose is reassuring to the listener, and expectation is important to the communication of musical meaning. Western theorists have tried to make a case for the necessity of this type of organization, yet the physics of sound offers little in support of the concept of tonal center as a natural phenomenon. There can be no doubt that Western ears tend to expect a tonic, but this must be credited to conditioning rather than to any underlying law of nature.

Tertian chords are usually composed of two or three different thirds—sometimes piling up as many as six—thus making available a great variety of harmonic color within the tonal system. (Anyone interested in experimenting with chord construction will find the piano a cooperative ally, and a variety of harmonic colors can be produced simply by combining assorted groups of alternate white notes.) The simultaneous sounding of chord tones creates *block chords,* whereas the sounding of these tones one at a time results in *arpeggios* or *broken chords.* The Western ear is so accustomed to harmonic music that when the tones are sounded successively, or even incompletely, the listener tends to combine them into familiar chord groupings. When tones of a broken chord are interspersed with tones foreign to it, the extended grouping is called an *ornamented or decorated* broken chord. The tonally conditioned ear has no difficulty in differentiating between the essential chord and its decoration, although this is usually accomplished subconsciously.

Quartal Harmony

Early in the twentieth century, many composers became disenchanted with the sounds of tertian harmony and found tonality restricting. They began to investigate the possibilities of chords based on intervals other than the third, and they found the fourth to be particularly viable. *Quartal harmony,* or harmony in which chords are built in fourths, has become a widespread means of pitch organization and continues to be used by composers in many different countries. A substantial body of twentieth-century music is cast in quartal harmony, some composers using it within a framework of tonality, and others using it in such a way that no tonal center can be heard.

Side 1 Band 5

Quartal harmony is an important organizing force in the "Entombment" movement of the symphony *Mathis der Maler* by Paul Hindemith. It begins with a solemn, sorrowful statement by

The Crucifixion, one of the panels of Mathias Grünewald's Isenheim Altarpiece, painted between 1510 and 1515. *The Entombment,* to which the Hindemith title refers, is the bottom panel.

the string choir, emphasizing vertical quartal sonorities; as the woodwinds enter, the interval of a fourth begins to assume melodic as well as harmonic significance. The second theme, played first by oboe, then by flute, opens with two ascending fourths, and the unifying interval recurs frequently as this plaintive melody unfolds. Toward the end of the movement, tertian harmony replaces quartal harmony, and the movement ends with an affirmation of the tonality that has been implied, but not made explicit, from the beginning.

Clusters

Another manifestation of the search for new harmonic colors is the *cluster,* which consists of the simultaneous sounding of several adjacent pitches. (On the piano a group of adjacent white notes, or adjacent white notes plus the intervening black notes are both called clusters.) Clusters are basically instrumental in concept, and they have been particularly associated with the piano, where they are performed with fist, flat hand, forearm, and, on occasion, even with a two-by-four. In both instrumental and vocal music, the directions for the performance of clusters range from very specific pitch indications for their outer limits, to unspecified pitches to be executed somewhere within an indicated pitch area.

Side 1 Band 6

In the second movement of the *Creole Dance Suite* by Alberto Ginastera, clusters are combined with conventional harmonies in a tonal pitch framework and a Latin American rhythmic format. The pitches within each cluster are clearly specified and can be played either with the fingers or a flat hand, but whichever method is used the pianist must give a slight emphasis to the top tone of each cluster in order to delineate the melody, which would otherwise be drowned in a deluge of sound.

REGISTER AND TESSITURA

In referring to a general pitch area, musicians commonly use the term *register,* accompanied by a qualifying adjective such as low, medium-low, middle, medium-high, or high. These descriptive terms are used both absolutely and relatively, because they describe both the entire gamut of audible pitch as well as the registers of a single instrument. For example, a solo violin passage could be described as being in the middle register of the entire pitch gamut; yet of the same passage it could be said that the violin was playing in its low register. Since the lowest tone of the violin lies within the average female voice range, it could never be described as absolutely low, but compared with the very high tones of which the violin is capable, it is indeed a low tone—for a violin.

The concept of register also includes the idea of *tessitura,* which refers to the "lie" (the characteristic or predominant pitch area) of a voice or an instrument in a given composition. A singer who is most comfortable in the high register (such as an "Irish tenor" or a coloratura soprano) is said to have a high tessitura; a solo trumpet piece calling for constant straining in the upper register would be said to have the same. A soprano may read the same notes that a tenor reads: either they sing an octave apart, matching tessituras (which is the normal way), or they sing in an identical register, in which case the soprano sings at a comfortable place in her voice range while the tenor is at the high edge of his. In that event the listener's attention will be riveted on the tenor, because the heroic vividness of his tessitura will eclipse the less intense sound of the soprano's.

In the nineteenth century, the ideal use of register was one in which all parts were in the same general register at any given moment. This uniformity was thought to be prerequisite to the blending of sounds, an important facet of the aesthetic goal. This homogeneous use of register does indeed facilitate blending, but it sacrifices the dramatic potential of contrast. Throughout the twentieth century, particularly since 1950, composers have shown great interest in using registers in new ways. With simultaneous sounds it is not uncommon to find tones separated by two or three octaves of "empty space," with the two registers thus thrown into sharp relief and the integrity of both tones maintained at the expense of blend. In the use of consecutive sounds, even greater extremes of register are exploited. Igor Stravinsky arranged the familiar tune "Happy Birthday to You" with such a technique as a greeting to a friend. The ear is hard pressed to shift octaves fast enough to recognize the tune. **Side 1 Band 7**

Violent dislocation of register may be accomplished without strain of tessitura. The jump from a low tone to a high one might be accomplished in an orchestra, for example, by a bassoon tone followed by one for the flute or piccolo, causing no great strain. But a similar progression might also use a growly, difficult horn tone and a tortured oboe tone above the normal range. For a singer to execute such a gymnastic leap demands extraordinary effort, thereby creating a sense of stress.

DENSITY

The *density,* or thickness, of a musical sound depends on the number of performers contributing to it, the number and vertical spacing of the different pitches, and the register or registers involved. When an orchestra tunes up before a performance, a single instrument sounds the official A; then all the violins take it up, increasing the density by number, and gradually each section of the orchestra joins in, sounding A in its preferred register, so that the density increases dramatically. Yet this procedure involves only one pitch (in various octaves). If the orchestra were to sound three pitches in different registers, the effect would be one of even greater density. Register alone has a powerful effect:

Carnegie Hall in New York, seen from a box seat; the Chicago Symphony Orchestra is on the stage. Carnegie Hall, opened in 1891, has proved one of the most successful modern halls acoustically.

Philharmonic Hall in West Berlin (below), set up for an orchestral concert. Many modern halls include ceiling baffles similar to those shown here, which can be moved to change the patterns of reverberation.

if the same three-tone chord were played in high, middle, and low registers, the low version would sound very thick and the high one quite thin. The fact that low tones produce a greater quantity of audible overtones accounts for this difference, but the contrast between the high and low chords illustrates the effect vividly.

SOUND ENVIRONMENT

Finally, musical sound is affected by the environment in which it is produced. The bathroom shower, with its humidity and close-set walls, provides optimum conditions for reinforcing sound—a sympathetic environment that clothes even the most undistinguished voice in a halo of reverberation. The great outdoors, on the other hand, is the most unsympathetic locale for music making. The open atmosphere swallows sounds so quickly that musical coherence is difficult, if not impossible to attain. Concert halls provide a more congenial ambiance, but they present an assortment of secondary acoustical problems that vary inexplicably from hall to hall. The professional musician is aware of "live" versus "dead" halls and the greater resonance with the audience present versus the dry sound of the empty hall during rehearsal. The size of the place is equally vital, and so is its physical nature—its materials, shape, proportions. Interestingly, although architects have long studied these elements, no one has yet devised a foolproof formula for creating the ideal concert hall. Acoustical excellence cannot be commanded; it eludes the best engineering skills, and the proportion of luck to know-how in its pursuit discomforts the wisest of architects.

2. Melody and Texture

MELODY

THE MUSIC OF ALL PEOPLES includes melody conceived as a linear progression with an appropriate shape. Certainly a succession of tones has no place to go except forward in time, and with this fact of life melodic universality begins and ends. Aesthetic ideals differ from culture to culture, and often from century to century within one culture; what constitutes appropriate melodic shape has changed in both time and place, and is unlikely ever to be a matter of general agreement. But joy in melody is universal, and the endless variety of melodic shapes, sizes, and effects is a special manifestation of the richness of the human spirit.

Vocal Ideals

Melody is vitally influenced by the medium in which it sounds. An effective melody is at one with whatever voice or instrument performs it; ideally, it fulfills the artistic potential of that medium, exploiting the medium's character, accepting or transcending its limitations. But whether a melody is sung or played instrumentally, the influence of the human voice is likely to be stamped upon it. Virtually all human beings have voices, and virtually all of us have made musical noises even in the cradle—more musical perhaps to our doting parents than to objective observers, but enough to give us strong internal yardsticks of our own vocal range and length of breath. We listen to melody with reference to our internal yardsticks: melodic register is often interpreted as high or low in relation to the listener's own voice; the extent of a melody's total range is often perceived as small or large according to our own capacities; and the speed at which a melody proceeds seems faster to a person with a pulse rate of 66 than to another with a pulse rate of 84.

A vocal range of about an octave is normal for an untrained voice. This means that melodies lying within a fifth or sixth are heard as restrained, those using an octave or so are normally active, while those ranging over a tenth or more seem expansive, adventuresome, or even reckless. An expanded range is characteristic of drinking songs, and the large range (a twelfth) of the tune of "The Star-Spangled Banner" doubtless reflects its origin as a men's-club song honoring the union of "the Myrtle of Venus and Bacchus's Vine."

In the same way, the capacity of human breathing has shaped punctuation in both speech and song: the length of one breath is a basic unit in mobilizing the flow of meaning. And similarly, the shapes of normal speech inflections have set up norms for melodic meanings. Both sentences and musical phrases tend to have an arc shape, with a gradual rise at the start and a drop in both pitch and intensity at the end of ideas.

For composers, melody relates to skilled singing technique. Even in instrumental music, the influence of the voice on the contours of melody is persuasive, no matter how great the range of the instrument. The limitations of the voice would seem to be many—the range of a single voice, when trained, is still normally less than two octaves; the necessity for breathing makes a long unbroken sound impossible; and the voice does not lend itself to the execution of a series of large leaps, but is more comfortable with small intervals. The vocal medium thus imposes formidable restrictions, but composers have managed to transform technical restrictions into melodic virtues. The limited range of the voice becomes a positive factor in melodic coherence by restricting pitch range to adjacent registers; the pauses necessary for breath bring about the creation of phrases (meaningful subdivisions of melody, comparable to clauses in language), and thus lead toward clarity of design; and the preference for small intervals gives a large leap an importance that it would not otherwise have, thereby creating focus and emphasis. As a performing medium itself, the voice stands foremost in its immediacy, its unity of instrument and performer, its enormous scope of tone quality and effect, and its unique potential for an intimate association with a text.

Melody that is sympathetically attuned to vocal frailty is categorized as *lyric,* whether it is intended for vocal or instrumental performance. Lyric style is characterized by moderate range, smooth, flowing connection, and simplicity of design. Although all cultures have maintained an art of lyric song, most have also supported another vocal art in which singers of practiced skill transcend the vocal norms and perform elaborate, often highly complex melodies that use the voice as a virtuoso instrument. Such performance often uses lyric materials as a basis of departure, keeping the original more or less intact but bringing to bear upon it whatever variations technique and imagination invoke. Thus the distinction between what is *vocal* and what is *lyrical* is a

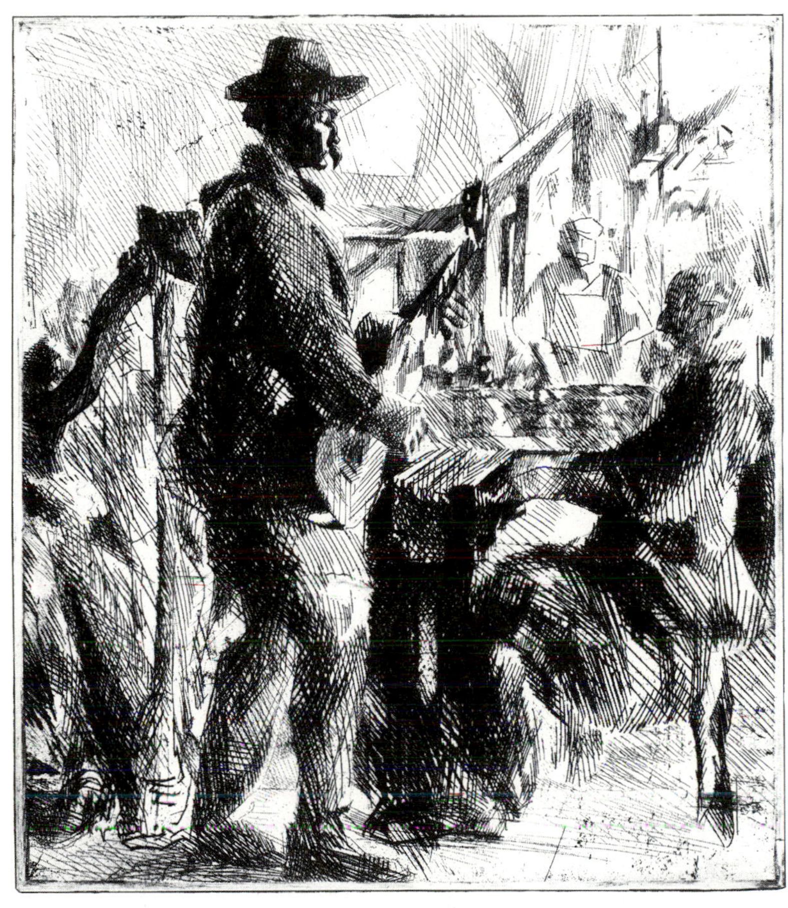

Musicians in a Bistro (1912) by Jacques Villon.

very important one. A simple song is most probably both, and a lyric song is a universal glory of the human voice; but a coloratura (highest soprano) aria or scat singing in jazz is vocal but not lyrical, whereas the theme of a slow movement of a violin concerto is lyrical but not vocal.

Important distinguishing features of vocal melody include *attack* (the manner of beginning and connecting tones), tone color, and tessitura. For example, the traditional blues song exploits the low tessitura of the female voice; in attack, a blues melody tends to slide from one tone to another; and the ideal tone color demands chest resonance. A coloratura aria, on the other hand, normally has a high tessitura, demands clarity and precision in attack, and favors a tone quality based on head resonance.

The ancient Incas showed a marked preference for high tessitura, both in vocal and in instrumental music.

> None of the archaeological instruments thus far inventoried blows notes lower than a violist's open C—a fact that may help to explain why the Spaniards found their vocal ideal so high and strident. For that matter, their only groups of professional singers at Cuzco before the conquest reflected a similar trend, since they were always composed exclusively of young girls not out of their teens.*

The Pygmies of the Itruri Rain Forest, in central Africa, use their voices in a number of effects, including a low, murmuring imitation of bees. They use this as they gather honey, a seasonal activity that they accomplish and celebrate in song. In the

Side 1 Band 8

recorded example of a honey-gathering song, the solo voice is accompanied by the steady pattern of musical rhythm sticks, the murmuring of the men as they sing of the bees, and extraneous noises, including a cock crowing, the motion of the prod-sticks, and a thunderclap.

The natives of Tahiti favor a breathy tone quality, a low tessitura, and an aspirated attack preceding vowels with an h-sound.

Side 1 Band 9

In the recorded example, these characteristics are readily discernible, as is the elusive, indefinite pitch of the recurring high note.

Nasal vocal quality is prevalent in both the Near East and the Far East, and it was standard in the West throughout the Medieval era. This quality sounds exotic to modern Western ears because it has been carefully avoided for centuries in the training of professional singers. Divergent vocal ideals are just as important in distinguishing the music of one culture from that of another as are different systems of organizing pitch and rhythm.

Some cultures are almost exclusively vocal in their concept of melodic performance: to the Arabs, music divorced from singing is all but inconceivable. Other cultures have made tone color a matter of preference, offering options and placing instruments and voice on an equal plane: music of the Renaissance period, for example, might bear the superscription "for voices or viols." Choice is also involved in the performance of Hindu ragas:

> A *raga* is the melodic framework established by tradition or born and inspired in the spirit of a master musician. One can theoretically

*Robert Stevenson, *Music in Aztec and Inca Territory* (Berkeley and Los Angeles: University of California Press, 1968), p. 273.

> perform any *raga* in any style of singing, or play it on any wind or stringed instrument, plucked or bowed. Only the drum is incapable of rendering a *raga* by itself; it must be used to accompany parts of a *raga* when sung or played by other instruments.*

Such dual-possibility music must, however, be vocal in concept. Since one of the choices is vocal, the basic idea cannot be otherwise. The option, however, does not imply that a uniform result is either expected or desired; each medium invests performance with its individual character and style.

Even in music of purely instrumental design, the influence of the vocal ideal is readily apparent. The success of the Swingle Singers, who vocalize chamber and keyboard music, is evidence of the music's vocal essence. But even the Swingle Singers would have trouble with music that exploits the full scope of instrumental capabilities. The range of the piano, for example, is something over seven octaves; a melody incorporating only half that range would be all but impossible for a singer. After centuries of vocally based melody, instrumentally conceived melody has come into its own. In fact, the pendulum has swung, and twentieth-century singers often find themselves struggling with songs whose concept is fully instrumental.

Melodic Structure

Music, whether vocal or instrumental, is normally composed of *phrases*—units of musical thought that group themselves into the musical equivalent of sentences. Punctuation is provided by *cadences,* points at which the forward motion slackens or stops, permitting breathing time in mid-thought, or indicating that a conclusion has been reached. Cadences clarify musical meaning, much as punctuation aids the comprehension of language. Melody, harmony, rhythm, and texture collaborate in the creation of cadences, and the degree of finality depends on the extent to which each element contributes to the cause. The most definitive cadence imaginable is a tonal one, in which all rhythmic activity ceases, following an active-to-relaxed chord progression that coincides with the melody's coming to rest on the tonic tone. Such a cadence is comparable to a period or exclamation point, depending on the degree of emphasis involved. But the noncoop-

*Ravi Shankar, *My Music, My Life* (New York: Simon and Schuster, 1968), p. 21.

eration of one or more elements—a relaxed-to-active chord progression, continued rhythmic activity within the texture, or any tone other than the tonic as the last tone in the melody—would create a more tentative cadence; this kind of cadence, like a comma or a semicolon, would suggest that further development or elucidation of the idea is yet to come. In composition, cadences are frequently marked by long notes (comparatively speaking); in performance, they are often clarified by breaks in tonal continuity in the same manner that a speaker takes a catch breath after a comma, a full breath after a period, and makes a substantial break before beginning a new paragraph.

In music of the West, the end of a composition has traditionally been marked by an irrefutably final cadence, sometimes repeated for emphasis. In the second half of the twentieth century, however, another type of ending, called the *fade,* has gained increasing favor in popular music as an alternative means of bringing a piece of music to a close. The fade has little place in live performance; it is a recording technique in which the final fragment of a song is repeated, while the engineer gradually turns down the volume until the sound fades beyond audibility. It is most effective in songs dealing with gentle sentiment—the wispy evaporation that characterizes the fade is particularly appropriate to casual amiability, but it would weaken a song of strong emotional commitment.

Melodic Shape

The shape of a melody can be represented visually, as in the graph below, which shows the shape of the song "Mary Had a Little Lamb." It represents in miniature some of the attributes of Western melody. The song is made up of two phrases, the first ending with a tentative cadence (comma), and the second ending with a conclusive cadence (period). The melody has a high point, which is reached only once; it builds toward a climax, attains it, then moves away from it to settle quietly on the tonic. It proceeds

"Mary Had a Little Lamb"

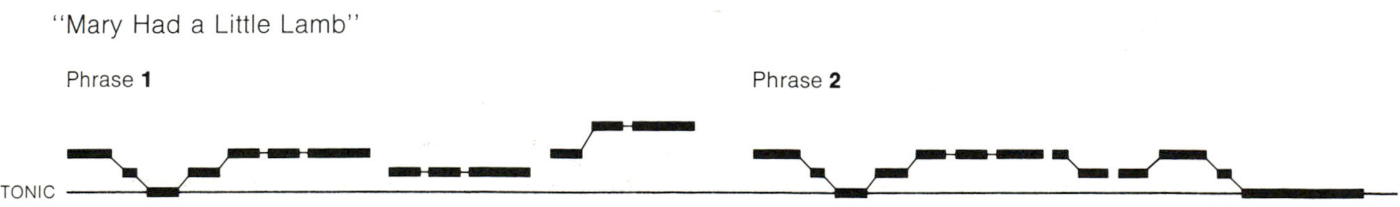

by small intervals (seconds) exclusively until the third statement of "little lamb," where there is an upward leap of a third, arriving at the highest pitch of the melody. So even this modest climax is emphasized in three ways: (1) a leap following a series of smaller intervals, (2) arrival at the high point in pitch, and (3) repetition of the verbal fragment "little lamb."

This type of graph indicates visually the character of a melodic line—whether it is curved or angular in shape, wide or narrow in range, convoluted or simple in design. The traditional vocal ideal has strong leanings toward curved lines with occasional shifts of direction. The melody of "Londonderry Air," shown in the following graph, typifies this ideal. The melody consists of four phrases

"Londonderry Air"

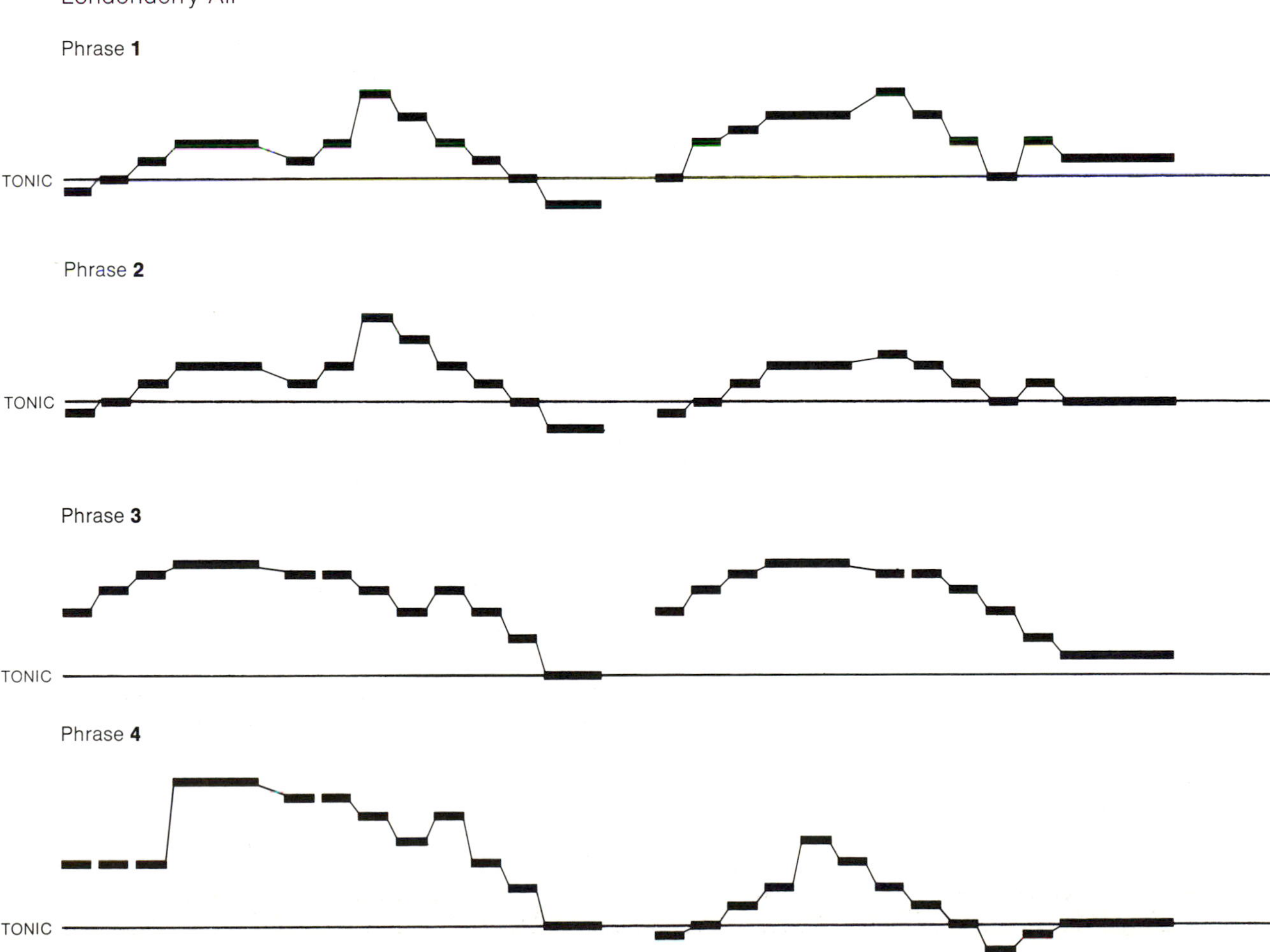

that combine to form two musical sentences. Modified and exact repetition of melodic fragments give shape to the melodic design of the first three phrases, and the very different contour of the fourth phrase sets it apart, paving the way for the climax, which is created by a large leap to the highest pitch in the song.

Melodies with angular outlines, frequently employed by twentieth-century composers, are unvocal in that they employ many large leaps, frequent shifts of direction, and a wide overall range. Such melodies exploit the potential of the instrument for which they are written and often rely heavily on the skill of the performer. "Polka," from *The Age of Gold,* a ballet by Dmitri Shostakovich, has an active, angular melody, as the following graph reveals: This melody would be difficult to sing, but it poses no great problem for the xylophonist who plays it.

Shostakovich: "Polka" (from *The Age of Gold)*

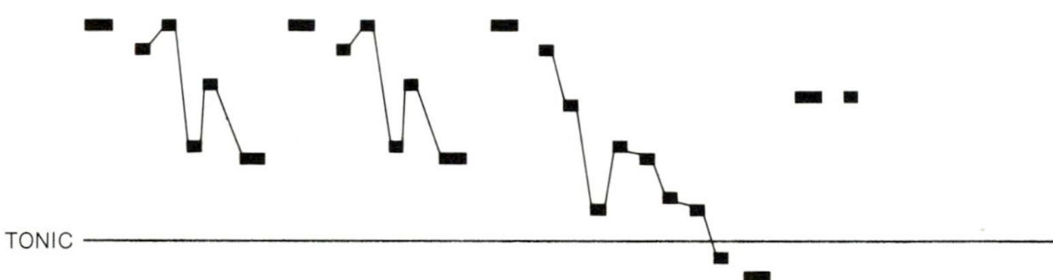

In cultures where melody allows no competition from vertical elements, melodic design is more intensively developed, and melodies are enriched with a high degree of ornamentation. Compared with Eastern melody, with its extensive embellishment and subtleties, Western melody seems simple and straightforward indeed.

> [In Indian music] the ornaments are not arbitrarily attached to a melody; rather, they seem to grow out of it. These embellishments are as essential to our music as harmony and counterpoint are to Western music. Just as there are no straight lines or strong contrasts in Indian art (as opposed, say, to classical Greek art), so Indian music is characterized by gentle curves, controlled grace, minute twining, winding whorls of detail.*

Side 1 Band 10 "Sanai Gath" *(Raga Kaphi)* is representative of this organic spinning-out of melody. Its slides, fast repeated tones, and irregu-

*Shankar, *My Music, My Life,* p. 23.

lar groupings are basic to Indian ornamental design in music. This design, too, can be represented graphically; the last section of the raga has the following shape:

"Sanai Gath" (*Raga Kaphi*)

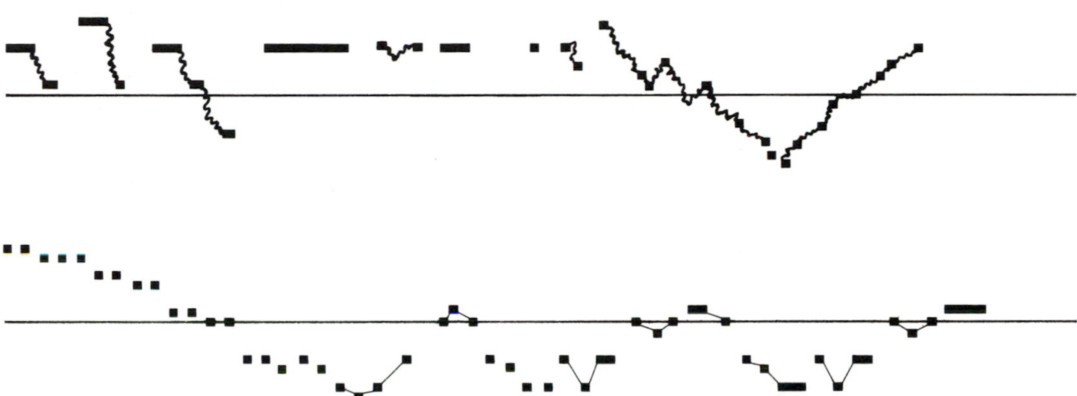

Occasionally one encounters a "nonmelody," a static line that yields center stage to harmony or rhythm. The beginning of the second movement of Beethoven's Symphony No. 7 illustrates this type. Following a sustained chord played by wind instruments, the low strings enter with the main theme, which combines a persistent rhythmic figure with ever-changing harmonies. Melodic interest is almost nonexistent; for some time the melody seems unable to break away from dead center, and throughout the theme repeated notes far outnumber those that move melodically. Subsequent repetitions of this theme add a countermelody of greater intrinsic interest, but, curiously, it is the static melody that the memory retains most vividly. In its final appearance, the main theme is fragmented, and each segment is assigned to a different combination of instruments playing in a different register. Then the movement ends as it began, with a sustained chord played by winds.

Side 2 Band 1

Another example of static melody is George Gershwin's "The Man I Love" (page 33). It is almost impossible to think of this tune divorced from the harmony that accompanies it. The isolated tune has little to recommend it, but the song as a whole is a beautiful one—its popularity has bridged an ocean and endured for over half a century.

PITCH SYSTEMS

In many ways, music reflects the culture that gives rise to it, and it almost inevitably bears the imprint of the prevailing method of pitch organization. Pitch systems are based largely on some division of the octave into small units, and such division varies greatly among the world's cultures. In the West, the division into twelve equal half steps, as represented by the tuning of a piano, is known as *equal temperament* or *tempered tuning* and has been commonly employed since the mid-eighteenth century. Within this system, however, string and wind players will frequently inflect, or alter, certain pitches so that some half steps are slightly smaller and some slightly larger than the tempered norm, and singers inflect pitches intuitively. But the division into twelve half steps, equal or not, is the basis of modern Western pitch organization.

Divisions of the Octave

Traditional Western *scales* are ordered listings of the pitches used in melodies. Most often they consist of seven tones, with half steps and whole steps distributed in different ways. Occasionally a scale may incorporate a step larger than a whole step but never one smaller than a half step, the smallest unit in Western scales.

Eastern scales also employ whole tones and half tones, but they go beyond this to include three-quarter tones, quarter tones, and occasionally microtones of even smaller size. Nor are these intervals always of uniform size; they may vary as melodic circumstances demand. This variety in step size gives Eastern music greater scope and subtlety than ours—it can cater to the preference of voices for moving predominantly by steps without sacrificing the diversity of interval size that so enhances melodic interest. Western ears have difficulty with the finesse of Eastern tuning because we tend to perceive anything smaller than a half step as being out of tune, and our imagination boggles at the prospect of dividing a half step.

In addition to these divergent pitch systems, there is another, which cuts across cultural lines—the *pentatonic* (five-tone) scale. This scale can be produced at the piano by playing only the black notes. It has no half steps, and between groups of black notes the distance exceeds a whole step. This combination seems to lend itself easily and naturally to melodic invention, as pentatonic

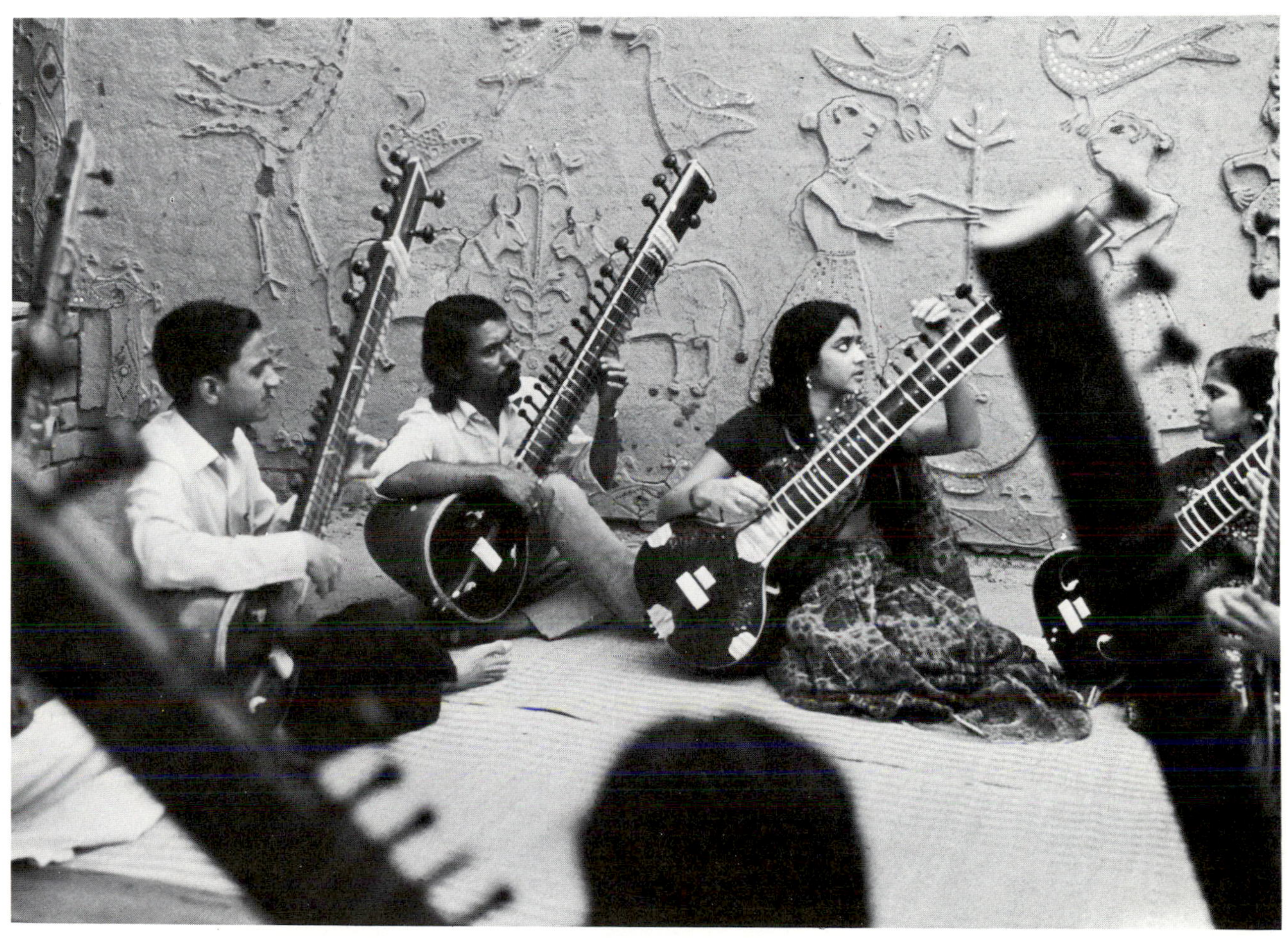

A group of sitar players.

melodies exist in the folk music of every continent, predating any influence of foreign cultures. Aztec melodies were predominantly pentatonic, treating any of the five available tones as a tonic, but using only the five tones melodically. Black spirituals, which must be recognized as African in influence if not in origin, are primarily pentatonic; "Swing Low, Sweet Chariot" is an example. The Scottish folk song "Comin' through the Rye" is a pentatonic melody, as are many of the Hungarian folk melodies discovered by Béla Bartók in his research. Modern China has rejected its historical musical heritage, and, in an effort to create music of the people, the Chinese have now turned to folklike tonal materials. The opera that was telecast during President Nixon's visit to China in

The Banjo Lesson (1894) by the American painter Mary Cassatt.

1972 gave ample evidence of the predominance of pentatonic melody. (But the harmony, oddly enough, represented an embrace of the Western world in being both tertian and tonal.)

Tonality and Modality

The seven-tone scales of Western music represent two types of pitch organization: *tonality* and *modality.* With tonality there is a sense of the inevitability of the final tone—a feeling of urgency about reaching it and a sense of repose once this has been accomplished. In modal music, on the other hand, reaching the final tone seems to be less crucial. A modal final tone, although it provides a perfectly satisfactory conclusion, has less authority than tonality's tonic, and demands less subservience from the other tones.

Modality flourished during the Medieval and Renaissance periods, declined during the Baroque era, and gave way almost completely to tonality during the Classical and Romantic periods. The twentieth-century revolt against tonality, however, brought about a revival of interest in the old system, and modal patterns, couched in the language of *neomodality,* are frequently encountered in the music of the first half of the twentieth century.

Atonality

Another, more drastic expression of antitonal sentiment has found shape as *atonality*—a manner of organizing tones so that no one of them has greater importance than the others. Both modality and tonality are based on a fairly predictable final tone, with the tones organized in such a way that the final or tonic tone outranks all the others. Not so with atonality, in which pitch organization is dedicated to the proposition that all tones are created equal and that they are endowed by their composer with equal rights under musical law. This sounds like tonal democracy, but to listeners in the early twentieth century atonality seemed more like total musical anarchy. The familiar expectations regarding resolution and conclusion did not apply. Instead, listeners were left in uncertainty, not knowing the probable direction and outcome of this music. Atonality, with its lack of tonal focus, does make great demands on the listener's powers of synthesis; but, as with any style, familiarity gives rise to a set of expectations, establishing a basis for communication of musical meaning. Fear and rejection of the unfamiliar may be natural, but they run counter to the spirit of adventure, the most important attitude in approaching a new musical style.

MONOPHONY AND HOMOPHONY

Single-line, unaccompanied melody is a worldwide phenomenon that cannot be delimited either in time or place. It has played an important role in both simple and highly complex cultures—and in some cases the simpler the culture, the more complex the melodies. Accompanied melodies have existed in many cultures, too, with types of accompaniment as various as melodic styles. Unpitched rhythmic accompaniment and one- or two-pitch drones have been almost universal in application, but beyond those, accompaniment styles have differed widely, relating specifically to an individual culture's own theories and aesthetics of music. In the West, interest in vertical sonorities has led to the development of accompanying figures based on chords—a basic format that has proved flexible enough to meet the needs of every generation from the Middle Ages to the present.

In describing one-melody music, two terms, *monophony* and *homophony,* are commonly used. Their etymological similarity is evident, but the different meanings that musicians have assigned to them are less obvious. Homophony is the more limited of the two: it applies only to Western music and is used to describe a melody supported by harmonic accompaniment. Monophony is a more comprehensive term: it has no stylistic connotations and it applies to any single melodic line, whether presented in solitary splendor or reinforced by any type of duplication or nonmelodic accompaniment. A Carole King ballad; a raga sung to the accompaniment of sitar, tamboura, and drum; a bugle call; and the chanting of a priest all fall within the category of monophony, but only the first piece could be called homophonic.

Within the Western tradition, accompaniments vary enormously. Chords range from bland to pungent in sound, and the choice of chords has a powerful impact on the emotional message of any song. The folk song "Shenandoah," for example, uses simple, ingenuous harmonies to underline its quiet, wistful mood,
Side 2 Band 2 whereas in "Solitude" by Duke Ellington, the poignancy of the chords suggests an intensity of loneliness bordering on despair. Chord progression normally involves a gradual increase in tension, then a sudden relaxation of that tension, as illustrated by the first section (ending with the words "so I just did") of Burt Bachar-
Side 2 Band 3 ach's "Raindrops Keep Fallin' on My Head." Each successive chord has greater energy than its predecessor. Tension builds to the very end of the section, where the music comes to rest on the same chord with which it began and repeats the section with different words. Less typical of tonal harmonic progression are the songs of Joan Baez. Her harmonies are often extremely simple, consisting primarily of three fundamental chords. The way in which she orders chords reverses the usual principle of chord progression to one of tension followed by gradual relaxation.

The simplest form of accompaniment, aside from a drone, consists of block chords (page 12), marking changes of harmony. This type is comparatively rare and is used principally for songs in which the words are more important than the music. Ideally, an accompanying medium should be capable of sustaining one chord until the next one is sounded, but this capacity is notably lacking in the most popular accompanying instruments, including the guitar and piano. A tone produced by struck or plucked strings decays rapidly; either repetition of a chord or some linear distribution of its tones is necessary for harmonic continuity.

But prolongation of chord color is only part of the problem. Accompaniment patterns influence the communication of mood; they must therefore be consistent with the emotional content of a song and must be designed to support rather than compete with the melody. In "Raindrops," for example, the steady, repeated chord accompaniment provides a gently throbbing pulse that lends stability to the freewheeling, uninhibited melody. Broken chord figures or embellished harmony would sound too busy and would contend with the melody, thus interfering with the relaxed good humor this song should convey. But Ellington's "Solitude" is very different. In this song the mood is uneasy, and harmony is equal to melody in importance, giving the accompaniment a strong role in communicating the mood. The undercurrent of unrest and the long sustained notes in the melody demand linear activity, and the accompaniment employs both broken chords and embellished harmony to heighten emotional intensity.

In the contribution they make to the effectiveness of songs, accompaniments range from insignificant to indispensable. "Sometimes I Feel Like a Motherless Child," for example, could easily stand alone; only a self-effacing type of accompaniment would be appropriate. On the other hand, in "The Man I Love," Gershwin entrusted essential materials to the accompaniment. Both the underlying harmony and the arabesques that lead into each successive chord are imperative to the impact of the song.

Side 2 Band 4

HETEROPHONY

In most of the world's music, melodies are presented singly. Some cultures cherish a technique of sounding two or more versions of a single melody at the same time. This technique, a kind of simultaneous variation, is called *heterophony.* It is usually improvised,

Drum and xylophone played in duet (Ghana). The drummer uses his fingers at the rim of the drumhead, producing sharp, well-delineated tones with the potential of great speed and intricate pattern. The xylophone is raised from the ground on a frame and has gourd resonators for pungency of tone, deepened by the stickheads, which are bound (probably in leather).

with one performer to a line, each line with embellishments independent of the others. A complex brand of heterophony is found in African marimba ensembles. The performers improvise their own variations within structural boundaries that must either be agreed upon in advance or arrived at, in performance, through what seems to be extrasensory perception. Emphasis is on rhythm rather than melodic shape, but the effect is one of complicated interweaving of multiple linear strands.

Heterophony is more common in non-Western cultures than in the West, but Dixieland and kindred jazz styles might be regarded as a kind of improvised heterophony, one in which there are both melodic and harmonic elements of unity. In Dixieland, each melodic line is basically a variation on the same tune with rhythmic alterations and embellishments, and the simultaneous presentation creates an exciting, often ecstatic free-for-all, which is kept from flying apart by the solidity of the harmony-rhythm section. Dixieland is less purely African in derivation than the marimba ensembles, but its heterophonic character, improvisatory style, and rhythmic originality make its ancestry readily apparent.

POLYPHONY

Combined Melodies

When at least one of the performers in a jazz group plays a totally different melody in combination with the original tune, the music takes on a polyphonic rather than a heterophonic character. *Polyphony* or *counterpoint*—the two terms are often used interchangeably—is a combination of two or more independent melodies, equal in importance and different in design. To retain individuality, the melodies must contrast in contour and rhythmic pattern, but for the merger to work successfully there must be some unity of overall rhythmic and harmonic scheme. Listening to this kind of counterpoint is something like listening to several simultaneous conversations at a cocktail party. Concentrated attention is required to follow two or more separate lines of thought, but with practice it can be accomplished—at least during the early stages of the party. Melodies that make their initial entrance together operate under a handicap: the ear normally refuses to accord them equal status and focuses on one to the detriment of the other—a form of auditory discrimination that only experience and concentration can eliminate.

Imitation

Another type of polyphony is found in the organization of two or more melodic lines around a single musical idea in an arrangement known as *imitation.* Each part sings or plays identical or similar melodic material, but because each part enters separately while the others continue the line, no two parts are ever involved with the same section of the melody simultaneously, and the melody is forever being combined with assorted portions of itself. Attention shifts constantly from one part to another as fresh entries demand to be heard. If a text is involved, its words may suffer some loss of clarity, but from a purely musical standpoint it is an exhilarating experience for both performers and listeners.

Rounds (such as "Frère Jacques") represent the simplest form of imitation, and at the same time they represent a strict form of *canon.* Canons are composed for a fixed number of parts, ranging from two to eight, and they are performed much the same as rounds: one part enters alone and continues the tune as subsequent parts enter, one after the other, with the same melody. Not all canons involve exact repetition. The basic melody may be imitated in another register, at another pitch level, or in different note values (each note receiving twice or half its original value, for example). The melody may be turned upside-down, or presented backward—last note to first. Interest in canonic composition has waxed and waned throughout the history of music. It reached a peak in the late Middle Ages and arrived at a second summit in the second half of the twentieth century, particularly in music based on the manipulation of tapes.

Canon is the most uncompromising and cerebral form of imitation—though its effect may be anything but. It flourishes only when composers are most concerned with the structure and organization of materials, and its periods of ascendancy have been few. When canon is ascendant, complexity is normally viewed as a virtue. Epochs in which canons have occupied center stage have usually been followed by reform movements waving a banner emblazoned *Simplicity,* musical fashion returns to one-melody music, and the cycle begins again.

Freer forms of imitation have had wider appeal, and, regardless of prevailing musical practice, some composers within every generation have employed imitative techniques to a greater or lesser extent. *Fugue,* for instance, has managed to hold its own in eras when canonic complexities were out of fashion. A fugue begins as if it had every intention of being a canon; once underway, however, the music alternates between passages in imitative style and less intense, more harmonic episodes. The form allows considerable latitude and flexibility in the organization of melodic materials.

TEXTURE

The polyphonic or homophonic character of music is a primary aspect of its *texture*—a term that refers to the facets of music not directly related to pitch, rhythm, or dynamics. A single vertical "slice" of music reveals its density (its thickness or thinness—one

Children in the Andes highlands, South America, playing small xylophones made especially for them. Miniature instruments for children are common throughout the world.

feature of texture), but both vertical and horizontal dimensions are required to determine its homophonic or polyphonic character. With the exception of unaccompanied melody, all music contains elements of both vertical and horizontal interest. There is no such thing as either pure harmony or unalloyed counterpoint. "Homophonic" and "polyphonic" are descriptive adjectives indicating relative emphasis rather than absolute entity. If one line is consistently in the spotlight while the others are subordinated, that music is homophonic. But if melodic supremacy is challenged by a second line, an element of contrapuntal interest enters the picture, and if two or more lines consistently vie for top honors, the music must be classified as polyphonic.

Surface Texture

Yet another aspect of texture in music is *surface texture*—a term that suggests an analogy with fabric. Technically, it concerns attack, the way tones are begun and are connected to or disconnected from succeeding tones. A phrase played on a violin with a single, deliberate stroke of the bow can be as smooth as silk, with one tone gliding so easily into the next that almost no distinction is possible between the starting and ending points of individual tones. If, on the other hand, a violinist changes the direction of the bow with each successive tone, the surface texture becomes

A wall in Pakistan, decorated with carved patterns of varying shapes and densities.

more prickly, giving each tone a definitive beginning and a measure of individual identity. And if the violinist puts the bow aside and plays the phrase pizzicato (plucking the strings with a finger), each tone becomes isolated from the others, creating a surface texture in which "holes" of silence are an integral part of the fabric.

Silence

Although sounds are the stuff of which music is made, some interlacing of silence is necessary to give those sounds clarity. Continuous sound, proceeding without any break in tone, would be both dull and incomprehensible. Density would be devoid of variety, musical meaning would be imperiled by lack of structural definition, and, being bereft of breath, such music would seem lifeless indeed. Silence plays a major role in the perception of texture—the tiny holes of silence in the pizzicato passage just described, for example, frame each tone and contribute to the distinctive character of the surface texture. Density, too, is affected by silence: when an inner part withdraws from activity, substituting silence for sound, the listener perceives a change in density—a thinning of vertical texture. For structural clarity, silence is imperative; the delineation of units of musical thought requires breaks in tonal continuity, and the strength of a cadence is measured in part by the length of the silence that follows it. Composers occasionally specify a prolonged silence following a crucial cadence, even a final one. Beethoven, for example, called for an extended silence after the last note of his Third Symphony, indicating that the symphony ends not with the final chord, but with the ensuing hush.

Emotionally, silence serves many moods. Sometimes its role is one of repose, but more frequently it is used to sustain tension. In building toward a climax, composers bring all the available resources of sound into play, usually combining the brilliance of high register and tessitura, a forceful dynamic level, and an increase in rhythmic activity. Having arrived at the peak of the climax, composers have three choices: (1) they can relax the tension by harmonic resolution, (2) they can sustain the tension through repetition, or (3) they can give added punch to the climax by suddenly introducing a silence in the midst of all that sound and fury. Suspense is created when silence delays the continuation of a musical idea, and, when alternating with restrained melodic fragments in a low register, such silences can be ominous. Sometimes silence contributes to the creation of humor. If a passage of music sets up strong expectations of a predictable outcome, and if at the moment of anticipated resolution nothing happens, the ensuing silence inevitably produces an "I've been had" reaction in listeners—to their almost certain delight.

3. Rhythm

TEMPO, BEAT, AND METER

THE PACE AT WHICH SOUNDS and silences move forward in time is perceived relatively, and this perception is colored by nonrhythmic elements as well as by the actual speed of rhythmic progression. The *tempo* (degree of speed) of an eight-note descending scale played in two seconds by a solo flute would seem quite leisurely. If several other instruments joined in and harmonized each tone with a different chord, however, the tempo would be heard as very fast. And if the flutist used a *staccato* (detached) attack, the impression of velocity would be even greater than that created by a *legato* (connected) version played at precisely the same speed. Sometimes the illusion of speed and its actuality coincide—certainly no sense of languor is communicated by a pianist rattling off fourteen notes a second. But when harmony, texture, and attack combine forces to create an effect of deliberation, a flute playing an eight-note scale in *one* second cannot offset the effect of slowness created by those combined nonrhythmic elements.

Individual units of sound and silence are also perceived relatively: a silence of one second's duration, for example, seems dramatically long when it follows a cascade of tones, but a one-second silence surrounded by slow-moving chords might be almost imperceptible.

The Western listener has a strong tendency to organize consecutive sounds into comprehensible groups and patterns and is inclined to shape the forward motion of music into symmetrical and predictable intervals of time. Not even the steady, noncommittal ticking of a clock or metronome is exempt. Many people feel compelled to group such regular, repetitive sounds into twos or threes, and sometimes this delusion becomes so real that they even "hear" a nonexistent accent at the beginning of each imaginary group. Such compulsive systemization of sound might be seen as symptomatic of a society tyrannized by clock time, but it seems more probable that the tendency stems from a musical culture in which regularly recurring pulse patterns are the most fundamental method of rhythmic propulsion. Or it might be both.

Regular pulse in music is called *beat.* It is by no means unique to Western cultures, but exists universally, particularly in dance music, for which rhythmic regularity is crucial. Response to a steady beat in music seems to be basic to the human condition, requiring neither formal instruction nor cultural experience. It is *meter,* the organization of beats into regularly recurring patterns, that represents the Western proclivity for measuring movement and circumscribing time with predictability.

Most metered music is based on groupings of two, three, or four beats, and those groups, called *measures,* normally remain consistent throughout a section or an entire composition. Groups of more than four beats are usually heard as compound units. A recurrent pattern of fives, for example, is perceived as 2 + 3 or 3 + 2, sixes as 3 + 3 or 2 + 2 + 2, and so on. The first beat of each measure is endowed with a *metric accent,* real or imagined, giving it added importance and reinforcing the sense of systematic recurrence of beat groupings. This framework of rhythmic organization has potential for deadly monotony, but for several centuries composers have eluded that hazard by using varied rhythmic patterns, by varying the subdivisions of the beat, or by defying the authority of the beat through evasion or ambiguity. The first of these three techniques—rhythmic variety within and between measures—is vital to musical interest and is common to all eras. But the second—variety of beat subdivisions—has been more cyclic, varying from one historical epoch to another. During the Baroque period, for example, beat subdivisions (normally twos or threes) were relatively consistent. During the Classical period they were variable, and in the Romantic period contrasting subdivisions (twos and threes and fours) were employed simultaneously.

The eye assembles data to form a unified object whenever it can. The horse and rider are easy to perceive, especially when squinting or from a distance.

Syncopation

Ironically, the most vehement challenges to beat authority depend totally on steadfast, regularly recurring pulse patterns. An example is *syncopation,* in which an unexpected strong emphasis is placed either on some other beat than the first or on a subdivision of a beat. It is characterized by anticipation of or tardiness in arriving at the beat. The visceral response elicited by jazz owes its being to the body's tendency to supply the beats that the music tantalizingly evades.

Identical metric groupings are the most usual, but not the only, manifestations of meter. Groupings that consist of asymmetrical units—such as 2 + 3 or 3 + 4, in which the pulse remains constant and the two units alternate in regular sequence—are common throughout the world and have appeared in the West with increasing frequency during the past hundred years. They provide enough vacillation to keep listeners pleasantly off balance and sufficient order to give them a sense of security.

Polymeter

Polymeters are more difficult to identify aurally, but the crosscurrents of tension that they set up are easily perceived. When groups of threes and fours, for example, are combined, their

A Korean dancer twirls and sounds the hanging gongs with wooden sticks. Such incorporation of musical elements into the dance has been common throughout the world for thousands of years.

Part of a procession in an Aztec victory ceremony, showing rattles and drums. The rattles are made of gourds and trimmed with feathers, showing them to be of royal provenance; the bowl drums are made of turtle shells. (Detail of an 8th- or 9th-century wall painting, Bonampak Temple, Mexico.)

respective strong beats are in opposition most of the time. Whenever these strong beats do coincide, therefore, they assume a rhythmic significance comparable to the resolution of harmonic dissonance:

1 2 3 | 1 2 3 | 1 2 3 | 1 2 3 | 1 2 3 | 1 2 3 | 1 2 3 | 1 2 3 | 1

1 2 3 4 | 1 2 3 4 | 1 2 3 4 | 1 2 3 4 | 1 2 3 4 | 1 2 3 4 | 1

Changing Meter

Meter without predictable pattern represents a form of organized chaos that many twentieth-century composers have found attractive. Measures of different lengths succeed one another in unordered sequence, and each strong beat comes as a surprise. Such music seems to meander, stream-of-consciousness fashion, without predictability.

Unequal Beats

Consistent, unchallenged pulse enables listeners to take rhythmic progression for granted and focus their attention on other elements in the music. But when pulse becomes variable, rhythm demands special consideration by virtue of its energetic unexpectedness. Uneven pulse results when uniform subdivisions of the beat march forward at a steady pace but are grouped, sometimes in twos, sometimes in threes, producing beats of different lengths. Variable pulse contributes significantly to the rhythmic vitality characteristic of Spanish music. A typical Spanish metric scheme involves the alternation of three fast beats, each embodying two subdivisions (2 + 2 + 2), with two slower beats, each equivalent to three subdivisions (3 + 3). Every measure is equal in time to every other measure, but the beats in the two-beat measures are half again as long as those in the three-beat measures—an irresistible rhythm, eliciting physical response in all but the comatose.

Unequal beats within a measure create still greater excitement; a repetitive scheme consisting of asymmetrical elements has a hypnotic force that is not easily ignored. One of the most widely used patterns is a three-beat measure based on a 3 + 3 + 2 arrangement of eight equal subdivisions. This rhythmic structure superimposed on a fast four-beat measure with consistent pulse produces a sound characteristic of American jazz. To hear these combined rhythms, establish a steady four beat with the left hand on a table top, then add the right hand, beating at twice the speed of the left and accenting as indicated by the underlined numbers below:

```
RH 1 2 3 1 2 3 1 2 | 1 2 3 1 2 3 1 2 | 1 2 3 1 2 3 1 2
   -     -     -     -     -     -     -     -     -

LH 1   2   3   4   | 1   2   3   4   | 1   2   3   4
```

Side 2 Band 5

The sixth of Bartók's "Six Dances in Bulgarian Rhythms" from *Mikrokosmos,* Vol. 6, is based on the three-beat measure just described, and it is a good example of the compelling rhythmic thrust of this pattern of asymmetric beats. The piece begins with rhythmic chords over an insistent repeated note and continues by capriciously reversing the registers of those two components. Suddenly the repeated note evaporates, the texture thickens, and a canon based on the rhythmic chords enters, takes over, and leads to a powerful climax. Following this, the dynamic level is sharply reduced, and the repeated note reenters, but with an amiable hint of whimsy replacing the relentless drive of the beginning. Approaching the final cadence the music becomes more resolute, and that cadence is a triumphant affirmation of both the key and the rhythmic pattern.

MUSIC WITHOUT PULSE

Unlike living organisms, music can survive with no pulse at all. The absence of pulse, however, can produce contradictory effects. The lack of pulse may serve to direct attention away from rhythm toward text, melody, or tone color; or, if the rhythm is aggressive, it can become the focal point, creating suspense through erratic behavior. Medieval plainchant (page 53) owes its serene, ethereal character in part to the pulseless flow of its rhythm; interest centers equally on text and melody, and rhythmic pattern does not intrude on the listener's consciousness. In operatic recitative (page 118), text must be paramount, and to that end all competing elements are shorn of fascination; rhythm is derived from language and is ungoverned by pulse, melody is reduced to perfunctory status, and the accompaniment, with simple block chords marking changes of harmony, offers no threat.

In the West, pulse has served most often as a point of departure, with rhythmic interest generated by some combination of evading and submitting to the beat. Pulseless music in which rhythm is central is primarily a product of the second half of the twentieth century and is still in the experimental stage. No longer the prime stabilizing agent, rhythm in this music becomes erratic, elusive, and unreliable—but never tedious.

It is impossible to overstate the importance of rhythm in music. Other elements may be altered without impairing the identity of a piece of music, but any significant change in the rhythm can render a composition unrecognizable. A sequence of pitches cannot exist without some form of rhythm, but rhythm has no corresponding dependence on pitch. Rhythm alone, although it can never be completely divorced from tone color, texture, and dynamics, can create and sustain interest, and can be manipulated to give a composition significant form without reference to or reliance on pitch.

The size of these gourds, wound in vines for both strength and embellishment, requires that they be played with both hands. The size means the sacrifice of some delicacy, but it compensates in depth of tone quality.

Les Percussions de Strasbourg, a contemporary French ensemble.

MUSIC WITHOUT PITCH

In Western cultures, pitch has exercised such a mesmeric influence that rhythm has all too frequently been forced into second place. Absorption with tonal relationships has placed pitch in the forefront of attention, with rhythm merely supporting and contributing to the melodic and harmonic splendor. In African music, however, the relative positions of pitch and rhythm are reversed.

Attention centers on rhythm, often to the virtual exclusion of all else; although pitch in some cases plays an important part, elsewhere it disappears altogether. African drum music is incredibly complex in construction, involving complicated linear patterns and combinations of contrasting rhythms that professional musicians would find challenging—if not virtually impossible—to perform. Pulse is basic to this music, and the subtleties of syncopation, coupled with crosscurrents of competing rhythms, command an interest and response that remain undiminished by repeated hearings. In the recorded example of African drums, "Like the Ocean," a steady, throbbing pulse asserts itself immediately. As the piece unfolds, subdivisions of threes emerge, while beats seem to group themselves in pairs, adding the stability of pattern to the solidity of regular pulse. Tone-color contrasts differentiate linear threads, which weave around the beats in fascinating aural designs, creating a rich musical fabric and a mood of sheer exuberance.

Side 2 Band 6

Ionisation by Edgard Varèse represents a very different approach to unpitched composition. It is scored for thirty-odd percussion instruments and two sirens, and tone color is as important as rhythm—occasionally more so. The sirens, for example, are exceedingly colorful, but from a purely rhythmic viewpoint they interrupt the proceedings and disturb continuity. Pulse is a sometime thing, remaining consistent for a while, becoming variable, and sometimes disappearing altogether. Technically, Varèse cheated a little: toward the end of the piece he introduced pitched instruments (chimes and piano), but there is no hint of pitch relationships, and tone color is far more important than any pitches the chimes and piano may produce. In its Paris premiere, *Ionisation* scandalized its audience, who felt that with its non-pitch format it qualified as nonmusic. Percussion ensembles, although still not a household word, have gained a measure of acceptance since then, and pitchless music is no longer regarded as a contradiction in terms. In France, the ensemble called Les Percussions de Strasbourg enjoys such popularity that the group is featured on prime-time television shows, and other percussion ensembles are proliferating throughout the Western world. The self-sufficiency of rhythm as a basis for musical organization has been amply demonstrated, and it may yet dethrone pitch as the focus for Western music.

Side 2 Band 7

4. Medieval Music

THE FACT THAT no evidence exists concerning the origins of music has in no way hampered writers, who have come up with a number of fascinating but contradictory theories on the subject. Writings about the beginnings of music go back to ancient times; Egyptian, Greek, and most other mythologies accorded music a divine origin, and tales concerning the magical powers of music are universal. The Arabs, with their interest in genealogy, have gone so far as to provide a family tree:

> Jubal the son of Cain (Qain) is credited with the first song, which was an elegy on the death of Abel. Bar Hebraeus the Syrian . . . tells us that the inventors of musical instruments were the daughters of Cain, hence the name for a singing-girl, which was *qaina*.*

Folk music is irrepressible; it exists everywhere and has existed since before recorded time. Formal music is less hardy; it requires careful cultivation and the climate of a civilized society. Historically, the development of formal music has corresponded to the value that society has placed on it. The ancient civilizations of the Far East were the first known to have cultivated music systematically. India today is heir to a continuous musical tradition that goes back at least four thousand years, and the music of China may be even older. The ancient Chinese developed a complex and sophisticated system of music, a tradition that continued unbroken until the second half of the twentieth century, when it was officially abandoned as incompatible with current political philosophy.

Early civilizations in the Near East, too, held music in high esteem and provided a congenial atmosphere for its development. Unlike the Far East, there was much cultural interaction, and the continuing effects of this early musical reciprocity can still be detected in melodic similarities in the music of Near Eastern nations today. Egypt, as matriarch of the Mediterranean, may have pointed the way, but musical influence was mutual rather than unilateral, and each of the ancient Near Eastern civilizations must be credited with having developed an intricate, subtle system of music.

As for Western Europe, it was culturally retarded. The great bulk of the continent remained uncivilized for an astonishing

*Henry Farmer, *A History of Arabian Music* (London: Luzac, 1929), pp. 6–7.

On this page of a 14th-century book, Jubal is pictured twice, with an organ and with a psaltery. The organ symbolizes instrumental music and the psaltery (which accompanied song) symbolizes vocal music. Thus Jubal is depicted as the originator of both types—hence of all music.

length of time. Even the regions along the Mediterranean were long unaffected by the highly developed civilizations bordering the same sea. Rome, the first great civilization to develop in Western Europe, was more notable for its politics and law, its technology and architecture, than for its fine arts. In this area, except for literature, the Romans were content to appropriate the accomplishments of the Greeks. Musically, the Romans embraced the Greek theoretical system; thus the first formal music of Western Europe had its origin in Near Eastern sources. Rome proved to be fertile ground for this Hellenistic transplant, and as the empire flourished, so did its music. With the decline of Rome the fine arts suffered an eclipse: as Europe fragmented into small feudal units, the arts fragmented as well. Music was left to the hazards of chance and memory. Only the Christian Church, as the single unifying institution, preserved and encouraged the development of knowledge and culture at a time when both were regarded as expendable.

EARLY SACRED MUSIC

We have only meager evidence concerning specific music used in early Christian services, but such music must have derived largely from the cantillation (chanting) of the synagogue and from folk materials. The fact that the first Christians had been Jews makes this a reasonable supposition, and similar melodic fragments still existing in both plainchant and cantillation give weight to the theory. Greece lent its language to the New Testament and gave sanctuary to early Christian leaders, so it seems logical to assume some Greek musical influence as well. In any event, the Church, having originated in the Near East, derived its music from that region, freely using both sacred and secular sources to serve its needs.

Plainchant

By about the year 500 a body of music called *chant,* or *plainchant,* had accumulated for use in Christian services. It was

Mounted musicians found in a T'ang Dynasty tomb (c. 750 A.D.). Their instruments are panpipes, recorder, and cross-blown flute. At the far left is a player who appears to have been holding a mouth resonator (Jew's harp).

melodic in concept and vocal in performance. Near Eastern influence was evident in the character of the melodies. The absence of instrumental accompaniment was an austerity imposed by the Church. (This rejection of instruments seems less reactionary considering that during the early years of Islam music was banned altogether.*) The eventual division of the Church into two separate bodies resulted in the development of equally distinct musical styles. The Eastern branch, which was to become the Greek Orthodox Church, retained an oriental flavor in its music, while the Western branch, which was to become the Roman Catholic Church, drifted away from Eastern ideals and subsequently contributed significantly to the development of a uniquely Western style of music.

Chant, as a musical expression of religious reverence, has had universal appeal and is a feature common to most of the religions of the world. Range, tessitura, and speed all vary enormously. The recorded example, the chanting of the Lament for the Dead by Tibetan Buddhist lamas, illustrates the combination of low range and tessitura with an extremely slow tempo. After an initial spoken phrase, the monks begin their intonation. The voices are joined by the sound of bells, which also are virtually universal in connection with sacred ritual. Although they are not part of the chant per se, they are intrinsic to the ritual and hence always accompany the Lament.

Side 3 Band 1

In the Roman Church there are two types of chant: that which is intoned by the priest, and that which is sung by choirs or soloists. The chanting of the priest is musically restricted to an extremely limited range, sometimes proceeding on a single pitch—not surprising, since priests are not selected for their musicianship. This type of chant proceeds very rapidly, one note per syllable, and the text is all-important. The melody—and it can be called that only in the loosest possible sense—serves solely to enhance the words; it seeks no musical merit for itself, and without the text it would perish of its own tedium. But this chant serves its purpose well by imparting to the text a fervor that prosaic speech cannot equal, and it has remained relatively unchanged throughout the past fifteen centuries.

The second type, the chant sung by choirs and soloists, has changed radically throughout its history. Prior to the ninth century,

*Farmer, *Arabian Music,* p. 39.

there was great diversity of melodic styles in the chant of individual churches, because their geographic isolation forced a measure of independence on them. Attempts at codification met with considerable resistance, but by the ninth century Roman practice was a norm within which certain differences persisted, especially in Milan, France, Spain, and the British Isles.

Early chant was rhythmic in that the duration of long and short notes was proportional: one long note was precisely equal to two short ones. The chant was not metered, and its rhythm derived from the flow of the Latin text. The range was normal, generally about an octave, and, unlike the chanting of the priest, the melodies had shape and musical merit in their own right. There were two types of text settings: *syllabic,* in which each syllable of the text was given one note, and *melismatic,* in which several notes were sung on the vowel of one syllable. The length of a melisma varied from a few notes to an entire musical phrase. These two types of text setting existed in combination more frequently than in pure form. Musical phrases paralleled text phrases and clauses, and therefore differed in length. Cadences normally ended on a long note, often preceded by a melisma, but final cadences were not notably more conclusive in character than other cadences. Melodic motion consisted primarily of steps, repeated notes, and thirds; a leap larger than a fifth was very rare.

Side 3 Band 2

The Kyrie of the eleventh-century *Missa Orbis Factor* ("Creator of the Universe Mass") consists of nine phrases: three of "Kyrie eleison," three of "Christe eleison," and three additional repetitions of "Kyrie eleison." Melodically, there are only three different phrases, which can be represented as *aaa bbb aac.* Each has a long melisma on the first syllable of the second word, and the final phrase contains an equally long melisma on the last syllable of the first word. All the "Kyrie" phrases have a range of slightly less than an octave, but with the word "Christe," the range is expanded, lending increased urgency to the supplication.

By the eighth century, the important choirs were found in monastery and convent chapels. Women had been included in early church choirs, but in the sixth century they were excluded, and the treble range was supplied by young boys. The choirs sang in unison (or octaves if men's and boys' voices were combined)—pure melody continued to be the order of the day. A single phrase or a complete section might be sung by one soloist or by the entire choir, or it might be sung *responsorially* (by soloist and choir) or *antiphonally* (by two choirs). The voices of men and boys were used separately for contrast and then combined to produce a different color. Space was exploited not only in the placement of choirs for antiphonal singing but also in processions, which sometimes involved impressive visual as well as musical effects.

Organum

By the tenth century, performance was based on the principle of contrasting consecutive phrases, and fourths or fifths were used to complement the traditional intervals of the unison and the octave. *Organum,* the practice of singing a phrase in parallel fourths or fifths, provided a tone color even more dramatic than the combination of men's and boys' voices in octaves. When phrases in organum were doubled at the octave, the sound must have seemed spectacular. The origins of organum may be uncertain, but its consequences are clear: the introduction of organum was a decisive step away from Eastern ideals and an early manifestation of our Western taste for vertical sonorities.

Sometime during or prior to the tenth century, the church lifted its ban on instrumental accompaniment. Instruments were added as a standard procedure in the performance of chant, thus extending both the available pitch range and the array of colors. Decisions regarding the distribution of phrases among soloists, choir, and choirs in combination, accompanied or unaccompanied, were entirely the province of the person who organized the performances. Composers continued to notate single-line melodies in the tenor register, leaving details of color, register, and number to choice.

In the eleventh century, parallel organum gave way to a style in which the added voice moved in contrary and oblique as well as parallel motion, thereby creating a second melody. The independence of this second line lay in its contrasting melodic contour rather than its rhythm. The two voices retained a basic note-for-note relationship, and although the tenor line, carrying the plainchant melody, was considered preeminent, the second voice added melodic interest as well as color.

In the twelfth century, a melismatic style of organum developed in which the tenor sang a plainchant melody in long notes while a higher voice, the countertenor, sang several notes—

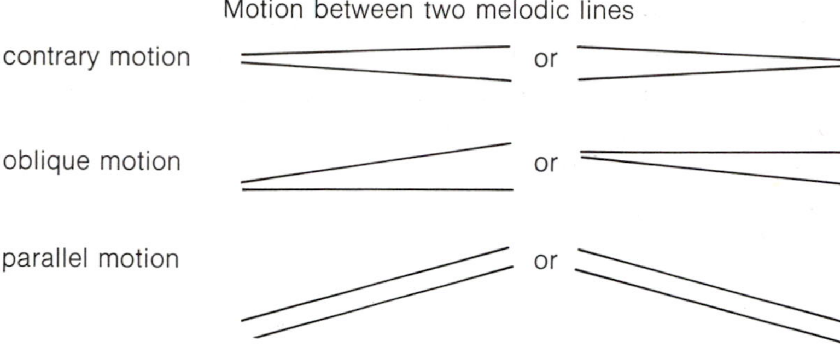

sometimes an entire musical phrase—around each tenor note. During the course of a phrase some startling dissonances might occur, but cadences were always reassuringly consonant. The tenor voice proceeded too slowly to establish any sense of pulse, so the upper voice, which moved more quickly, assumed rhythmic responsibility. The music had a regular pulse with a subdivision of three, and to our ears it sounds metered. This adaptation of chant was unique because interest centered on the florid upper voice rather than on the chant itself. The music was more monophonic than polyphonic, because the slow-moving tenor could not sustain melodic interest. The tenor's musical function was to accompany the more active line, often turning into a series of drones.

Polyphony

During the eleventh and twelfth centuries, Medieval musicians had been flirting with polyphony, but by the thirteenth century they were ardently committed to it. Monophonic composition continued, as it always has, but interest in polyphonic sound was central to the music of the Gothic era, and increasing attention was devoted to the combination of multiple melodies. Two-voice organum continued to flourish, with the tenor part becoming more active, resulting in dual melodic interest. And three-voice organum came into being, allowing both greater density of texture and further linear activity. In this three-voice texture, both upper voices were more active than the tenor, but all three voices had a measure of rhythmic and melodic independence. Triple subdivision of the pulse continued to be the norm, and pulses most frequently occurred in pairs. Phrases tended to be more equal in length than they had been in pure plainchant, and cadences were customarily followed by rests that definitively punctuated the phrases. Sharp dissonances within phrases were less frequent than in melismatic organum, and cadence combinations were limited to intervals of the unison, octave, and fifth.

The Motet

In addition to organum, another multivoiced form that gained great popularity during the thirteenth century was the motet—a composition characterized by short melodic figures in the tenor voice, all based on the same rhythm and separated by rests. Above this voice were one or more countermelodies which were rhythmically more active and melodically wider ranging than the tenor. Each part had its own text, and not only different texts but even different languages (most often Latin and French) were combined in the same motet.

In early performances of motets, the slower tenor line was sung by the choir, played on instruments, or both, while the more active upper lines were assigned to soloists. As the motet form developed and the tenor became more active, a soloist was used for each melodic line, and the choir ceased to have a role in motet performance. As in organum, instruments were sometimes used to double or even substitute for voice parts. But unlike organum, the motet was sometimes performed by instruments alone. Such instrumental performances would have been unlikely in church services, but by the end of the thirteenth century, the motet was no longer exclusively church property; many were secular, and sacred motets were frequently performed in secular settings.

Like most Medieval music, motets were composed in layers, most frequently from a previously known melody placed in the tenor. In many cases, a two-line motet was used by a later composer as two of the lines of a three-line motet. The recorded example, by an unknown composer, is treated as though it had existed first in a two-line form. The tenor and one added line begin alone, and then both these lines are performed again with a third line added to them. The pungent rhythmic character is emphasized by the addition, for the second line proceeds with two notes to each one note in the tenor (though with a beat in threes), and then the third voice adds further rhythmic motion, giving a three-speed effect to the combination.

Side 3 Band 3

SECULAR MUSIC

The Church had no monopoly on the development of music in general; the secular sector had been equally creative and had progressed at a faster pace in the imaginative use of instruments. Unlike plainchant, secular song normally assumed the presence of instruments—to support the voices, to alternate with them, to provide simultaneous variations, or just to play.

Manuscripts of secular song in Europe before 800 are virtually nonexistent. Folk music, being by definition an oral tradition and largely improvisatory, left no written heritage for posterity. Even secondary sources yield little specific information. References to music in writings of the period concern sacred more than secular music—which, since the writers were monks, is neither remarkable nor conclusive. That secular song existed is certain, but firm knowledge of its rhythmic and melodic shape is beyond reach. We can be sure only that these songs took shape from the poems to which they were set—one phrase for each line of poetry.

Jongleurs dancing to the accompaniment of two horns.

Minstrels and Jongleurs

The earliest professional music makers of historical record in Medieval Europe were the minstrels and jongleurs, documented in detail only from the tenth century. *Minstrels* were full-time performers in the employ of noblemen. They were not expected to compose—a fact that suggests a preexisting body of well-known musical compositions. *Jongleurs* were all-purpose entertainers: in addition to singing and playing several different instruments, they were expected to have a repertoire of vaudeville acts such as juggling, performing acrobatic feats, and presiding over trained animals. These men and women led a precarious and transient existence, traveling about in search of an audience in castle or town, often unprotected by civil law and always subject to economic uncertainties.

Troubadours and Trouvères

Toward the end of the eleventh century, however, the jongleurs' lot improved dramatically. A new lyric art, that of the troubadours, created a new demand for their services, and with more secure employment they acquired economic stability and a measure of respectability. Many of the early troubadours were noblemen who

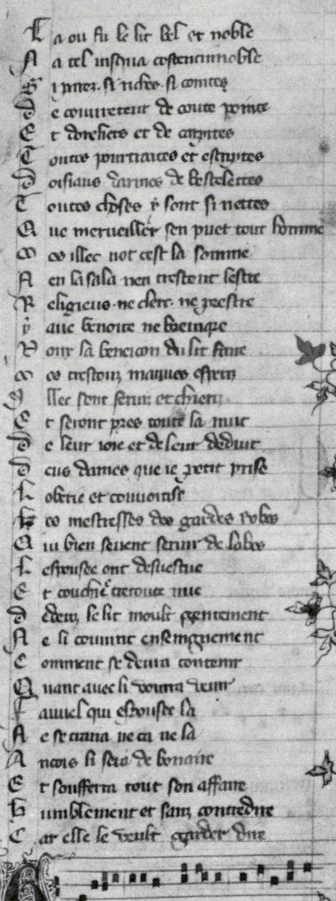

An ivory casket carved in the 14th century depicts scenes of a tournament. Virtually all such ceremonies featured music, with singers before and trumpeters during the jousting.

turned their attention away from the more rigorous aspects of knighthood toward the gentler, more chivalrous side. They occupied themselves with the writing of lyrics—frequently in praise or persuasion of a lady fair—and with the composition of melodies to turn these lyrics into songs. The noble knights, however, were far from self-sufficient in this endeavor. They were often illiterate, requiring assistance in recording their poetic efforts, and certainly they needed help in transcribing their melodies. Further, if not blessed with a beautiful voice and instrumental skill, a troubadour required the services of a professional performer, and the many-talented jongleur was well equipped to supply these needs.

The troubadour movement originated in the south of France, reached its height late in the twelfth century, and then gave way to the *trouvère* movement of northern France. The two movements had much in common both socially and musically; they were separated more by geography and differing dialects than by stylistic dissimilarity. Songs of both the troubadours and the trouvères were of necessity rhythmically regular because they often served as music for dancing. Existing manuscripts give little or no indication of the intended rhythm, but it is known that the Medieval preference for a pulse subdivided in three applied equally to secular and sacred song. Melodies rarely exceeded an octave in range, and motion consisted primarily of steps,

(Opposite) French dancers in masquerade, from a 14th-century manuscript.

These 13th-century chess players are sustained through the long waits between moves by their minstrels.

repeated notes, and thirds. Phrase structure corresponded to the lines of poetry, but these songs—particularly those of the trouvères—indicate that great attention was given to organizing musical materials. The songs of the troubadours placed the entire burden of structure on the text. The songs of the trouvères gave music its share in this responsibility, however, with phrases organized in groups that formed clear sections, giving the music its own overall shape. Thus, although melody supported the poem in rhythm and mood, it no longer depended on language for its organization. Having form in itself, the melody could stand alone.

Dance Music

Dance, as always, availed itself of any existing music that served its purpose, and it was not uncommon for songs so used to receive purely instrumental performance. A Medieval dance band had much in common with contemporary jazz groups: drums were prominent, the beat was relentless, and arrangements often included a featured singer. In "Kalenda Maya," a dance song by the troubadour Raimbaut de Vaqueiras (c. 1155–1205), the instrumental group and the vocalist share honors equally, alternating in irregular sequence throughout the arrangement. The strong Medieval flavor of this song is enhanced by the nasal quality of the voice and the persistent instrumental drone.

Side 3 Band 4

Music composed expressly for dance was rare. For the most part, Medieval music was vocally conceived and linked with a text from which it drew its basic rhythm. One form, however, was constructed especially for dance: the *estampie,* an instrumental form that based phrase lengths on the requirements of the dance rather than on poetic lines. To be coherent, instrumental music must have pattern in its structure, and the estampie was given shape by the pairing of phrases: an initial phrase was repeated, each time followed by a different cadential phrase (abac). The first ending (b) was marked by a light cadence, the second (c) by a more solid one, so that the four phrases formed a comprehensible musical section. Subsequent sections substituted a new phrase for (a), repeated as before, with the same ending phrases as were used in the first section (dbdc, ebec, and so on), thus relating and contrasting the sections simultaneously—an organizational principle that is still valid today.

An 11th-century dancer twirls her veil.

Medieval Instruments

A large variety of instruments was available in the thirteenth century. Many, unfortunately, are unknown to us except for tantalizing references without description in the literature of the period. Others have survived in art, giving us their appearance without their sound, and a few have survived in actuality. The string family included both bowed and plucked instruments. In the latter category, the small harp appeared early, stayed late, and was something of a staple throughout the period. Fiddles (*fithels* in England, *fidels* in Germany, and *vielles* in France) were common and were played with a bow, although neither the bow nor the fiddle had the physical shape to which we are now accustomed. The woodwind family included recorders (as we know them) in all registers, and oboes, brought back from the Crusades. Brasses were represented primarily by trumpets, although larger horns similar to the French horn were also used. Drums of various types and sizes, cymbals, bells, tambourine, and triangle constituted the principal percussion instruments. The bagpipes was very much on the scene, although it came to be regarded as a country cousin. Keyboard instruments as we know them were yet to come, but two zither-type instruments were common: the plucked psaltery and the struck dulcimer. The pipe organ existed, but instead of sounding single tones it produced composite sounds consisting of six pitches related to the overtone series. Contemporary descriptions of the magnitude of sound produced by this instrument make it sound fairly frightening.

The 13th-century *cantigas* (songs) of the Spanish king Alfonso the Wise were illustrated with pictures of instrumentalists who might play the songs. Top left and right, bells and rebecs; below, lute.

The Medieval use of instruments, like the organizing of organum, centered upon the principles of combination, contrast, and alternation. Combination involved the use of different rather than similar instruments; clarity of individual colors rather than homogeneous blend was the goal. Contrast concerned color, register, and number. Whether combined or alternating, tone colors were individually distinct—as were contrasting registers—

and textural variety was produced by alternation between individuals and groups. Dynamic variety was achieved primarily through number and instrument type—one performer alternating with a group of four, or two trumpets alternating with two recorders, would naturally produce dynamic contrast. All these decisions were made by the person in charge of a performance, whose function was comparable to that of a modern-day producer.

NOTATION AND *ARS NOVA* IN FRANCE

The Medieval pitch system, being relative rather than absolute, allowed great latitude in the distribution of musical phrases among instruments and voices. Pitch relationships rather than specific pitches were crucial in performance, and the prevailing notation, called *neumatic* notation, was adequate to the needs of a monophonic, improvisatory art. Early *neumes* were no more than graphic representations of musical gestures. They conveyed the direction and the approximate distance of melodic motion, but

One of the earliest representations of a pipe organ—a 12th-century copy of a 9th-century picture. Organ pumpers were employed until well into the twentieth century.

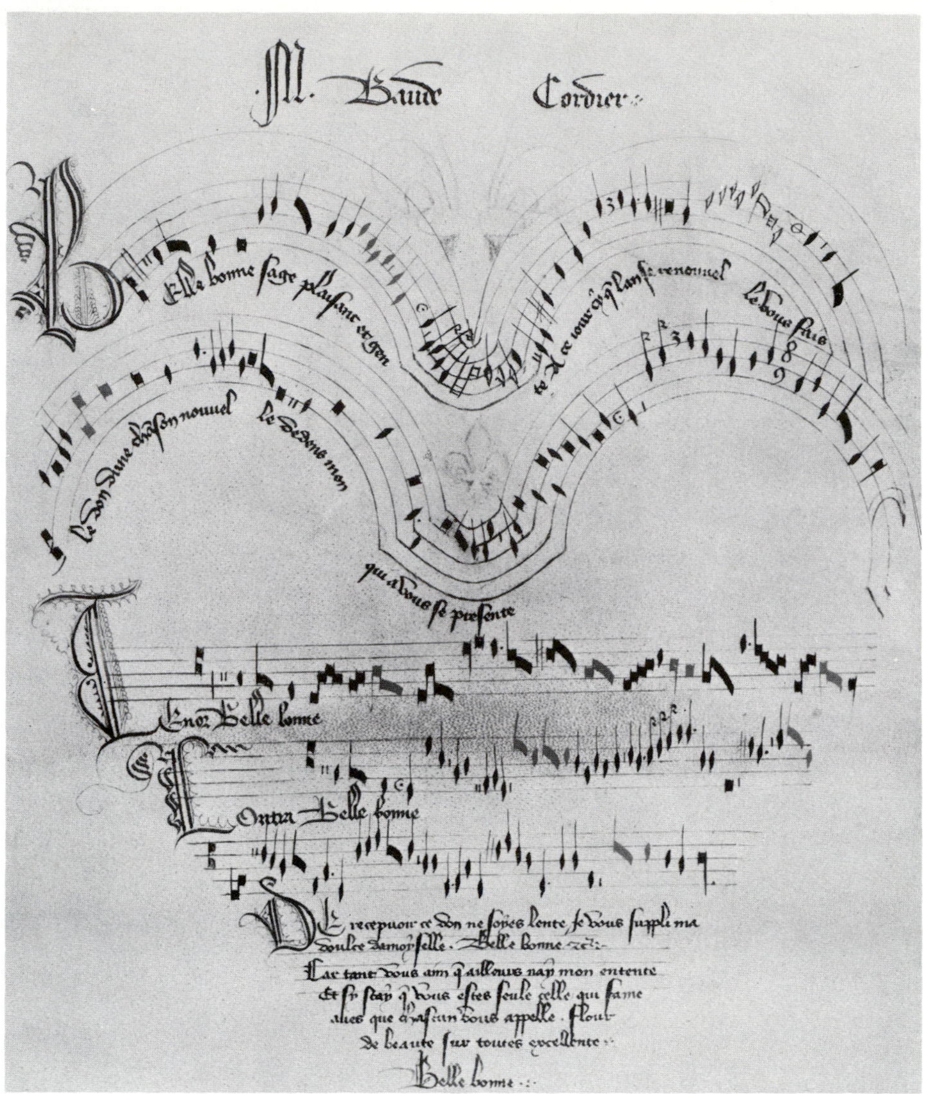

An early 15th-century popular song. The composer's name, Cordier, means "of the heart," and he has notated the three-part song with the tenor across the middle, the ornate solo voice in the top two lines, and the slower bass (marked "contra") at the bottom, with text below—all in such a way as to incorporate the shape of a heart.

they did not indicate precise pitches and, in the beginning, were altogether vague as to rhythm.

By the end of the thirteenth century, a high degree of rhythmic independence in combined melodic lines had developed and, at the same time, the melodies themselves had become more ornate. As the style became too complex for improvisation, the organization of melodies became the responsibility of the composer, not the producer. This was a formidable responsibility because neumatic notation—more an outline than a blueprint—

was inadequate to the task. Development of a new notation was crucial to representing this new kind of polyphony—so crucial that Philippe de Vitry's book detailing it, *Ars nova* ("New Art"), named the entire epoch. Ars nova originated in Paris, thus assuring French leadership in music for the next hundred years.

Rhythmic developments of the fourteenth century were indeed complex. Subdivisions of the pulse, while equal to one another, varied in number, thereby creating an illusion that the pulse itself was variable. The effect of each line was one of changing meter; combined lines produced the sound of polymeter as well. The richness of rhythmic invention in late Medieval music remained unparalleled until well into the twentieth century.

In Medieval popular songs, the roles of beat and subdivisions were often reversed: beat remained constant, and variable subdivisions were obliged to conform to it. "Par maintes foys," a late-fourteenth-century chanson by Vaillant, is propelled by a solid beat, while subdivisions of that beat shift unpredictably from threes to twos or fours. Changes in subdivision patterns are dictated not by caprice but by the natural lilt of the language. Rather than forcing the words into a metric mold, the melody accommodates itself to the intrinsic rhythm of the text.

Side 3 Band 5

Perhaps the most popular ars nova rhythmic device was the *hemiola.* The literal meaning of the word is "one and a half," and it describes an arrangement of pulse subdivisions first in threes, then in twos. To get an impression of this rhythm, repeat rapidly and evenly the following formula, feeling a pulse on each "one":

| 1 2 3 | 1 2 3 | 1 2 | 1 2 | 1 2 | 1 2 3 | 1 2 3 | 1 2 | 1 2 | 1 2 |

The hemiola has never lost its appeal; it has appeared in the music of every century, and today it is associated with Latin American rhythm, providing much of its charm.

Ars nova was predominantly a secular movement—its characteristic rhythmic vitality and animation were hardly conducive to the creation of a reverent atmosphere. The Church disapproved of such rollicking complexities in liturgical music, and early in the fourteenth century, a papal decree forbade any musical elaboration of the mass that might compromise the integrity of the basic chant. This decree somewhat discouraged church composers from employing polyphonic intricacies in sacred music. But the secular influence was too strong to be abolished by edict; it manifested itself in sacred music in increased use of instruments and extensive use of accompanied solo voice as well as in the continued use of illicit polyphony.

Isorhythm

The popularity of the motet remained strong in both sacred and secular music. In fact, motet style found its way into the mass and brought with it some elements of ars nova rhythmic innovation. Motets at this time frequently employed a rhythmic device known as *isorhythm.* The term denotes a rhythmic pattern in a single voice, generally the tenor:

> Some melody repeated itself in equal sections (stanzas or verses) while the rhythmic pattern was shorter or longer than the melody and therefore did not coincide with the melody on its reentries. If, for instance, the rhythmical pattern was one note longer, the melody, repeated for the first time, would set in on the last note of the not-yet-repeated rhythmical pattern, while its second note would be given the metrical value of the first note of the repeated pattern and consequently would shift the metrical values of all its notes by one digit.*

With letters representing the melody notes, and numbers the rhythmic pattern, the procedure might be symbolized thus:

A B C D E F G | A B C D E F G | A B C D E F G | A B C etc.

1 2 3 4 5 6 7 8 | 1 2 3 4 5 6 7 8 | 1 2 3 4 5 6 7 8 | etc.

This complex process was a kind of intellectual game. Each "repetition" created a new melodic pattern, and only the initiated were aware of the actual repetitions involved in the musical structure.

Canon

Rhythmic intricacy was vital to the style of fourteenth-century polyphony, but it was by no means the only kind of intricacy in ars nova music. The complexity of melodic organization equaled and

*Curt Sachs, *Our Musical Heritage,* second edition (Englewood Cliffs, N.J.: Prentice-Hall, 1955), p. 98.

perhaps exceeded that of rhythm. Originating as an art in which different melodies were combined, Medieval polyphony developed into a highly unified structure in which a single melody was combined in a time lag with itself. The Medieval mind, which willingly embraced authority, delighted in the rigors of the canon (page 36), and composers devised complex forms to captivate the mind and the eye as well as the ear. Some of the self-imposed complications that composers brought to canonic writing included the "crab" canon, in which a basic melody is combined with a version of itself that proceeds backward from last note to first; the "mirror" canon, in which a second voice presents the melody upside-down and backward; rhythmic canon, in which one voice sings the melody faster *(diminution)* or slower *(augmentation)*, or in which all voices sing the pitch sequence using different durational values. All this artifice tended to obscure rather than clarify melodic relationships, but the Medieval mind cherished subtlety and secret meaning—even at the cost of creating a musical enigma. The rise of such canonic convolutions depended on the development of a precise system of notation, one that conveyed specific pitches and exact rhythmic relationships. Many of these musical riddles were designed to be solved by eye rather than by ear.

Hocket

One quite different device depended for its effect entirely on the ear. A melody was apportioned, note by note, between two vocal parts, so that the total choral effort produced one single melodic line. With this technique, called *hocket* (meaning "hiccup"), each vocal line consisted of alternate notes and rests, the notes of one coinciding with the rests of the other. Neither line made musical sense alone, but their alternate tones, when combined, reconstituted the dismembered melody. Hocket is a lighthearted, playful treatment of both melody and vocal resources. It can be fiendishly difficult to perform, but it places only minimal demands on the abilities of the listener. Hocketing was practiced in both Europe and Africa long before any known cultural interaction between the two continents. The only explanation of this phenomenon must be the basic appeal of the technique itself.

The leading exponent of ars nova was the French trouvère priest-musician Guillaume de Machaut (c. 1300–1377), a versa-

MACHAUT

tile cosmopolitan whose influence extended well beyond his lifetime and the borders of his native land. Scholars credit him with the first complete, polyphonic mass setting by a single composer. Throughout the Medieval period, music for the mass had been compiled rather than composed as a unified whole. Choosing specific music from existing (often anonymous) sources was part of the job of the producer, along with the distribution of performance responsibilities among soloists, choirs, and instruments. The idea of a complete mass written by one composer was novel—and an idea that represented a lessening of autonomy for the producer-organizer of church music.

Machaut's motets, written early in his career, were typical in their use of hocketing, isorhythmic structure, and multiple texts. His trouvère works are more remarkable for their modernity. As a trouvère, both poet and musician, he found song a congenial medium of expression; most of his surviving works are secular poems, many with music. These settings are extraordinarily varied, including monophony, a style bordering on homophony, and complex polyphony. A vocal solo with two accompanying instruments was Machaut's standard combination for polyphonic songs. As well as being the leading ars nova poet-composer, Machaut represented the culmination of the trouvère movement.

MUSIC IN OTHER COUNTRIES

France was the musical hub of Medieval Europe. Sacred monophony developed primarily in French monasteries (including those of Gallic Switzerland), and the Cathedral of Notre Dame in Paris was probably the single most important Medieval center. The troubadour and trouvère movements had provided French leadership in secular music, and French style continued to be imitated throughout Western Europe. It was not until the fourteenth century that other countries asserted their musical independence and developed stylistic self-sufficiency.

Italy

In Italy, the trend was toward a simpler style in which an ornate solo line was combined with one or more accompanying voice parts, thus producing a clear, uninvolved texture. Fourteenth-century musical thought was linear, but Italian composers, in practice, were moving in the direction of chordal thought, not only in their melody-plus-accompaniment style but also in their treatment of the lowest line as a *bass*—a foundation for the musical structure. The Italians tended to reject rhythmic and canonic complexity in favor of one beautiful melody supported by non-competing lower voices. Their comparatively few excursions into canonic writing were limited primarily to simple two-voice canons supported by an instrumental bass line, often in the form of an *ostinato* (repeated melodic figure). Even these minimal canonic pursuits were occasionally abandoned in midstream in favor of dialogue or hocket. Northern polyphony was not unknown in Italy; the difference in style was a matter of preference, not cultural backwardness.

LANDINI

Francesco Landini (c. 1325–1397), a blind organist, was the leading Italian composer of the century. Along with his compatriots, he evidenced little interest in composing sacred music; his surviving works are mostly secular songs, with two or three separate-but-unequal vocal lines. In performance, the principal melody was sung by a soloist and the supporting melodies were performed by instrumentalists, by singers, or by both in combination. These songs normally followed a single metric scheme. Each had an established pattern of pulse and subdivision that was maintained throughout. Landini showed a definite preference for an ornamental type of cadence in which the upper voice approached the cadential tone by an upward leap of a third. He was not the first and certainly not the last to use this formula, but he employed it with such frequency that it is commonly identified as the "Landini cadence."

Side 3 Band 6

Landini's ballata "Gram piant'agl'occhi" illustrates all of these characteristics. It is a soulful love song, whose pliant solo line is taken here by a soprano, while two simpler lines are sometimes taken by voices, sometimes by viols, and sometimes by both. The ballata proceeds in a leisurely count of three throughout, with rhythmic complication lying chiefly in varying subdivisions and occasional off-beats. The balance between linear and harmonic interest is beautifully maintained, but overall interest remains with the solo vocal line. The Landini cadence appears at lesser, interior points, adding its turning figure to a line of elegant grace.

Germany

Unlike the Italian practice, German Medieval music was a far cry from stylistic independence. Composers in the German-speaking countries were still occupied with imitating the French style—and an archaic French style at that! The *minnesinger* movement, which paralleled that of the troubadours in style if not in time, began in the thirteenth century and continued through the fourteenth. A minnesinger, like his French counterpart, was most often a knight who sang in praise of his lady. His songs were monophonic—generally slower and more somber than troubadour songs—and in subject matter might include religion as well as love. Despite these differences, however, the lineage of the minnesinger's art was unmistakably French.

German composers continued to lag a century or more behind the French as the *meistersinger* movement supplanted the minnesingers. The meistersingers were from the middle class rather than the nobility, and their songs, for the most part, represented a giant step backward—from an already lagging position—for German music. They created no new style, perhaps because the elaborate organization of their guilds had encouraged musical formulizing, stunting the creative urge. Surprisingly, this movement persisted through the fifteenth and into the sixteenth century, with a durability all the more difficult to understand in light of the magnificent folk song tradition of the German-speaking peoples.

The British Isles

Perhaps the strongest national music of the fourteenth century was that of the British. The early bards of Ireland and Wales had been a potent influence in Europe, and English choirs were famous on the Continent. By the end of the ars nova period, the spontaneous singing in thirds (as versus fifths on the Continent) for which the British were famous began to influence French and Flemish composers, and thirds were to be conspicuous in the ensuing style. Musical trends on the Continent had little impact on British music until late in the Medieval period, when the French trouvère texture was taken into the English church. English sacred music, in the style of French popular songs but also incorporating the English love of harmonic thirds, became extremely popular. Masses in this format, performed in Lady Chapels, comprised one of the loveliest of the musical tributes to the Virgin and one of the summits of the history of music in Great Britain.

(Opposite) Durham Cathedral, England—an outstanding example of medieval architecture.

5. Renaissance Music

IN RETROSPECT, the fifteenth century seems to have been, musically, an extremely untidy one. On the one hand, it cannot easily be classified as either Medieval or Renaissance, and on the other, there is good reason for it to be counted as both. It includes the span of time that witnessed both the climax of the Medieval era and the start of the Renaissance—not consecutively, but simultaneously.

MUSIC IN BURGUNDY

Early in the century, the musical center of the Western world moved northward from Paris to Burgundy, an area including what are now the northeastern provinces of France, Belgium, and the Netherlands. The dukes of Burgundy were politically independent, vastly wealthy, and enthusiastic patrons of the arts. So important was the cultivation of music in the Burgundian court that a sizable group of musicians were employed solely to provide music for the chapel, and a separate band of minstrels were maintained to supply secular music. Generous remuneration and professional prestige attracted the finest artists and musicians of the day to the service of these dukes, and the court of Burgundy became internationally renowned as a cultural center. The outstanding Burgundian composers were widely known and admired, with rival courts, great cathedrals, and even the Papal chapel competing for their services.

The Chanson

BINCHOIS

Among Burgundians, the French *chanson* was the most popular of secular forms, and the leading chanson composer was Gilles Binchois (c. 1400–1460). To refer to the chanson as a "form" is somewhat misleading. The term was applied to any song with a French text, and its style varied from century to century in conformance with changing musical ideals. With the troubadours and early trouvères, the chanson was monophonic; with ars nova composers, it was a polyphonic work resembling a motet in style and structure, sometimes with highly complex rhythms. The only features that remained constant throughout the centuries were the language of the text and the fact that the chanson was sung, with or without accompaniment.

In the early Renaissance, biblical scenes were given a contemporary appearance. Here the artist Israel van Meckenem has depicted the dance of Herodias as a Burgundian court scene. A pipe-and-tabor player is in the center, with two companions playing the sackbut (right) and the cornetto.

Binchois's chansons were three-line polyphonic works that frequently used hemiola rhythms to create varied rhythmic effects. In performance the upper voice was sung as a solo, with instruments playing the lower two lines. In texture, rhythm, performance practice, and range, Binchois's chansons were all typically Medieval. They departed from the older style, however, in their poetic forms, as well as in the melodic contours of their instrumental lines. The solo part was exquisitely vocal: stepwise motion predominated, and the line was graceful in shape. The lower two lines, however, often were less vocal in concept, more angular in shape. Melodic leaps abounded—sometimes one right after another—and rhythm was used in contrast and opposition to the melody. Linear integrity was maintained, but through rhythmic independence rather than through equivalent melodic interest. Binchois's handling of the lower lines strongly suggests that he thought about the total harmonic result as well.

Binchois's "De plus en plus" ("More and More"), one of the most popular chansons of the period, incorporates the chanson style at its loveliest. In this recording, the soloist is a soprano and the accompanying instruments are a flute, a viol, and a lute. The bell sound at the beginning indicates that the arrangement was for dancing; it was customary for a woman to set the tempo of dances with a handbell.

Side 3 Band 7

The chanson gained such supremacy that it invaded the sacred precincts of the mass and motet. Tradition had long placed the chant melody in the tenor, but Burgundian composers, infatuated by the beauties of chanson style, often assigned the melody to the top voice and adorned its simplicity with melodic embellishments. Aside from this unusual treatment of plainchant and the somewhat jagged shape of accompanying melodies, masses composed for the chapels of Burgundy at first resembled polyphonic settings of the fourteenth century. Although based on chant, they employed the chanson's three-part texture, and they were performed in the manner of the chanson, with the relatively ornate top line sung and the two less interesting lower lines taken by instruments. But in the middle of the century more dramatic changes occurred altering the style and the form of the mass.

DUFAY

The leading figure in mid-century developments in church music was Guillaume Dufay (c. 1400–1474). A native of Burgundy, he received his musical education there and spent much of his creative life in the service of the dukes. His early works are similar in style—though often superior in quality—to those of his contemporaries, while his later works represent a style more consistent with Renaissance ideals than with those of the Medieval era. It seems probable that his various sojourns in Italy, where he held both sacred and secular posts, influenced the development of his style. His repeated exposure to the burgeoning Italian Renaissance may have been his source of inspiration; but whatever the source, Dufay's techniques became common practice among later Renaissance composers.

Fundamental to all his other stylistic modifications was Dufay's use of four vocal lines as the basic texture in sacred music. The fourth voice was added *below* the tenor, which had for centuries been the lowest voice and the organizing force in coordinating all other voices. In this new texture, the bass served as primary support, and the tenor became the next-to-lowest voice. The use of four voices meant also an increased attention to vertical sonorities and their continuity, thus strengthening harmonic interest. The concept of vertical combinations as a decisive force in shaping music had been alien to the Medieval ideal. In this respect Dufay anticipated the harmonic style that was to become so basic in Renaissance music.

In Dufay's secular works, thinner textures often prevailed. Two vocal lines with instrumental accompaniment constituted a frequent combination, and he occasionally indicated three voice parts. "Ce jour de l'an," a song in celebration of New Year's Day, is an example of the latter category. It was evidently intended for male trio—one bass in normal range and two tenors in high tessitura. Following an instrumental introduction, the voices enter one by one in quick succession, establishing a linear texture that is maintained throughout the song. There is little competition from harmony, which seems almost incidental to the interweaving of the melodies.

Side 3 Band 8

Instrumental Music

The fifteenth century was not a propitious time for the flowering of instrumental music. Instruments were used primarily to double or accompany voices, as they had been throughout the Medieval era; dance provided the principal occasion for performance by instruments alone. In dance music the art of improvisation continued to flourish. The "score" from which performers read consisted of the sketchiest of outlines, and players improvised melodic phrases in rhythms appropriate to currently popular dance steps. (The proclivity of dance bands for improvisation seems to be timeless. Twentieth-century dance bands, for example, frequently play from "lead sheets," which provide little more than a common harmonic background for individual flights of fancy.) Medieval ensembles were usually quite small, often consisting of two related instruments and one of a contrasting type, but utilizing a larger group at court. The composer Marie de Bourgogne compiled the *Livre de Basses-Danses* ("Book of Low Dances") about 1450. The basse-danse was the most popular court dance, called "low" because its steps kept the feet close to the floor in a series of slow slides that allowed for the heavy, ornate garments worn at the Burgundian court. Although Marie's book, untypically, presented all the parts and not only the lead melody, it did not specify the instrumental group. In this recording, the first phrases

Side 3 Band 9

A 15th-century miniature shows a funeral procession led by minstrels with vielle, lute, and harp.

are played by recorder and lute and the continuation by viols; the entire group combines at the end. In a dance, the piece would have been repeated several times, most probably with variations.

During the last quarter of the fifteenth century, the last Burgundian duke died, leaving no male heir, and the political entity of Burgundy ceased to exist. The subsequent loss of ducal patronage and the demise of the brilliant court had surprisingly little effect on the development of music in that region—the new generation of composers came primarily from the Low Countries (the Netherlands and surrounding areas). By virtue of holding most of the important musical posts on the Continent, these Flemish composers were the principal shapers of music of the Renaissance.

Art and science met in the many nature studies made during the 16th century. Observation was keen and the pen skilled, as in this watercolor study of a gentian by Conrad Gessner.

THE EARLY RENAISSANCE IN ITALY

The Renaissance began in Italy in the mid-fifteenth century as a secular movement that gloried in Man—not as a creature of his Creator, but as an individual capable of shaping his own destiny. (Renaissance Woman, if considered at all, was not similarly regarded.) Italian art and literature were quick to respond to this new humanistic philosophy, but no comparable trend existed in music, which, far from being heroic, centered its secular development on the ephemeral arts of the street song and improvisation. The enormous wealth of the Italian city-states enabled their citizens to seek out the finest talents of the day, and the first great Renaissance music in Italy was written by Franco-Flemish composers. Thus Italy found itself in the somewhat anomalous position of assuming cultural leadership while importing its composers.

The Mass

Since the transplanted Netherlanders were charged with the responsibility for providing music for private chapels, it is not surprising that most early Renaissance music was devoted to settings of the mass. Yet the chapel services represented a secularization of the mass, for the chapel was used as a social and political means of entertaining and impressing important visitors. Chapel musicians worked also as accountants, secretaries, counselors, and negotiators for those they served. Part of the pageantry of the chapel mass was the use of two or even three men or boys on a single musical line. It is curious that a secular movement that honored the individual should be represented by sacred music written for chorus. The Renaissance spirit resided not in the music itself, but in the character of the men who wrote

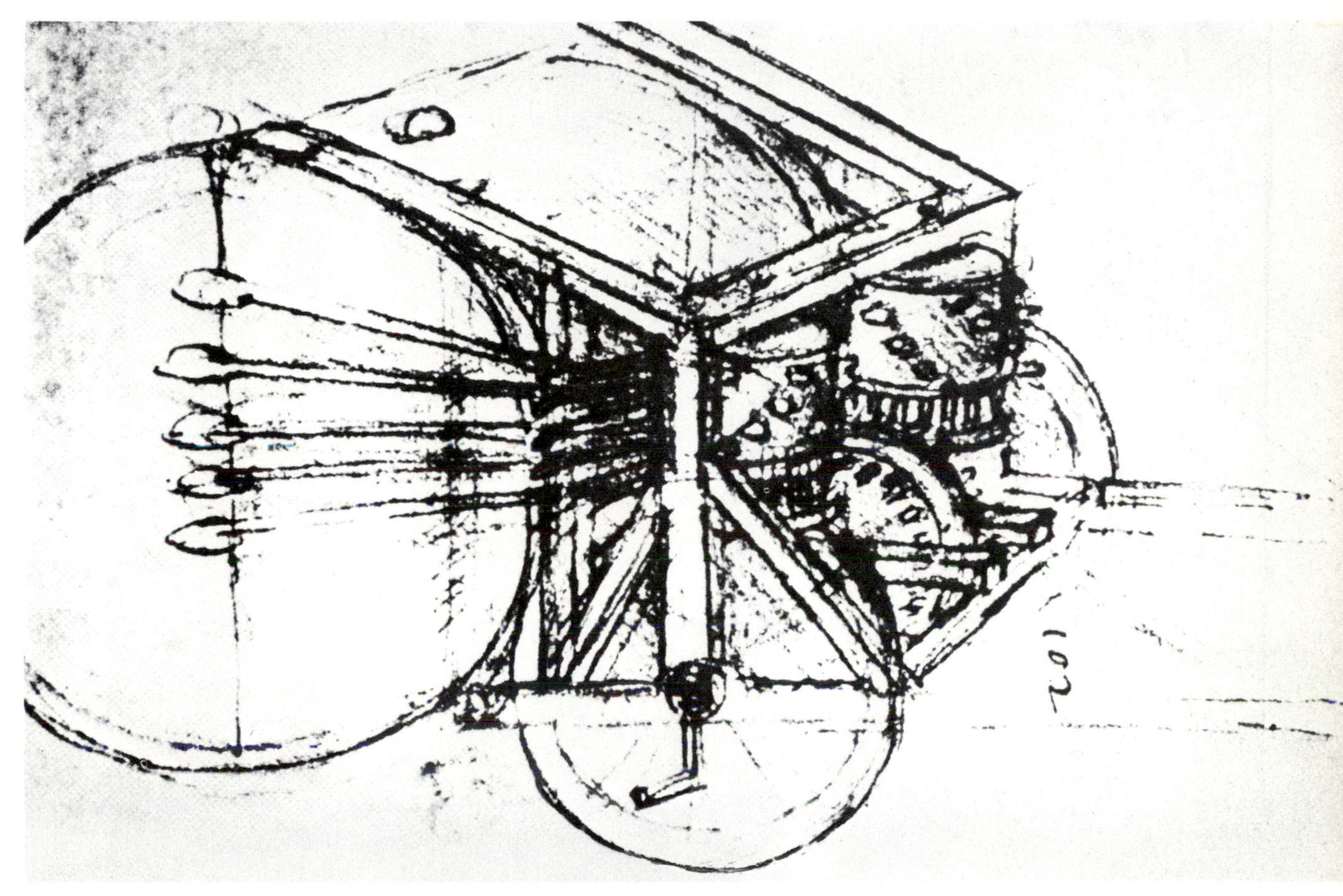

Leonardo da Vinci included many musical projects in his notebooks, such as the caisson above, whose wheels activate cogs that cause drumsticks to strike both heads of a mounted drum.

it—independent men who created a new style and who shaped their music and their careers with equal care.

By the end of the century, the break with the Medieval era was nearly complete; the Flemish composers were working in a new style, motivated by different musical ideals. An overriding concern for musical momentum was reflected in their style: the strong progression of successive vertical sonorities, the interweaving of distinctive melodic lines, and the irresistible impetus of rhythmic thrust. Even the act of composition proceeded along new lines. The Medieval approach had involved writing one line at a time, but the new style—blending harmonic and melodic elements—demanded that all voice parts be considered simultaneously. Harmony, once admitted as a partner, has a tendency to seize

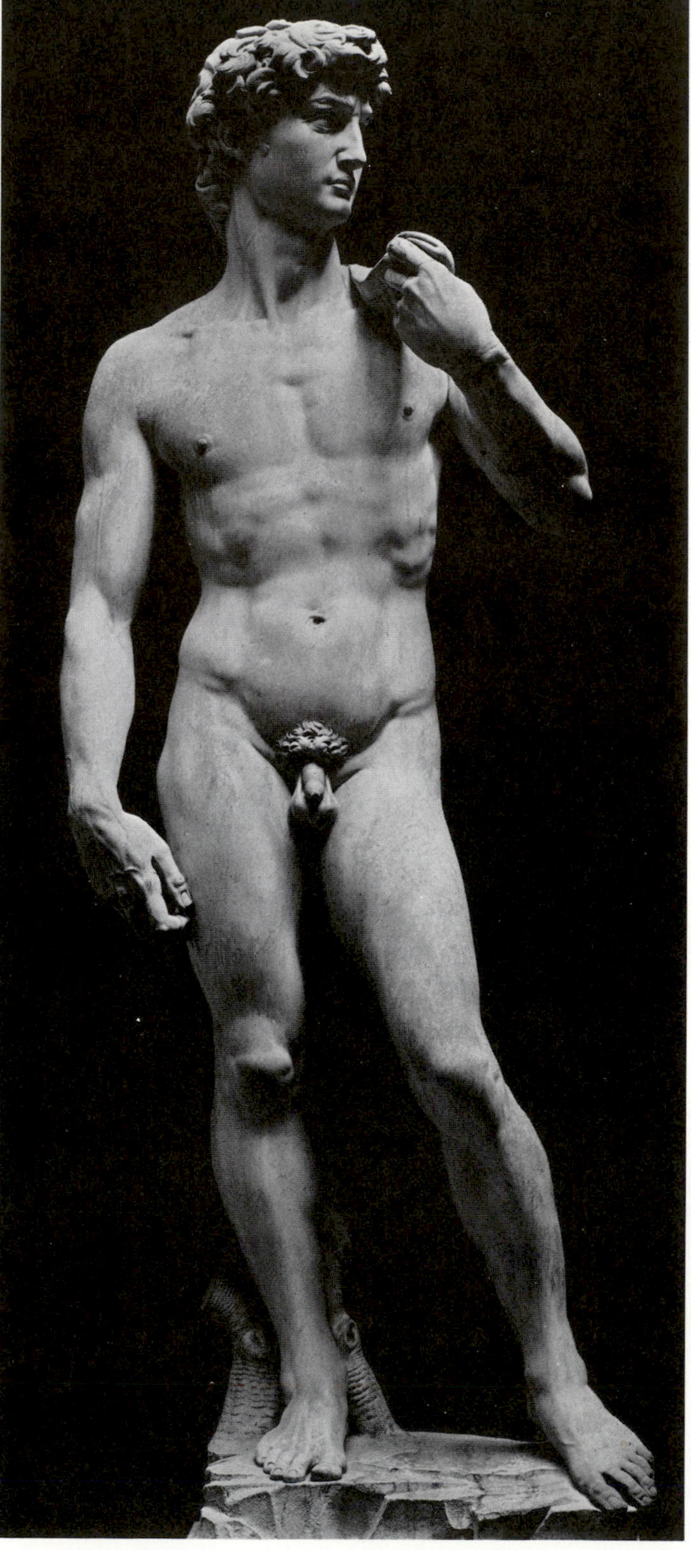

Michelangelo's giant (18-foot-tall) statue of David (*c.* 1504) symbolized the new heroic ideal—the young David, a humble shepherd had slain the fearsome Goliath.

center stage and relegate the vocal lines to subsidiary roles. This imperils melodic integrity—the harmony may demand a series of repeated notes or a series of leaps for one part or another, resulting in lines with no redeeming melodic significance. Maintaining a balance between vertical and horizontal features is a noble goal, but it is exceedingly difficult to attain.

The mass continued to receive preeminent attention throughout the rest of the fifteenth century and into the early sixteenth century. It was polyphonic in character with strong harmonic implications, and a variety of polyphonic techniques were employed within a single work. Canons, both plain and fancy, were used, but were normally limited to short sections and to two vocal lines. Within the four-voice texture, which had become the norm, polyphonic treatment tended to be less strict. In a free form of imitation, a phrase might begin with the voices entering separately in imitative fashion, and be completed as they continued their separate ways to a cadence. But there were also phrases in which all the voices shared a single rhythmic pattern, each singing the same text syllable simultaneously. This technique, taken over from the popular street songs, was called the *familiar* style. In the hands of the imaginative Netherlanders, it became a powerful contrast to the *learned (or imitative)* style, and was used at moments of climax or to emphasize important words of text. In other techniques, different melodies might be combined, or similar melodies might be set to different rhythms.

Renaissance scientific study included optics, which entered painting through the use of unusual perspectives. In 1524 the young artist Parmigianino painted a self-portrait showing himself in a convex mirror.

Later, the goal of musical momentum led to the weakening of interior cadences. Instead of all the voices coinciding rhythmically at the end of every phrase, vocal lines were phrased individually. A seamless fabric was thus created, which extended—sometimes without break—to the sectional cadence, or even to the final cadence. Sectional cadences frequently used chords with thirds, but the final cadence, representing a last link with the Medieval era, most often avoided the third and culminated in a sonority of intervals of the unison, octave, and fifth.

Each line of a Renaissance mass was melodic; linear independence was maintained through contrasting contours and rhythms, and through varying the vertical intervals between each pair of voices. Parallel fifths—the backbone of early organum—were shunned as if they threatened the body politic. Melodic independence might be established at the beginning of each

In glorifying the humble, the Renaissance artist also faced and accepted the homely. Durer's charcoal drawing of his mother (1514) is as candid and truthful as a snapshot.

section by staggered entries, or the four voices might enter either simultaneously or in pairs. The range of most lines was at least an octave and a half, and the combined ranges generally exceeded two and a half octaves. This extension in total range was primarily in the lower register, reflecting the new prominence of the bass.

The bass line, functioning as harmonic foundation, was superseding the tenor in the organization of pitch materials, but the tenor still retained possession of the *cantus firmus*—the plainchant melody that unified the structure. Plainchant itself, however, was encountering strong competition from secular sources; in many instances, the chant melody was supplanted by a popular tune or a chanson melody, which assumed the role of cantus firmus and formed the melodic basis for an entire mass. Chant had suffered distortion at the hands of composers of melismatic organum, but its exclusion from any part in a musical setting of the mass was a radical departure—indicating, perhaps, the extent to which musical concerns had overpowered liturgical tradition in the minds of composers. To the twentieth-century mind, the use of any preexisting melody as a basis for musical creation may seem strange. Originality in the early sixteenth century, however, was measured in terms of the imaginative selection and treatment of a known melody rather than the invention of a totally new work. Masses were named for the source of their materials, so a mass might have a highly secular title (*Missa Baisez-moy,* for example, to be translated as the "Kiss Me Mass"). Or, strangely, when the mass was not based on any prior material (a new but increasingly popular practice), it might have the name *Missa Sine Nomine,* or "Mass without a Name."

Performance focused on the sound of voices in combination throughout the mass. The Medieval ideal of color contrast, both by juxtaposition and by combination, was replaced by a desire for consistency in color and blend of combined sounds. Contrast was achieved through changes of density (varying the number of vocal lines), changes in tessitura, and the use of different styles of polyphony. Choruses were small by our standards, with only two or three men or boys singing each line. Instrumental doubling of voice parts for certain sections provided additional contrast, and often proved a practical solution to pitch problems as well.

JOSQUIN

The leading Franco-Flemish composer in Italy was Josquin des Prez (c. 1445–1521), usually called "Josquin." His life span paralleled that of Leonardo da Vinci, and his fame was comparable. Much of his career was spent in Italy, where he served in Milan, Florence, Modena, Ferrara, and at the Papal chapel. He gave definitive shape to the early Renaissance mass, and his works were held to exemplify the ideal of choral sound throughout most of the sixteenth century.

In his secular works, Josquin often used his great contrapuntal skill to promote the cause of fun and frolic. "Baisez-moy" is one such song. In this performance, an instrumental quartet, consisting of treble recorder, minstrel's harp, and two tenor viols, begins the song and continues in an accompanying capacity after the entrance of the solo tenor voice. A vocal quartet (soprano, two tenors, and baritone) then takes over and subjects the frivolous text to rigorous contrapuntal treatment. In listening to this song, one tends to focus on linear progression, but vertical interest is strong, and at times harmony becomes a competing factor. Rhythm is less complex than was often the case in late Medieval music, and the beat subdivision of twos is characteristic of Renaissance rhythmic preference.

Side 4 Band 1

Music for instruments, having languished in neglect for centuries, began to receive a measure of attention from composers in the first half of the sixteenth century. Instrument-makers prospered as the new ideals of blend and homogeneous color demanded the creation of families of string groups or wind instruments. Each family, or *consort,* consisted of graduated sizes of a single instru-

Monks singing in choir. The volumes from which they read were often much larger than the one in this 15th-century woodcut.

ment type, corresponding in range generally to the various ranges of human voices. Performance of vocal pieces by these consorts was nothing new in principle—instrumentalists had been doing just that for several centuries. The difference was that, in the sixteenth century, they were *invited* to perform—on the printed page. Title-page indications such as "to be played or sung" suggested that instruments and voices possessed equivalent musical potential.

Solo Instrumental Music

Perhaps the most radical change in instrumental music was the new popularity of solo instruments. This phenomenon had no counterpart in the Medieval period; its appearance during the Renaissance, and its focus on an individual performer, was consistent with—if not inspired by—Renaissance philosophy. Foremost among solo instruments was the lute, which had been used extensively in Spain since the eleventh century. Its use slowly spread across the continent, and it became the most widely performed instrument of the sixteenth century. Medieval musicians had known the lute and used it as a linear instrument; Renaissance musicians were attracted to it because its ability to articulate several melodies simultaneously made possible the performance of a polyphonic work in a homogeneous sound, by one player. It was remarkably well adapted to the polyphonic-harmonic style of the century, and its importance is reflected in the large quantity of music published for it. This music was not "for voices or lute," but specifically and only "for lute."

The organ had developed apace during the fifteenth century, and by the start of the sixteenth it had become a formidable instrument. Like the lute, it could play single tones, multiple melodies, or chords. It had an array of contrasting tone colors that could be used separately or in imaginative combinations. In dynamic potential the organ ranged from a soft, flute-like tone to a full-throated roar that could startle resident cathedral bats into daytime flight. Because an organ had both manual and pedal boards, the organist activated tones with both hands and feet, so the organ could (and still can) produce more simultaneous notes and melodies than any other instrument. Composers were keenly aware of the polyphonic potential of this instrument, and a sizable body of organ literature accumulated during the century. Northern countries led the way in enlarging the scope of the organ, both in developing the instrument itself and in creating music designed for it.

The invention of processes for printing notes gave strong impetus to the growth of instrumental music, and "how-to-play" books came along soon after printed music appeared. These, in turn, further encouraged nonprofessionals to try their hand at playing an instrument, and amateur music making thrived in small homes as well as in elegant courts. The advent of music printing advanced the cause of music by making it widely available. But it must also have contributed to the gradual decline in improvisation that eventually led to the printed-page paralysis that afflicts so many performers today.

The increasing prominence of instrumental performance led to the development of forms appropriate to a nonverbal medium, and one of the most important of these was the *set of variations.* Medieval performers had presented variations on a melody simultaneously, but a succession of several variations was an innovation. The usual procedure involved a straightforward presentation of a theme (often a popular song) followed by a series of variations that were often cumulative in rhythmic activity, so that each variation was more active than its predecessor. Basic pulse and harmonic structure were maintained throughout; melody was the primary subject for variation, and embellishment and elaboration were the principal techniques employed.

Another type of variation was based on an *ostinato* (p. 71), repeated throughout the work, above which a series of contrapuntal variations were constructed. The ostinato was the constant factor, and normally it remained unchanged; the variations consisted of polyphonic elaborations in the upper voices. Variations were composed throughout Western Europe, primarily for lute and keyboard instruments—and, of course, master performers continued to improvise them. The form has proved durable—every generation of composers from the sixteenth through the twentieth century has written one or both types of variation.

Secular Vocal Music

The Flemish domination of sacred music was Continental in scope—every major country felt this influence, either directly through resident composers, or indirectly, through knowledge and use of Flemish music. Secular music, on the other hand, developed somewhat independently in each country, and by the mid-sixteenth century, distinctive national styles were beginning to take shape.

Italy, although continuing to import Flemish composers for important chapel positions, was developing a measure of musical self-sufficiency. A new generation of native-born musicians, many of whom were students of the Netherlanders, was providing Italian courts with secular music in a style quite different from the prevailing polyphony. Early in the century, the most popular Italian song form was the *frottola,* a somewhat formalized homophonic setting with a melody in the upper voice and harmonic accompaniment in the lower voices, in the manner of the older street song. Performance was by soloists; the top line was probably sung, and lower lines were sung or played, but by individuals in either case. Frottolas were simple and direct in their appeal, and those written by Flemish composers suggest that in a small way the form reversed the usual flow of musical influence.

By mid-century, the frottola had given way in popularity to the *madrigal*—a type that has come to be as closely associated with Renaissance music as is the lute. Renaissance madrigals were vocal music, sung one person to a part; instruments and chorus were equally inappropriate to their performance. The recorded example, "Saccio na cosa" ("One Thing I Know"), by Roland de Lassus, exemplifies the early ideal of the madrigal when it was still close to the frottola in style. For four voices, this piece is in the familiar style, with all parts singing the same words in the same rhythm. It is fleet, light, and delightfully energized.

Side 4 Band 2

The madrigal text was most often a love poem (often erotic), and an important facet of the style was a constant musical allusion to individual words—high notes for the word "heaven," for example—that delighted the performers, who sang only for themselves. The number of performers corresponded to the number of voice parts, and five lines was the norm at the madrigal's height of popularity. Madrigals were polyphonic in that no one line predominated in interest; all lines were melodic, and imitation was a prominent feature of the style. But harmony was not absent; some madrigals had contrasting sections in familiar style, and, even in polyphonic portions, melodic interest was sometimes sacrificed for the sake of rich harmonic progressions. Madrigals were designed for amateur singers and for performance in the home, so women were not excluded. The inclusion of female voices made possible an upward extension of range, resulting in a wider total vocal range than ever before. The madrigal was a uniquely Italian development that found eager acceptance throughout the Continent, by both importation and imitation.

Surrounded by courtiers, instruments, and singers, Emperor Maximilian I has a music lesson.

MUSIC IN GERMANY

Early in the sixteenth century, prospects for music in German-speaking countries brightened considerably. The meistersinger guilds persisted in their unrelenting pursuit of codified mediocrity, but, hermetically sealed off from change, they neither influenced nor were affected by the rise of a national style. Two circumstances contributed significantly to the vigorous growth of a German style: resident Franco-Flemish composers at noble courts, and the grass-roots music of the Reformation and the Lutheran church.

The Lied

During the fifteenth century, the *lied* (plural: *lieder*), a secular song with a German text, based on Germanic folk melody, had developed apart from the music of the minnesingers and meistersingers. In style, the lied was Medieval; that is, it was either monophonic or, if polyphonic, it was cast in a three-voice texture dominated by the tenor line. The old-fashioned settings, however, did not detract from the inherent beauty of the German melodies, which lured resident Netherlanders away from their preoccupation with sacred music. In their ventures into the composition of lieder they applied their highly developed contrapuntal skills to the creation of polyphonic part songs, transforming the texture of the lied while maintaining its basic German character. The wedding of the lied and the madrigal occurred shortly after mid-century, largely in the songs of Roland de Lassus (c. 1531–1594), the last of the great Netherlanders. His early sojourns in Italy (where he was called Orlando di Lasso) acquainted him with mid-century developments in Italian music, and when he accepted a ducal post in Bavaria Lassus brought the Renaissance with him. His lieder represent a fusion of the best in Flemish polyphonic technique, Italian madrigal style, and German melodic expression.

LASSUS

Lutheran Music

Since their noble patrons were Catholic, the Netherlanders were in no position to contribute directly to the development of Lutheran music. But they may have affected the movement obliquely through Luther's admiration for Flemish polyphony. It was Luther's associates, however, who influenced most profoundly the direction taken by music in the Lutheran church, especially with their adoption of the *chorale* (hymn tune) as an integral part of the service, and with their emphasis on singing by the congregation. Group singing presupposes familiarity with the melodic material, so the use of folk and popular melodies as chorale tunes was a natural result of congregational participation. Originally sung in unison, chorales soon received both harmonic and polyphonic settings; thus the course of the chorale paralleled the earlier course of chant. Germanic in both origin and character, the chorale was conducive to the development of a national musical style, and it was to serve continuously as a melodic basis for instrumental and choral works throughout the future of German music.

MUSIC IN ENGLAND

In England, the Reformation played a less prominent role in the growth of a national style. The creation of the Anglican Church had occurred through political decree rather than doctrinal dissidence, so there was less reason to replace plainchant as the musical mainstay. Only through the addition of the *anthem,* a motet in familiar style with an English text, did the Anglicans depart from Roman Catholic musical tradition. English congregations did not participate in the Anglican service; anthems were composed for trained choirs of men and boys and were an ornamental rather than an integral part of the service.

British composers, by and large, were an insular lot. Even in Medieval days, they had frequently disregarded Continental trends and had gone their separate way, happily indulging their natural penchant for vertical sonorities. When the Italian madrigal reached England at the end of the sixteenth century, however, it captivated the English immediately, and they were among the most enthusiastic imitators of that genre. So popular was madrigal singing in England that the ability to read a part ranked with the ability to sit a horse well as a social requirement among the gentry. English madrigals were, not surprisingly, somewhat more harmonic than their Italian counterparts. Frequently they employed nonsense syllables, such as "fa-la-la" and "hey-nonny-nonny"—English expressions of exuberance that found their twentieth-century voice in the "Yeah, yeah, yeah" of The Beatles. "My Bonny Lass She Smileth," by Thomas Morley (1557–1603), is typical, with a basic chordal five-part texture and a fa-la-la refrain that gives lip service to imitation but quickly returns to pure harmony. The basic metric grouping of fours is interrupted by a short section in threes—also typical of this style. The second verse repeats the music of the first. **Side 4 Band 3**

Madrigals were for amateurs to sing; professional singers specialized in solo songs, accompanying themselves on the lute. The English language was producing poetry and drama of transcendent value—this was the time of Shakespeare—and it was natural for lyric song to flourish as well. John Dowland (1563–1626) was a poet-composer-singer-lutenist whose lute songs were among the most popular ever written. His "Come Again! Sweet Love" begins with two graceful phrases that yield to a gently insistent rising sequence, and that in turn yields to a concluding line; both the sequence and the concluding line are repeated. The whole is repeated for six verses, of which three are included here. This performance, by a countertenor, is appropriate, since that voice was the most highly prized in Elizabethan England—as it had been for the previous three centuries. **Side 4 Band 4**

Solo lute pieces were also popular. These were often improvisational (like the *fantasia,* or, in English, the *fancy*), or else they were stylized dances. Dowland's son Robert Dowland (d. 1641) published *A Variety of Lute Lessons,* a volume for amateurs of unusual skill. "Queen Elizabeth's Galliard," one of the lute pieces in that volume, calls for near-professional dexterity and speed. The form is simple: two short sections, each of which is repeated with embellishments—the same dance form that was by then a long-established tradition. **Side 4 Band 5**

But the great love of amateur instrumentalists was the harpsichord, especially the small, portable models called virginals. A large quantity of lute music was transcribed for it, and more important, British composers had a strong affinity for the harpsichord, and it was their music that first exploited the full potential of this instrument. Their harpsichord writing was genuinely idiomatic—it contained chords and running passages encompassing the full available range. Many pieces, especially those of John Bull (c. 1562–1628), were vehicles for the virtuoso, containing displays of technical derring-do designed to astound and delight the listener. Other pieces were simple, both in technique and in form, and were readily accessible to the amateur. This music continues to have an important place in harpsichord literature and is occasionally programed by pianists—a fact that inevitably causes a debate between those who welcome any opportunity to hear seldom-performed music and those who feel strongly that the piano is totally inappropriate for music conceived for harpsichord.

The British were also mavericks in their treatment of instrumental ensembles. Rather than the homogeneous consort (page 85), they sometimes favored a "broken" consort, which included one contrasting instrument in an otherwise unified combination. The unrelated instrument was usually high in pitch. Its melodic role was an active one, and by virtue of its differing tone color it stood out in sharp relief from the basic group. Broken consorts were more ideally suited to a homophonic texture than to separate-but-equal-voiced polyphony—the disproportionate amount of attention attracted by a contrasting color inevitably makes that part more "equal" than the others.

THE LATE RENAISSANCE IN ITALY

Throughout the sixteenth century, musical innovation increasingly centered in Italy, and by the end of the century Italy was universally acknowledged as the leader of the West. Important musical posts on the Continent and in Britain were filled by Italians, and with the exception of keyboard music, Italy set the trends.

The Polyphonic Madrigal

Having captivated Europe with the part-song madrigal, Italian composers moved on to develop the madrigal form along different lines. The "new" style, cast in the prevailing polyphonic idiom of five or six linear parts, was designed for solo voice and an accompanying instrument, usually the lute. This combination was a sort of two-performer broken consort: the lute, playing four or five parts, served as a basic "group," and the voice, having sole possession of the text and offering contrast in color as well, assumed a position of dominance that exceeded any inherent importance in its melodic line. The solo madrigal, which was

principally a performance style rather than a new form at the end of the sixteenth century, foreshadowed an emphasis on the accompanied solo voice that was to dominate the seventeenth century.

Renaissance power was represented architecturally in size, weight, and symmetry—a symbolism carried into the 17th century, when projects achieved monumental size. The Basilica of St. Peter in Rome, already the most immense church in Christendom, was given a piazza to match its splendor, designed by Bernini and begun in 1656.

Instrumental Music

Italian influence on forms of organ music was found primarily in the *fantasia, toccata,* and *canzona.* These were works in which imitative and chordal sections alternated, often connected by running passages in improvisatory style. Changes in tempo were characteristic of such pieces, and they frequently offered the organist an opportunity for a display of virtuosity. The organ *ricercar* originated as a comparable form, but toward the end of the century this term began to be associated with imitative works based on one melodic idea.

Dance music continued to enjoy great popularity throughout the Renaissance, and as instrumental ensembles began to perform for listeners, they naturally drew on this source for their repertoire. Contrasting dances were combined into *suites,* which could be tailored to any desired length by the simple expedient of including more or fewer dances. As these suites became divorced from actual dancing, the musical organization of their separate movements acquired increased importance, resulting in the development and adoption of *binary form* as the norm for a single dance. At the end of the Renaissance, binary form consisted of two sections of equivalent length, each of which was repeated, and each of which was marked by a cadence of appropriate weight. Dances chosen for inclusion in a suite might be only loosely related. Normally they were all in the same key, but the process of organizing a suite was one of selection rather than of composition.

Late Renaissance practice extended polychoral principles to apply to instrumental ensembles as well as choirs. Antiphonal use of instruments developed primarily in Venice, and normally involved two consorts, blended or broken, which played both alternately and in combination. One performer for each line of music continued to be the rule, and all instruments playing together produced polyphony of eight or more parts. (The number of parts was even more impressive in choral music, which occasionally featured linear combinations in excess of twenty.)

Sacred Music

By the last quarter of the sixteenth century, Italian domination of music extended even to music for the Catholic Church. The dethroning of the Netherlanders in Italy was undoubtedly hastened by the decision of Lassus to leave Italy and make his career elsewhere. Roland de Lassus, more than any other composer, typified the best in both sacred and secular late Renaissance music. Had this last—and perhaps greatest—of the Netherlanders remained in Rome, his influence might well have delayed or diluted the totality of Italian dominance in musical style.

Another event that served to end Flemish musical supremacy in Italy was the Council of Trent (1545–1563), convened by the Roman Catholic Church as the chief arm of the Counter-Reformation in acknowledgment of the need for reform. The Counter-Reformation gave the Council of Trent a broad mandate concerning the removal of abuses within the Catholic Church, and music was among the subjects that came under scrutiny. For a while, the

Council considered outlawing polyphony altogether, but musicians who participated in the final decisions quite naturally opposed any such reactionary step. The final decree was something of an appeal to composers to shape their music with the needs of the Church in mind; no specific techniques were forbidden, but the appropriateness of a reverent spirit was strongly underscored.

PALESTRINA

The ideals of the Counter-Reformation are best represented in the music of Giovanni Pierluigi da Palestrina (c. 1526–1594). His career centered in Rome, and he devoted himself almost exclusively to sacred vocal music. A wide array of styles can be found in his compositions, ranging from canonic writing in the best Flemish tradition to simple harmonic settings; but most of his works are freely imitative, organized on a phrase-by-phrase basis for greater clarity of text. Stepwise motion predominates in his melodies, which are usually little more than an octave in range; his sympathetic handling of vocal lines made the ideal of *a cappella* (unaccompanied) performance a practical reality. Palestrina reinstated plainchant as the cantus firmus, enhancing it only with simple, diatonic harmonies. The sensual chord progressions so beloved by Italians are conspicuously absent from Palestrina's music. Rhythmically, the music is simple and straightforward, giving the impression of regular meter with consistent subdivisions, usually of twos.

Side 4 Band 6

The Kyrie of his *Missa Ascendo ad Patrem* ("I Go to the Father") typifies the reverent spirit of Palestrina's choral music. Elements associated with stress—wide range, extreme tessitura, loud dynamic level, rhythmic conflict, and so on—are avoided; tension intrudes only in the harmony, and harmonic dissonances are both introduced and resolved with consummate smoothness. Five-voice texture predominates, but textural variety is introduced through occasional reductions in the number of voices and, as the work progresses, through increased contrapuntal activity. The construction of the music belies its effect: the structure is very solid, but the sound it conveys is ethereal.

Palestrina was no innovator—there are, in fact, hints of Medieval style in his use of a limited melodic range, his return to plainchant, and his diatonic harmony. That he is today the best-known, most frequently performed composer of the late Renaissance period is a tribute to the timelessness of his somewhat eclectic, personal style.

COMPARATIVE STYLE CHARACTERISTICS

	LATE MEDIEVAL PERIOD	TRANSITION AND EARLY RENAISSANCE	MIDDLE AND LATE RENAISSANCE
TEXTURE	three-voice texture linear concept	four-voice texture primarily linear concept; some harmonic emphasis	five-voice texture equality of harmonic and linear concepts
CADENCES	long note in all voices octave, unison and fifth used as cadential intervals	long notes in some voices held while others begin a new phrase many cadences using octave, unison and fifth; some including the third	lines cadencing separately rather than simultaneously, creating a "seamless" effect the third as standard in coinciding cadences
POLYPHONY	canonic combination of different melodies	canonic combination of different melodies entry in pairs	free imitation, sometimes occurring only briefly
HARMONY		harmony in some popular music (familiar style)	harmonic passages used in contrasting sections
RHYTHM	cross-rhythms variable pulse variable subdivisions distinctive rhythm in each voice	less use of cross-rhythms pulse more regular some rhythmic patterns occurring simultaneously in two or more voices	uniformity of pulse uniformity of subdivisions
RANGE AND TESSITURA	high men's voices, tenor, and countertenor high tessitura	range extended downward to include bass high tessitura	range extended both upward and downward more natural tessitura
VOCAL FORMS	organum motet chanson mass	motet chanson mass frottola	motet chanson mass madrigal lied

	LATE MEDIEVAL PERIOD	TRANSITION AND EARLY RENAISSANCE	MIDDLE AND LATE RENAISSANCE
USE OF VOICES	ensemble singing—multiple performers for each line of music, alternating with soloists	ensemble singing—multiple performers for each line throughout an entire work variety in the number of lines present	ensemble singing—one performer for each line of music (madrigal) multiple performers (mass)
INSTRUMENTAL FORMS	estampie	estampie	set of variations dance suite
USE OF INSTRUMENTS	instruments combined and alternating with voices little instrumental music except for dancing and instrumental performance of songs heterogeneous groups	instruments combined with voices, doubling vocal lines, or with independent parts instrumental music for dancing and instrumental performance of songs mixed groups	unaccompanied voices the ideal instrumental music for listening as well as dancing homogeneous consorts
INSTRUMENTAL TONE COLOR	contrast, whether used simultaneously or consecutively	contrast in dance music, both blend and contrast	blend homogeneous consorts
SOLO INSTRUMENTS	none (except within a work involving other performers or in folk performance)	lute organ	lute clavichord harpsichord organ guitar in Spain

6. Instruments

THE LUTE

THE AMAZING POPULARITY of the lute in Western Europe in the sixteenth century was part of a web of interacting musical, social, economic, cultural, and other aspects of European life at that time. The lute was, in that sense, a phenomenon of its time and place.

First, of course, were the musical factors at the end of the fifteenth century: the host of well-known street tunes, generally played by ear in the popular tradition; a new fashion of homogeneous sound that was soon to produce the ideal of the consort; and a sudden musical concentration on exactly the kind of vertical sonorities that the lute could produce easily and idiomatically, incorporating the full bass-to-soprano range of human voices.

But of course there was more to the lute's popularity than that. New ideas were creating social patterns new to Europe. Perhaps the most revolutionary idea was the establishment of a new kind of family life in a new kind of environment. Whereas the Medieval pattern had been castle or hovel, feast or famine, unreasonable wealth or squalid poverty, too much leisure or no leisure at all, the new ideal of the family was of something between those extremes: enough to eat but not enough to waste, a reasonable amount of money, a balance of some leisure with a good deal of work, and a small but comfortable kind of dwelling eventually to be called a house or home. It is not hard to imagine what a difference a few seemingly simple changes in living arrangements would make in the daily round—wood floors, for example, and glass windows, which would let in light but keep out cold and damp. The acoustical change from an open hut to a wood-floored room was tremendous, so that the gentle lute could be savored in a Renaissance living room as it could not have been in either a hut or a huge, high-ceilinged castle hall.

Lute playing by ordinary people, then, had not been possible socially in the Medieval era; it would not have been economically possible, either. The economic setup of Medieval Europe allowed the commoners only the instruments they could make for themselves out of materials ready at hand. They could knock the pith out of a good slender branch of a birch or pear tree and make a pipe, they could use the bladder of a slaughtered animal for bagpipes, and go to the river to find a reed for it; they could hammer scraps of metal into finger cymbals; and they could use

A lute made in 1607 by a Flemish artisan, Magnus Tieffenbrucker II. The central hole on the face of the instrument, which aids resonance, has grillwork insets called rosettes. In Renaissance lutes these were often extremely beautiful. The rosette of this lute is shown in detail below.

anything, from discarded cooking pots to molded clay, from wood to metal, to fashion drums. And, of course, they were born with voices to sing with, hands to clap, and feet to stamp—all of which they used constantly and inventively. The other end of the economic ladder found kings and lesser nobles buying musicians as well as instruments—housing an entire musical retinue to whom a variety of instruments were furnished. There were the minstrels, whose duties were various and who were expected to play a number of instruments well and, of course, to recite and sing. Since the recounting of noble deeds in song was politically important to the musicians' employers, minstrels who performed those songs held the most prestigious jobs. For these performances, the lute was a purely supportive instrument, used by the singer as the harp or lyre had been since ancient times.

Economically, the Renaissance offered conditions favorable for the development of a solo art for the lute. The new kind of family had a business or vocation that provided the basic frame of daily life necessary for such an art. First, although these families could not afford to maintain musical retinues, they could afford the purchase of a lute and the services of a teacher to help them learn to play it. And they had enough time for practicing to acquire amateur skills—literally, the skills of one who plays for the love of it.

The implications of this development were enormous. First, of course, the number of lute players multiplied rapidly. This in turn created both a group of highly intelligent listeners—an audience of amateurs who could fully appreciate the skill of the professional performer—and a market for the purchase of sheet music, just at the time that the techniques for printing music had been developed to the point of practicality.

Second, the establishment of the first businessmen and their amateur enjoyments led to the need for still other businesses. The need for a great many instruments led to the profession of *luthier,* or lute-maker (a name kept even when, later, he became a violinmaker). The need for teachers led to the concept of a tutor, who made his living not in one household but piecemeal in a number of households—and lo, the modern music teacher had appeared. And the need for multiple copies of easy and popular music led to the development of the professions of music printing and publishing. All these professions were new in the Renaissance, adding ascending rungs to the socioeconomic ladder and extending purchasing power downward.

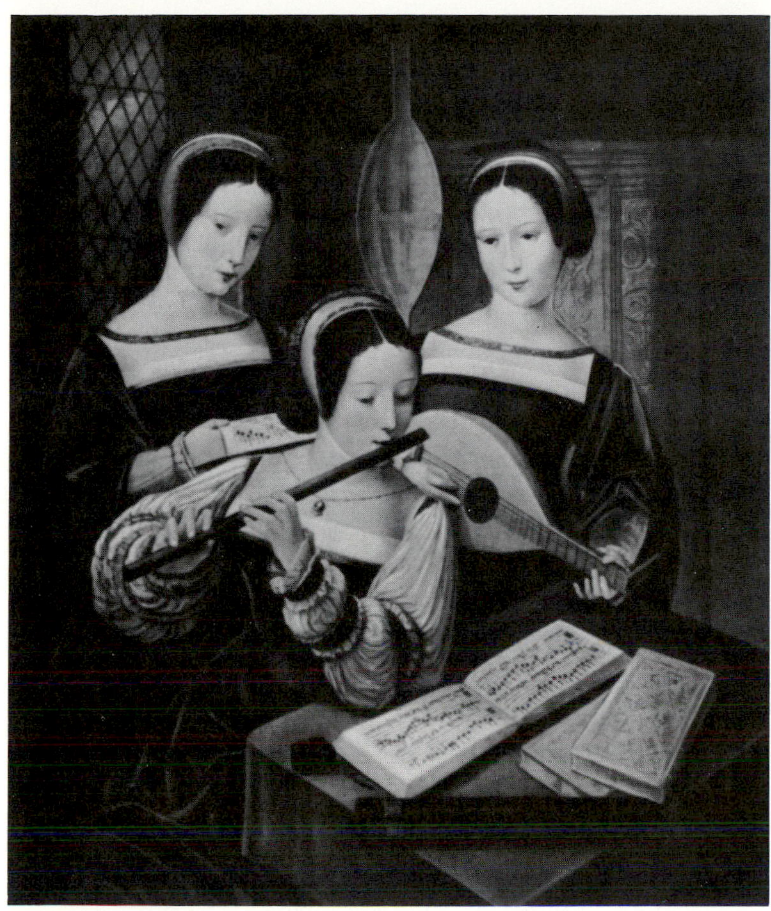

An anonymous English painting shows three women making music with contrasting sounds of voice, flute, and small lute.

Thus the lute, in the Renaissance, had both musical and economic clout; it was important culturally as well. The Renaissance was a time of experimentation. It was an era that delighted in any union of art and science; it was a period of veneration and imitation of ancient Greek ideas; and it was a period of humanism, when Man-as-Hero—a standard of accomplishment rather than noble birth—was the central focus. Instrument-making was experimental, and the lute was seen as an instrument of antiquity, equated with the lyre of classical Greece; its vogue was in large part associated, in the Renaissance mind, with its supposed heritage. Both lute making and lute playing were held to be blends of science and art—a concept that remains today in regard to performance, in which technique and interpretation are the two interdependent criteria of excellence in performance. And finally, the humanist ideas of the time opened vistas not only for amateurs—who could feel that their own talents (given by God) and their own work (brought about by their own efforts) were enough to make them lutenists—but more importantly for professionals, whose skills, fully appreciated by their audiences, were

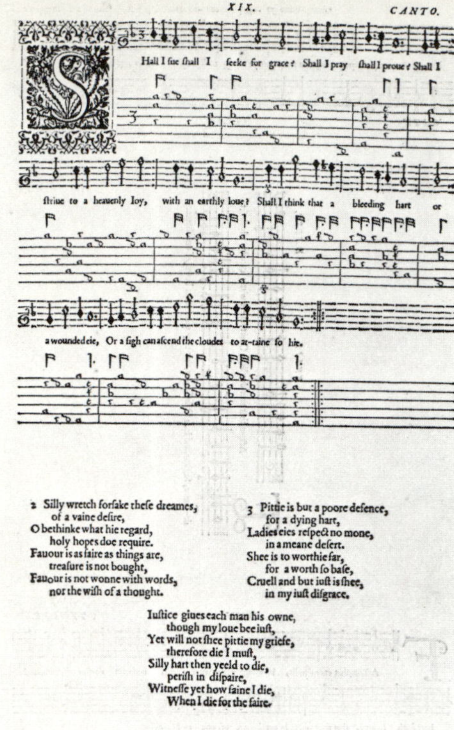

John Dowland's lute song, "Shall I Sue." The placement of the three lower parts is for the convenience of singers seated around a table.

seen as superhuman, heroic. In Italian, the term describing such skills is *virtuoso,* a word coined by awe-struck Renaissance audiences in admiration for the science-art of the great lutenists of the sixteenth century.

The history of every instrument can be discussed in similar terms, although few instruments have ever enjoyed the popularity of the lute in the sixteenth century. In the West, only the lyre in Greece and the piano in nineteenth- and twentieth-century Europe and America have enjoyed comparable careers. Beyond the Western tradition, a variety of equally popular instruments have flourished, and several of these—notably panpipes, natural flutes, drums, and bagpipes—have surpassed the lute both in longevity and geographical scope.

THE SANSA

The enduring popularity of the versatile African *sansa,* or thumb piano, spans many centuries and continues unabated. Basically, the sansa is a box, to which anywhere from five to twenty narrow split-cane or metal "tongues" are fastened over a narrow stick. The sansa is played by holding the box in both hands, pushing the tongues down with the thumbs, and releasing them suddenly, causing the tongues to vibrate. Because the tongues vary in number and can be adjusted in sounding length (hence in pitch), no standard of tuning for the sansa exists. Sansas vary not only in size and shape: some are attached to resonators to make them louder, and some have *mirlitons*—"windows" on the sides, filled with spider webs or bark or membrane, for added buzz. But they all have tongues, and they are all played with the push-and-release technique.

The social, economic, and cultural history of the sansa is as interesting as that of the lute. The African societies that popularized the sansa were those in which skill on a musical instrument could be encouraged on an individual basis. In ancient days, these included the herding and food-gathering peoples whose members could play while on a long hike or while guarding animals or crops. Like the shepherd's pipe, the sansa is a good instrument for a person to play on solitary marches or on a lonely evening in the field. But unlike the pipe, the sansa can also be used to accompany the player's own singing, and unlike the lute, it can be played easily while standing or walking—children play it while

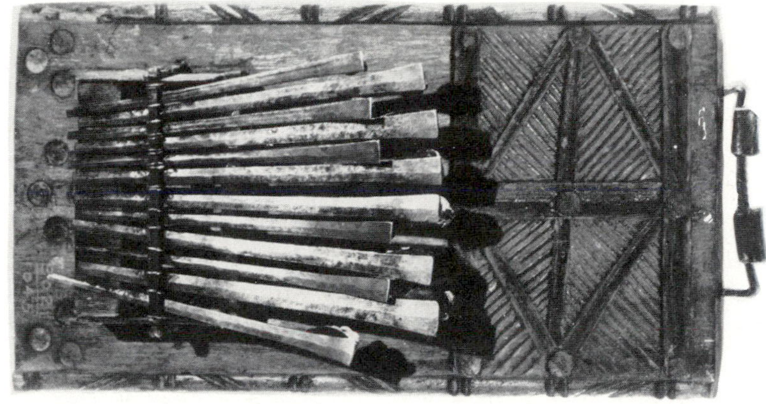

A twelve-tongued sansa. The depth of the box adds resonance, and the attached spool rattles add a mirliton-like effect.

running. It thus can claim a great versatility of musical usage duplicated only by the piano—which, to use an understatement, is not particularly portable. The sansa is a unique instrument, capable of both deep introversion and stunning virtuoso extroversion. Techniques of performance are highly individual, so that the art of the sansa is a particularly rich one.

The Nyari people of Central Africa are one of many who use the sansa. Like the lutenist-singer of Renaissance England, the Nyari singer is a poet, melodist, and instrumental virtuoso. In the recorded example, he begins with a short introduction that displays the pitch potential of his sansa and establishes his considerable skill on the instrument, and then he sings his song, continuing the accompanying pattern during phrases and between them. The sansa in this recording is tuned in thirds, and the singer uses them in a descending pattern that he also imitates in his vocal melody. The use of his thumbs limits him to two notes at once and easily produces a quick steady beat, which in this song accumulates in fours. The buzz on the highest pitch indicates that this sansa utilizes a mirliton.

Side 4 Band 7

THE VOICE

People throughout the world have always made music by singing, but the human voice is not a single type or a single sound. Even in our own culture, many ideals maintain separate vocal traditions, associated with a variety of musical styles and, even more important, with a variety of social functions. The dramatic soprano singing an operatic aria, the ingenue in a Broadway musical, the folk singer doing a ballad with his guitar, the rock lead singer

Small bowl or kettle drums, called *nakers*, are played by an angel carved at the entrance to a church in Italy. Another angel plays a triangle.

backed by a group, the soloist in an anthem in church, the monk or nun singing in chapel, or the cantor chanting in temple—each has a distinct vocal sound, repertoire, technique, and style, and each tradition has its own distinct place of performance and its own audience.

The history of our culture includes vocal types seldom or never heard now: the boy soprano, the countertenor, the castrato, and the coloratura alto and tenor. Moreover, if we go beyond the concert and the formal popular arts, we get to the twangy mountain voice, to field hollers, and to the storytelling vocal types that are as much speech as song. And beyond our culture lie rich vocal techniques—often related to language—of clicks, fricative sounds, yodels, drones, and decorative snaps that are impossible for singers of all but a few cultures.

Because so much music making, in world terms, takes place outdoors, a penetrating nasal quality is common virtually throughout the world. The nasal voice, which European singers shared with much of the world in the Medieval era, is a different type of instrument. It lies best in the upper register; it tends toward an attack not smooth but extremely clear; it is without vibrato; it is versatile in rapid embellishment; and it can be an almost perfect vehicle for the singing of a text.

Thus the human voice is multiple in types, techniques, and styles. Further, it is uniquely fascinating in its intimate link to human personality. Because of this, no two singers—not even two singers of the same type—are really the same.

OTHER INSTRUMENTS

Throughout the world, musical instruments have existed in such an enormous variety that classification by genus and species poses problems. Although no system of grouping is entirely satisfactory, most classifications center on kinds of sound production—either in terms of the physical entity that vibrates (column of air, string, and so on) or the means the performer uses to activate the sound (bowing, plucking, blowing, and so on).

Percussion Instruments

The most universal type of instrument may well be *percussion,* which is usually defined as the category in which tone is produced by striking the instrument. The most widely used percussion instrument is the drum, which is not just one instrument but a variable and diverse series of instruments, having little beyond their percussive nature in common. No single feature of construction is common to all drums, so that the typical definition of a drum as an instrument played by striking a stretched skin or membrane is far from satisfactory. Many drums do have skins, which are pulled across hollow logs, holes in the ground, empty gourds, hollowed-out rocks, or pots of clay or metal. But other drums are made completely of wood or other substance, or have cloth heads instead of skin, or no heads. They range incredibly in size and shape; they are one-headed or two-headed; they often contain seeds or a stone; they are played with sticks, fans, brushes, mallets—and these have heads of leather, wood, wound cloth, reed, or rubber—or by hand, in a host of positions and techniques. Although the sound of a four- or five-inch gourd drum is very high compared with that of a four- or five-foot log drum, few drums have specific pitches. Notable exceptions historically have been Aztec drums, tuned in pairs a fourth or fifth apart; pairs of pot drums like the bongos of Latin America; the *nakers* of Medieval Europe; and the kettledrums (timpani) of the modern symphony orchestra.

This south Indian medieval carving shows a double-head drum, played with the hands. Below, a military drum used during the American Revolution.

Around the world, bells, rattles, gongs, and drums provide basic ceremonial percussion. The practical demands of ceremony have created instruments and have even determined their physical as well as musical nature. The staff rattle of pre-Columbian America, for example, combined the scepter (a symbol of authority and power) with a means for rhythmic pacing of an entrance of dignity. In a march, two men with staff rattles might precede the chief dignitary, pounding the staffs on the ground at each step and turning them between pounds—in either case activating the rattles in rhythmic patterns. An idea of their effect remains in the now-soundless art of baton twirling.

The drums used by mounted soldiers also have a relation to ceremony. Fifteenth-century Polish envoys to France brought mounted drummers with pairs of kettledrums, and created something of a sensation. With one great drum slung on each side of the saddle, the riders were a feast for both eye and ear in their display of crossing hands and twirling sticks. By the beginning of the sixteenth century, such displays were mounted by royalty in

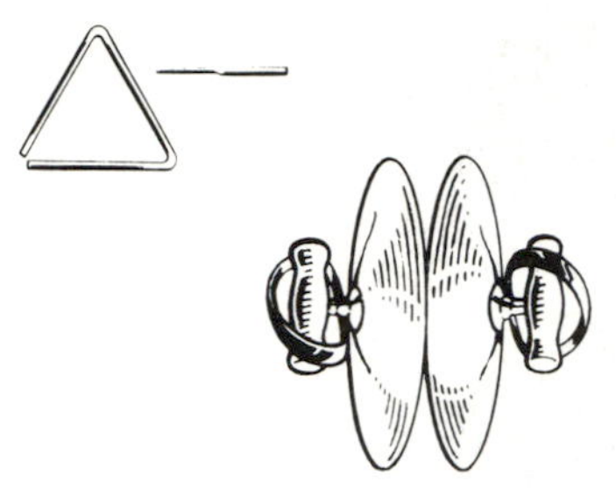

Some percussion instruments. From the top: triangle, cymbals, snare drum, kettledrum.

most European countries; the dignity thus obtained by the kettledrums enabled them to enter and remain in the prestigious world of the symphony orchestra.

Also in worldwide use today are notched scrapers of wood or bone, stick beaters (known in the West as wood blocks), rattles of seemingly endless ingenuity—anklets, bracelets, pendants, cogs, frames, sticks—and gongs of stone or metal whose forms defy categories, except that in each case the whole instrument vibrates. The instruments are scraped, rattled, or struck, as their names suggest, and many of them are tuned.

Inventive peoples all over the world have combined sets of sticks, gongs, or bells of varying sizes to achieve a musical scale. A set of such instruments is used in melodic music, so that its membership in the percussion category is somewhat weakened. Sets of gongs are pictured in paintings from ancient China, and sets of small bells in Medieval illuminations. Sets of great bells or chimes (chimes are tubular and have their own characteristic sound), called *carillons,* are hung in towers. These carillons, which have a range of an octave and a half or more, are made of metal, are hung stationary, and are played by bellropes, by pneumatic levers, or, more recently, from an electric keyboard.

Wood blocks and gongs are put into rows, most often in more directly manageable sets that can be played by a single player. The hugely popular African marimbas (called xylophones in Europe) are, like the sansas, of great variety—most often with a resonator for each slab of wood and sometimes with mirlitons. African marimbas are usually set on low stands or simply on the ground, and the player (or, for large instruments, players) sits in front of it. The marimba is generally a stationary instrument and thus cannot be played as freely as the sansa, but this very quality makes the marimba well suited to group performance and formal occasions.

The essence of percussion instruments is clarity and fascinating sound. Castanets, cymbals (from two inches to two feet or more, made of pounded metal or wound wire), clappers, bull whips—every kind of shape and material that the imagination can devise has provided riches for the ear. And daily objects have served their turn too: in the West, we can still find washboards used as scrapers, and bones or spoons played with verve and style in country dances.

Wind Instruments

Wind instruments, no matter how diverse, share one common factor: a tube or shaft in which an air column vibrates regularly. Subcategories of wind instruments are determined by the method in which air is forced into the shaft and the tone activated. Two methods use the player's lips: flute tone is activated by blowing across a hole that has an angled edge; trumpet tone is activated by stretching the lips across a hole and controlling the flow of air, so that only a part of the air column vibrates. It is possible to duplicate these procedures by blowing across a pop bottle and blowing into a rubber hose.

Natural flutes are made from lengths of bamboo and other branches; natural trumpets are found as shells, often the large marine shell called the *conch* (pronounced "conk"). Conch shells have remarkably loud, coarse voices—often of almost fierce aggressiveness—a quality that has given them universal use as signaling devices. Marine-shell trumpets date from beyond history and have turned up in archaeological digs far from the sea—facts leading to speculation about travel and trade in prehistory. Both flutes and marine-shell trumpets require tooling: the flute needs proper edging, and the trumpet needs a proper blowhole at the end or on the side. The same is true of animal-horn trumpets.

Characteristically, flute tone is as gentle as trumpet tone is stirring; technically, it is close to a *pure* tone, one with few strong overtones and a clear fundamental (page 4). Nonetheless, the flute and the trumpet were closely related in prehistory, for wood trumpets were also made, and in a few cases, instruments were invented with characteristics of both. The "stamping tube," for example, which was common on virtually every continent but Europe, was a long wood or bamboo shaft played by beating against the ground, up and down, striking exactly across the endhole. It was a one-pitch instrument, but could be played in pairs for variety of pitch.

A natural trumpet can sound a number of pitches through the use of varying lip tension; a natural flute can sound only one pitch or, at the most, a fundamental pitch and its octave or fifth. Thus almost all flutes have fingerholes, which enable the player to achieve a variety of pitches by shortening or lengthening the air shaft.

Two ancient instruments. Above, Japanese bowl gongs; right, a Tibetan brass horn.

Some woodwind instruments. Top, flute; right, oboe and clarinet; bottom, bassoon and saxophone.

Unlike marine-shell and horn trumpets, examples of which have occasionally survived over the ages, natural flutes perish easily, and ancient ones are now gone. A second kind of flute—the whistle-head flute—also predates history. Its tone is activated by blowing through a channel that directs the air against a sharp edge. This device was in early days associated with bone flutes. Bones, although providing good shafts once the marrow was removed, are splayed at both ends, thus making it impossible to blow across them successfully. A bone whistle-head flute survives from thirty thousand years ago—it is perhaps the oldest remaining melodic instrument. In modern times, the whistle-head flute is most often made of wood; we call it the recorder.

The flute is the only Western wind instrument to have achieved success in ranks. These rows of tubes, made of wood, clay, stone, or metal, were called panpipes. They enjoyed widespread popularity on all continents, but most especially in ancient Greece and pre-Columbian America.

Instruments that depend on vibrating reeds to activate the air in the shaft have no counterpart in nature. They were first fabricated in the cane-growing areas of the world, and a pair of reeds (called "double") was used to set the air column in vibration. Such instruments were common in both the Near and the Far East in ancient times, but were introduced into Europe only after the Crusades—which broadened the musical horizons, if not the religious tolerance, of the participants.

Two double-reed instruments, the oboe and the bassoon, were charter members of the symphony orchestra. The English horn and the contrabassoon were developed later and did not join the double-reed orchestral section until the mid-nineteenth century.

Single-reed instruments have been slow in gaining entrance to the orchestral inner circles. The clarinet was occasionally included in late-eighteenth-century symphonies, but did not win permanent membership in the orchestra until the dawn of the Romantic era. The saxophone, invented in the nineteenth century, has yet to achieve orchestral respectability. Snubbed by the prim orchestral reeds, this instrument first found welcome in the bordellos of New Orleans, and has attained eminence in jazz.

In the West, wind instruments are categorized either as woodwinds or brasses. These terms serve in describing the wind choirs of the symphony orchestra, in which woodwinds include both flutes and reeds, while brass indicates instruments played with the aid of a metal mouthpiece (trumpet, trombone, French horn, and tuba). Both names are more archaic than accurate; comparatively few modern woodwinds are made from wood, and many of the brasses are fashioned from other metals.

Not all wind instruments are blown outward. Free reeds (that is, a double reed fixed at one end but free at the other) can be blown either outward (by exhaling) or inward (by inhaling). The prototype of free-reed instruments was the Chinese *sheng,* generally made of thirteen sounding pipes (with four silent pipes added so that the instrument could resemble a phoenix), described as early as 1100 B.C. and used into this century. Each of the thirteen sounding pipes had a fingerhole just above the gourd-shaped air reservoir. The player, by covering holes, could prevent a number of pipes from sounding, thus filtering out the unwanted pitches and leaving the rest. Another outward- or inward-blown wind instrument was the small mouth organ, which was common in the Near and Far East by 600 A.D. but which was not made in Europe until the nineteenth century, when it received its modern name, the *harmonica.* The later, larger type was given a keyboard and was called the *harmonium.*

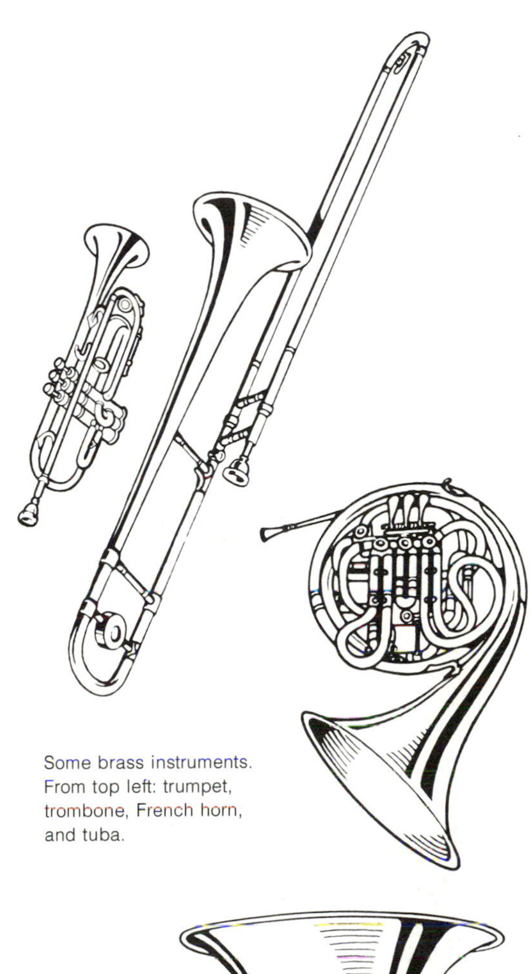

Some brass instruments. From top left: trumpet, trombone, French horn, and tuba.

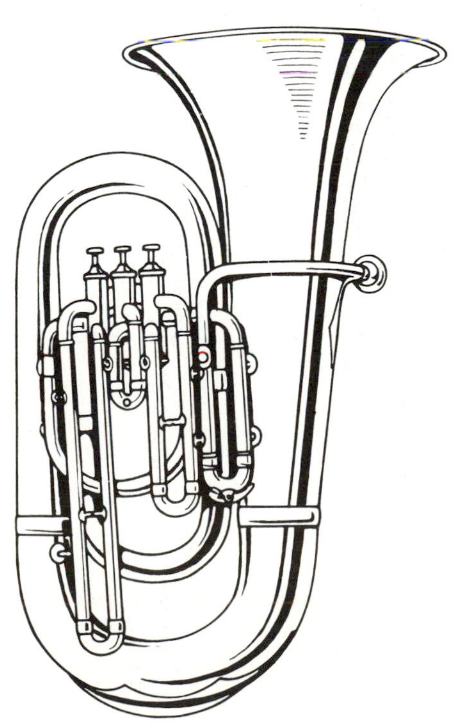

Another free-reed instrument with a keyboard, also European, is the "hand harmonica," better known as the *accordion,* invented in the 1820s. This instrument supplies air to the free reeds by means of a reversible bellows that works by either expansion or compression, the equivalents of inhaling or exhaling. Melody and harmony keys (or buttons) enable the performer to sound both single tones and chords.

Although it is not normally numbered among members of the woodwind family, the organ is, in a sense, simply a gigantic collection of panpipes. This mammoth instrument, which has always been so large that it required a mechanism to activate the flow of air, was the glory of the Baroque era, when it was held to be a veritable miracle of compounded complexity. The pipes—both flutes and reeds, set in ranks—are the sounding body of the organ, with air from the wind chest forced through them to activate the tone. The organist controls the entire mechanism from the console, which consists of an array of stops for selecting individual ranks of pipes in addition to the manuals and pedal board. More than any other single instrument, the organ demands space, for a thousand or more pipes are not unusual, ranging in length from under two inches to sixteen (rarely, thirty-two) feet.

A 16th-century German engraving showing dancers with recorder and bagpipes.

A wind instrument known throughout the Far East, Europe, and North Africa since ancient times is the bagpipes, which is named for its air reservoir, or bag. In its early days, this bag was most often made from an animal bladder. Holding the bag under his arm, the player supplies air to the bag by blowing into a one-way tube and activates the sound by squeezing the bag with his arm, forcing air out through the pipes. Once it has been started, the instrument sounds constantly, a feature that has been exploited by adding drone pipes to the single melody pipe (the "chanter").

Stringed Instruments

The third large category of instruments is made up of those with sounding strings. The classification of stringed instruments is based on the means of activating the tone rather than on the material from which they are made; the greatest number, therefore, are classified as *plucked strings*. Perhaps the earliest and most widespread was the archer's bow, used as a musical instrument. Such a bow appeared in a wall painting of about 15,000 B.C. in a cave in southwest France; it is shown in the illustration at the left. The bow is the simplest of the plucked stringed instruments, both because it has only one string and because some bows have no resonators. The player then uses his mouth by

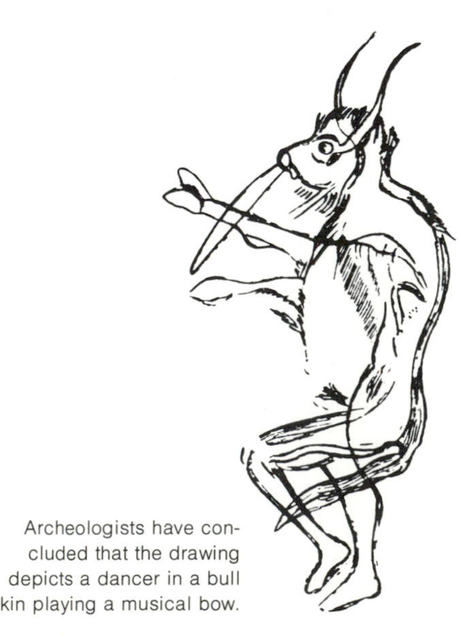

Archeologists have concluded that the drawing depicts a dancer in a bull skin playing a musical bow.

placing one end of the bow in it, or by holding the instrument against his cheek.

In its simplest form, the harp is a multiple musical bow—a fact that may be a key to its origin. Members of the harp family vary in their details, but they all have a resonator and a neck with strings stretched parallel between them. The number of pitches a harp can produce corresponds exactly to its number of strings—one pitch per string. The strings are graduated in length, and except for the concert harp, the pitch of individual strings cannot be altered during performance.

The lyre, closely related, was constructed with two arms and a crossbar; the body was often a tortoise shell. Harps are pictured frequently from about 3000 B.C. on, and were common in Assyria, Egypt, and the rest of Africa, where lyres were also popular. Small harps and lyres were used by storytellers, but the larger types soon became associated with instrumental performance. The *nebel,* or "angular harp" of the ancient Hebrews (of the Levites in biblical times), was the "instrument of ten strings" mentioned in the Psalms.

A harp from the Ivory Coast, Africa.

The lyre and its larger counterpart, the *kithara,* have given their names to such words as "lyric" and "zither," testifying to an unbroken heritage of use over the centuries. The lyre became the national instrument of ancient Greece; the harp, of Medieval Ireland and Wales.

The *zither,* or *psaltery,* belongs to another category of plucked stringed instruments, in which a simple wooden box, board, tube, frame, or stick is strung with as many strings as convenient. The stick zither with one or two strings is very much like a musical bow, except that the stick is rigid, whereas the bow is flexible. But box and board zithers can be ornate and technically complex. Perhaps India has granted the greatest honor to the zither: although the modern Indian *vina* and *sitar* have taken on certain characteristics of the lute, they still retain their zither heritage.

The zither in modern times is a folk instrument. The "mountain zither" popular in the United States is generally a three-stringed instrument, with one melody string and two drone strings. The *Autoharp* is a chord zither of recent origin, which uses a device for damping various combinations of strings, allowing chords to sound.

Early in the Christian era, an Egyptian instrument is thought to have been taken to Spain by the Arabs. This instrument had a

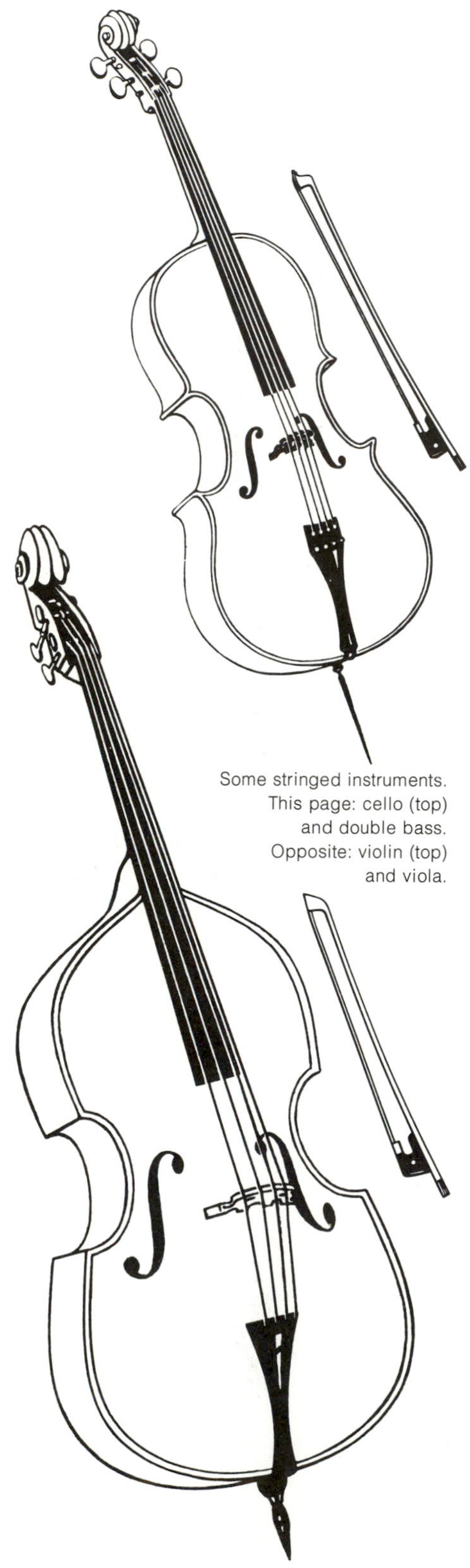

Some stringed instruments. This page: cello (top) and double bass. Opposite: violin (top) and viola.

bowl resonator with a long neck attached, and three or four strings, stretched between a raised piece of wood called a bridge and the end of the neck, where the strings were tied to pegs. Attaching the neck to the resonator body added a crucial element to the plucked string: readily variable pitch. By depressing a string at any point on the neck, the performer shortened the sounding length of the string and raised its pitch. Thus the neck was also called the *fingerboard.* The Arabs used the Greek term *kithara* for this instrument, spelling it *qitāra* and giving it to the Spanish as *guitarra* (guitar). In the fifteenth century, the neck was fitted with bands of gut to indicate the divisions for fingering. These bands, called *frets,* were the final addition to the guitar. Lutes and guitars are both tuned in fourths with a third in the middle, giving them a natural facility in playing chords. Like harps and lyres, lute and guitar types have been played since ancient times either with the fingers or with a plucking device called a *plectrum.*

The *violin,* like the Medieval fiddle, is tuned in fifths and has no frets. Well into the sixteenth century, the instrument was not consistently named, and it is impossible to sort out its early history. Yet by 1600 the violin was specified in consorts (as the single treble with trombones in a broken consort), and was a popular accompaniment to dance. Miniature versions, called *kits* or *poches* (pockets), were developed for the use of the dancing masters who provided increasingly important musical and social services after 1600. The violin (along with a new kind of singing voice) was to be the single most important instrument of the emerging Baroque style, and it would remain as the basic sound of the modern orchestra. The orchestral strings are the violin, viola, and cello—all of the violin tribe and all tuned in fifths—and the double bass or bass viol, which is tuned in fourths.

Keyboard Instruments

The only instruments that competed with the violin for popularity in the eighteenth and nineteenth centuries were three stringed instruments that are played indirectly, with a keyboard—the *clavichord,* the *harpsichord,* and the *pianoforte* (*piano* for short). They are very different in both mechanism and effect, in spite of their common keyboard: the clavichord strings are touched by tangents (small brass blades attached to the backs of the keys); the harpsichord strings are plucked by jacks (with plectrums); and the piano strings are struck by hammers.

The clavichord is unique in more than one respect. Depression of a key sends a tangent up to touch and remain upon the string; this touching tangent serves as a bridge and determines the sounding length of the string. By varying pressure on a key, the player can slightly modify this length and hence the pitch of the string, making a true vibrato (see page 204)—impossible on any other keyboard instrument. (Interestingly, it is only the Japanese *koto,* a board zither that is the national instrument of Japan, with which the clavichord shares this characteristic, though it achieves it in a very different way. The koto is fitted with movable bridges for the individual strings, controlled by the left hand while the right hand plucks the strings.) But in the clavichord, the more crucial characteristic is the continuing pressure on the strings by the tangent, which so dampens the tone that the instrument has too delicate a sound for use in concerts. Yet within its tonal compass, the clavichord is perhaps the most versatile of the keyboard instruments. Its silky sound and its immediate responsiveness give it a very special place among instruments.

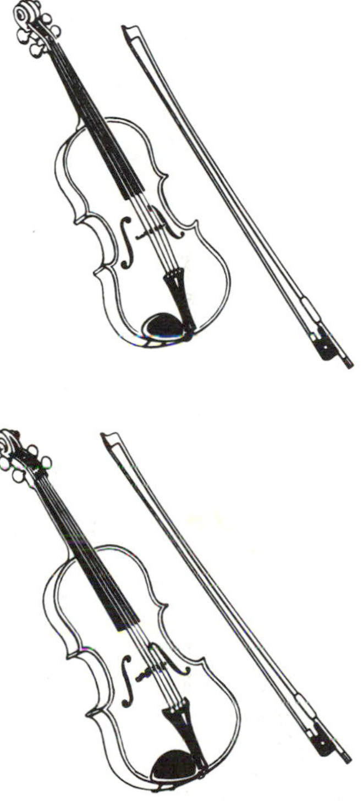

The harpsichord, like the organ, is a composite instrument, with independently controlled sets of strings (often with two manuals) that can be activated separately or together; larger models, with as many as five sets of strings and over eight feet in length, have good contrasts in tone and considerable power. The instru-

A 16th-century legless French clavichord, played on a table top.

A detail of a 17th-century Japanese scroll. The instrument on the left is a lute; on the right is a koto, the most honored Oriental stringed instrument.

ment had its small forms (the spinet, for example) for the amateur, and this popularity with amateurs, like that of the lute two hundred years earlier, provided a market for harpsichord music and also a fully appreciative audience for professional performers.

The wide swaths of tonal color of the harpsichord, along with its affinity to the organ, were Baroque in essence; the new spirit at the end of the eighteenth century demanded the suppleness of the clavichord with the power of the harpsichord. The piano furnished the answer to this demand, and it was to be the standard family instrument from that time on. Though not as responsive to delicate pressure as the earlier pianos (or the clavichord), the modern piano has greater dynamic potential and a good deal more resonance. The double and triple stringing that crosses the middle- and bass-range strings and the addition of several inches of length to the concert grand have created a marvelous instrument, capable of massive sound and suited to the delineation of grand ideas. Piano delicacy requires great skill and is not impossible to achieve, but it is not as idiomatic to the modern piano as it was to earlier models.

The percussion, wind, and stringed instrument categories contain almost all instruments of music, but there are a few that defy classification. The sansa, for example, does not belong to any of the principal categories; its means of tone production involves the release of tongues—a technique shared by music boxes. Several instruments, such as musical glasses and the hurdy-gurdy, rely on friction for the activation of tone. The musical saw, which is actually an ordinary carpenter's saw, is in a class by itself. Pitch is controlled by bending the saw, and tone is produced by drawing a cello or violin bow across the arc. Only in recent decades has the musical saw overcome its homespun image and been elevated to the status of a concert instrument.

During the twentieth century, the inventory of available musical sounds has been enlarged electronically. The mutation of instrumental tone color through amplification and distortion has become common practice in live performance, and the manipulation of tape has added a new dimension to recorded music. The synthesizer holds enormous potential for the creation of new sounds, and its versatility holds promise of its becoming an important concert instrument as well as an indispensable tone generator in the recording studio.

In addition to blazing new trails in the world of sound, the twentieth century has also witnessed an unprecedented interest in instruments from other times and places. Unhampered by nineteenth-century notions of evolutionary progress and Western superiority, twentieth-century music lovers are becoming remarkably cosmopolitan in their tastes. The recorder and harpsichord revivals bear witness to an interest in instruments from other times, and the growing popularity of the Indian sitar is symptomatic of the dissolution of musical insularity in the West.

7. Baroque Music

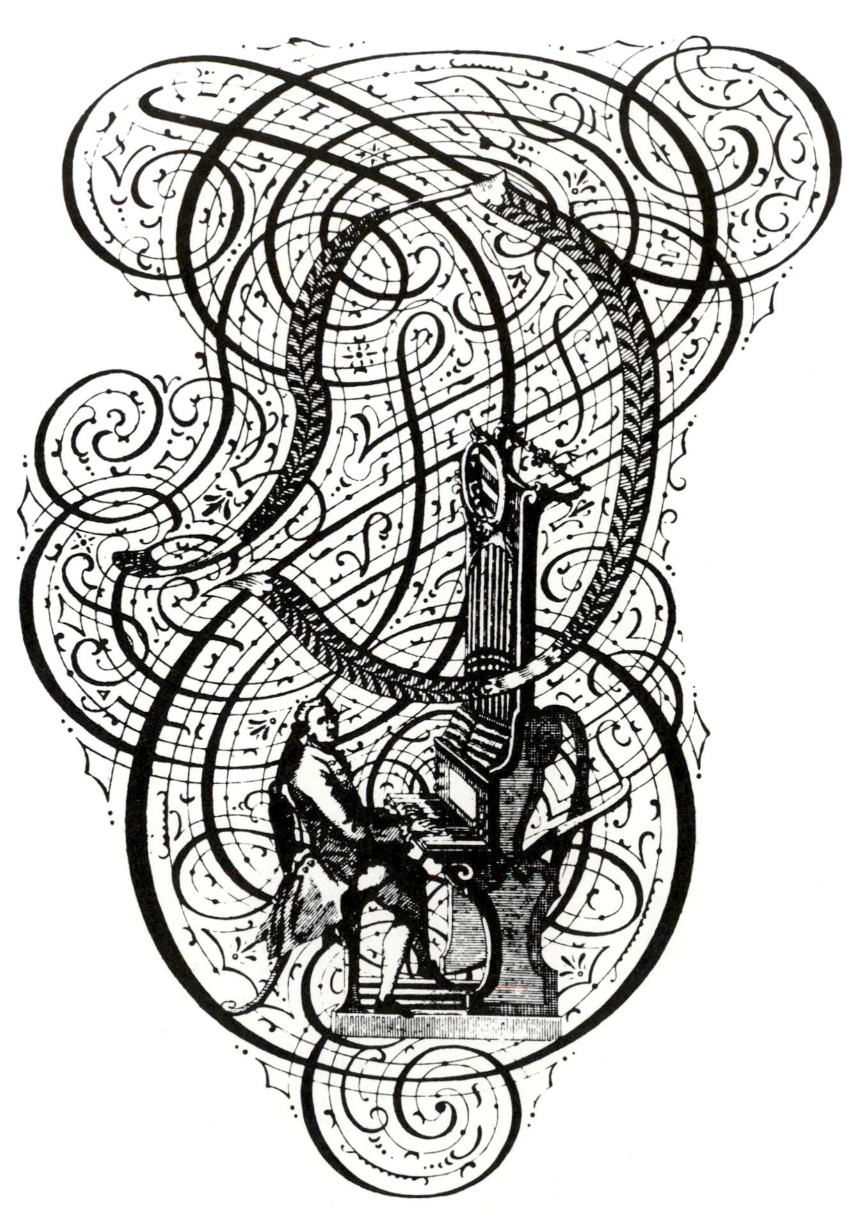

THE BEGINNING OF THE SEVENTEENTH CENTURY was dominated by the musical offspring of the Italian solo madrigal. Solo voice with lute accompaniment was a favorite medium, and lute songs proliferated in France, Spain, and England. A desire for dramatic style had given rise in Italy to the solo madrigal, but in these other countries, the lute songs were committed more to lyricism than to drama. Melodies were graceful in contour, and both melody and accompaniment were shaped to reinforce expressive elements in the poems. Accompaniments were primarily supportive; contrapuntal activity frequently occurred at important cadences, but aside from that, any linear competition with the melody was rare. In performance, a singer frequently served as his or her own accompanist, thus achieving greater subtlety of expression and balance than was possible in ensembles.

THE EARLY BAROQUE IN ITALY

Monody

In Italy, however, avant-garde composers were caught up in an exciting new movement that had its basis in a passionate commitment to the dramatic integrity of the text. Throughout the Renaissance, composers had attempted to enhance the poetic significance of their texts through musical word painting; the words "to soar," for example, were invariably expressed with an ascending melodic line, and "anguish" was harmonized with appropriate dissonance. Inevitably, exaggerated stereotypes developed, which—coupled with the textual chaos of polyphonic setting—did violence to the very text they were intended to enhance. The new technique, called *monody,* was proposed in reaction to musical concentration on individual words. A sense of righteous indignation was eloquently expressed by Vincenzo Galilei (father of Galileo) in his *Diálogo della musica antica e della moderna:*

> It is meaningless and ridiculous how they do justice to the words of the text and depict them, as children would, with dotted notes and syncopation (as if they had the hiccups) when the text speaks of a limping ox; they mimic drums and trumpets; to the words "he descended to Pluto," the singers grumble as if to scare the little ones; to "he ascended to the stars," they scream as if they had the colic;

> indeed, they have their ready-made symbols for crying, laughing, singing, shouting, clamoring, deceit, hard chains, harsh fetters, raw mountain, steep cliff, cruel beauty. Had Isocrates or any great orator stressed an individual word in a similar way, he would have been stopped by angry and laughing listeners.*

This late-sixteenth-century "reform" movement was one of the most improbable in the annals of music history. Its inspiration, the Renaissance concept of Greek drama, was nonmusical; its goal, to duplicate the inflection and rhythm of speech, was nonmusical; and many of those who helped to formulate its philosophy (it came into being by committee) were nonmusicians. In zealous adherence to their ideals, composers of monody avoided melody in favor of declamation, a kind of song-speech. Communication of the emotion inherent in the text was crucial, and nothing was allowed to impede the natural flow of language.

Imitation of speech resulted in melodies with a limited range, a tendency toward pitch repetition, and nonmetric rhythm characterized by rapid syllabic articulation. Performance included gestures and, in some cases, actions; in monody, therefore, singers did not accompany themselves. This declamatory technique was given the theatrical term *recitative.* It demanded a flexible accompaniment to accommodate its rhythmic freedom—an underpinning of chords that were designed to change at specific points in the text rather than to progress with rhythmic regularity or predictability. In practice, such accompaniments were sketched in musical shorthand; the bass line was provided, and chords were indicated by number symbols that referred to intervals above the bass. For example, the numbers $\substack{6\\3}$ denoted a chord consisting of the bass tone plus a sixth and a third above it. Range and spacing were left to the inclination of the individual accompanist, so they varied from performance to performance. Besides the bass line, composers provided a written line only for the soloist's melody. Polyphony was remote indeed from a style in which composers disregarded the inner voices, relegating them to the discretion of performers! A figured-bass accompaniment was called *basso continuo* ("continuing bass"), and it was a standard feature in most music from about 1600 to the mid-1700s. Most frequently, a harpsichordist translated the musical shorthand into chords (a

*Quoted in Curt Sachs, *Our Musical Heritage,* second edition (Englewood Cliffs, N.J.: Prentice-Hall, 1955), p. 164.

Panpipes player, silver, 8¼″ high. (Peruvian, Chimu period, 1000-1450 A.D.)

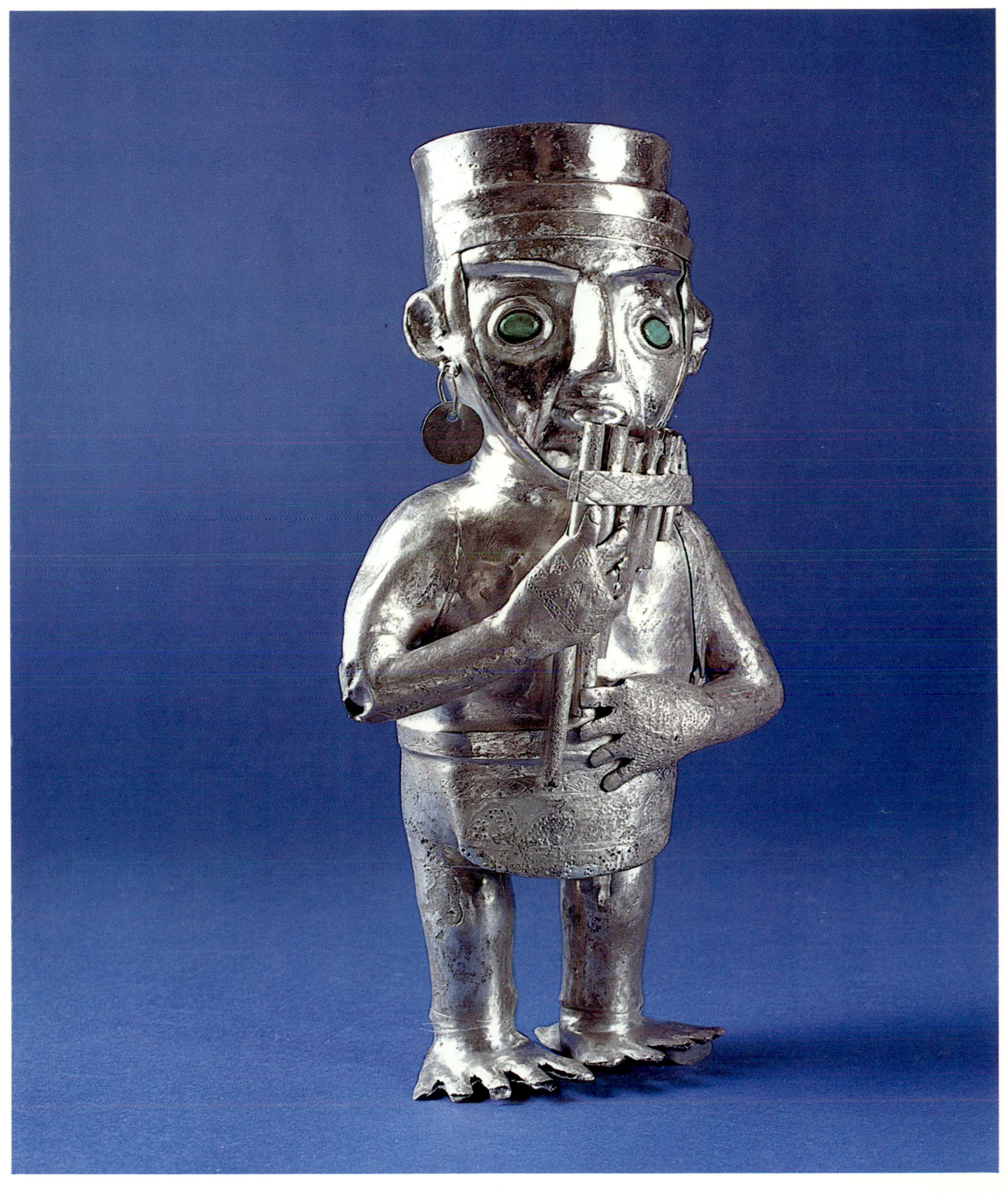

King David playing the harp; from a 12th-century English manuscript.

A design for a water clock from a 12th- or 13th-century Islamic manuscript.
At the base are horns and three kinds of drums.

Spring Morning in the Palace of Han (detail); a Chinese painting on silk from the Ming dynasty, 14th-17th centuries. The instruments are lute, table zither, and guitar.

(Opposite) Musicians at the court of Angevin, c. 1375; from the court copy of Boethius's *De Arithmetica et Musica*.

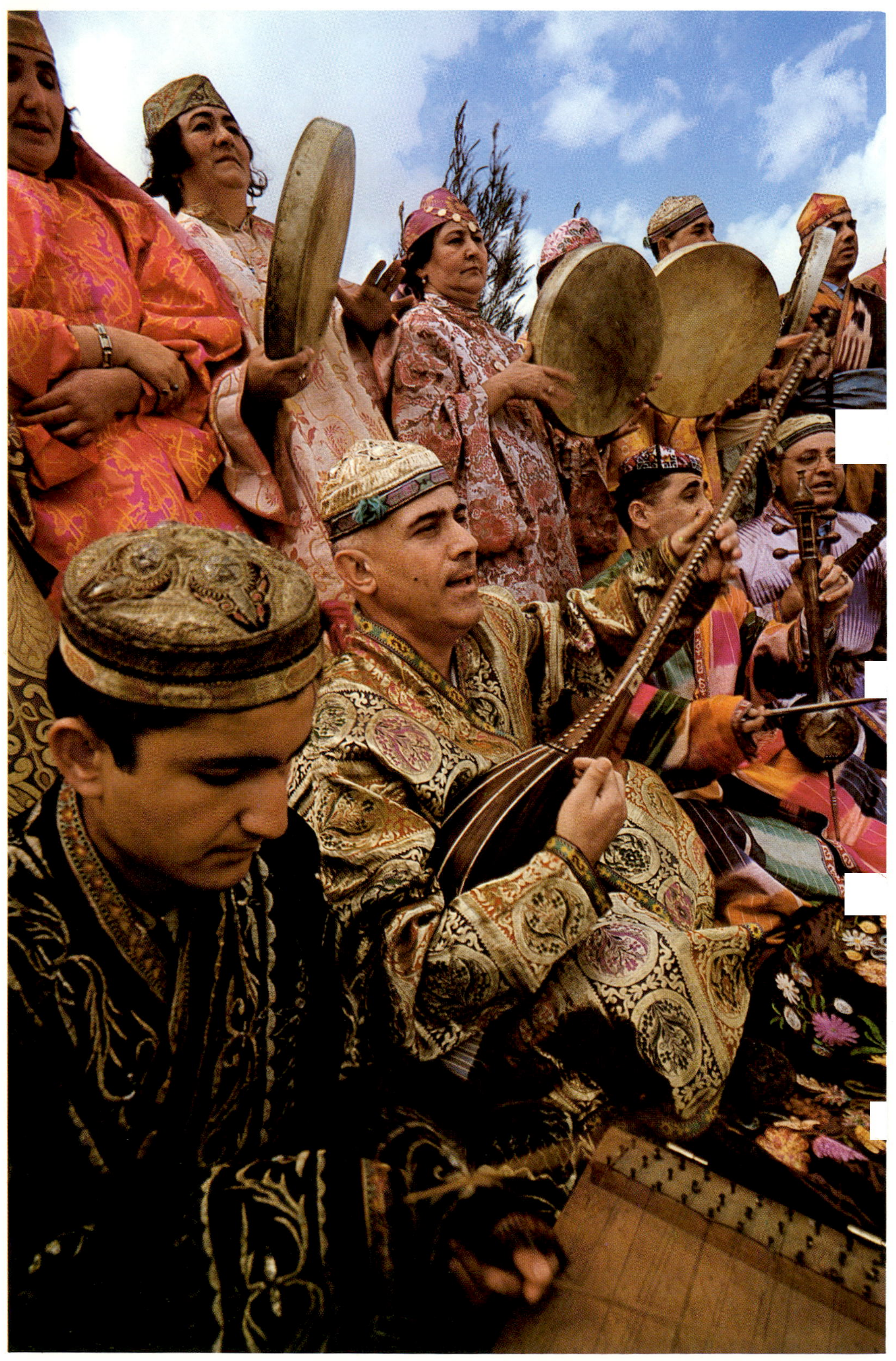

(Opposite) Uzbekistan Jews, playing traditional instruments. The large hand drums, the dulcimer (foreground), and the plucked strings are all mentioned in the Old Testament.

An illustration from a 15th-century Psalter (or book of Psalms, sometimes with music) that belonged to René II of Lorraine. The inscription reads, "Here are those men and women who performed the Psalter."

A Spanish royal wedding banquet. The dogs, the musicians, and the high style are representative of Renaissance court life. From *Histoire d'Olivier de Castile,* 15th century.

Isolated and given splendor by its height, the Benedictine Abbey at Melk, Austria, rises above the river; it was begun in 1702 and represents Baroque architecture at its apex.

process called *realization*), although an organ or an outsized lute with added bass strings could serve as the accompanying instrument. In any case, the bass line itself was played by a linear bass instrument (generally a cello or bassoon), so that two people were required to play the single part. The linear bass instrument gave equal weight to the bass line and emphasized the polarity of the outer voices.

Early Opera

The Italian passion for drama, which had sired the movement dedicated to naturalism and emotionalism, was not satisfied by isolated, unconnected recitatives. Nothing less than the total union of drama and music could satisfy that appetite. Historically, music was no stranger to the theater; its inclusion in theatrical enterprises dated back beyond classical Greece, but its role had been incidental—supportive or diversionary. Never before in the memory of the West had music united with drama as an equal partner in a joint enterprise. The earliest attempts to create *dramma per musica* resulted in somewhat diffuse works in which the singers maintained a declamatory recitative style throughout. It is probable that the tedium of an entire evening of nonmetric, nonmelodic, musically unrelated recitatives was responsible for the virtual oblivion that was the fate of these first music dramas.

MONTEVERDI

The first composer to integrate music and drama with enduring success was Claudio Monteverdi (1567–1643). Unlike his predecessors, he did not hesitate to clothe his text in beautiful melodies and include ensemble singing for variety, along with instrumental dances and interludes. By alternating emphasis on text and emphasis on music, and by focusing the audience's attention on the stage at all times, he kept the dramatic action moving forward without diminishing the importance of the music. His operas *Orfeo* ("Orpheus") and *L'incoronazione de Poppea* ("The Coronation of Poppea") are part of the repertoire of several present-day opera companies, and Monteverdi remains one of the very few composers who have combined music and drama without sacrificing the integrity of either.

Monteverdi personified the transition from the Renaissance to the Baroque not only in time but also in the forms and styles of his music. His early madrigals, published before 1600, epitomized the late Renaissance amalgamation of homophony and polyphony; the later madrigals and his operas, published after 1600, reflected the emotional extravagance that characterized the early Baroque.

By the third decade of the seventeenth century, enthusiasm for recitative had begun to fade, and the Italian love of beautiful melody had reasserted itself. The return to favor of melody coincided with a shift from Florence to Rome as the center of operatic activity. Roman composers modified both the style and the function of the recitative; it became a quick, dry articulation of the text with no melodic pretensions whatsoever, and it was used primarily to further dramatic action. Alternating with it and serving as a vehicle for communication of emotion was the melodic *aria.* This was a fortunate coupling; the recitative aided the unfolding of the plot, and the aria satisfied the musical cravings of performer and listener alike.

The delicate equilibrium between music and drama was short-lived; by mid-century the aria had tipped the scales, and drama was found wanting in the balance. Opera became a musical production staged in a theater, but with no legitimate claim to dramatic validity. (Musical and dramatic elements are rarely in perfect balance; full enjoyment of opera frequently depends on listeners' willingness to shelve temporarily their sense of dramatic verity.) The aria had assumed a definite three-sectional shape; it was called *aria da capo* (literally, "air from the beginning"), taking its name from the composer's direction to return to the beginning and perform the first section again. The middle section of this ABA form contrasted in key and melody, and the return of A gave stability and symmetry to the form.

The development of the aria gave rise to a new style of singing, because neither the nasal quality of the Medieval era nor the neutral tone of the Renaissance was appropriate to the rhapsodic and brilliant character of arias. The new style was called *bel canto* ("beautiful singing"), and it demanded warmth and clarity of tone coupled with accuracy and flexibility in technique. Bel canto has endured as a vocal ideal for more than three hundred years, and its twentieth-century adherents are no less passionate in their advocacy of this style of singing than those who formulated it in the seventeenth century.

Another aspect of the Italian vocal ideal that has, mercifully, disappeared from the musical scene was an overwhelming preference for the voice of the *castrato.* A castrato, having been gelded before his voice changed, had the barrel chest typical of the eunuch and a soprano (or contralto) range. Female sopranos could not compete with castrati in resonance, staying power, and breath control, and, with ever-increasing vocal demands on performers, women were temporarily displaced from the operatic stage. Judging from contemporary accounts, the castrato voice must have been magnificent. The greatest castrati became enormously wealthy and were the subjects of universal adulation. But by no means all the mutilated boys developed great voices; literally thousands of them were left without hope either for a musical career or for anything resembling a normal life. This unconscionable practice flourished primarily in the seventeenth and eighteenth centuries, after which it declined but did not totally disappear. Alessandro Moreschi, the last of the great Italian castrati, died in 1922.

Cantata

A contrast to the dramatic scope of opera was the more intimate form of the *cantata* (meaning "to be sung"). This manifestation of monody was conceived as chamber music, more appropriate to the salon than to the stage. The cantata was a secular work for solo voice and basso continuo, usually a setting of a dramatic love text, most often with prose for the recitatives and poetry for the arias. Its format was one of pairs of recitatives and arias, and, like opera, it was a uniquely Italian development. Cantatas were produced in great numbers by Italian composers throughout the seventeenth century, culminating in those of Alessandro Scarlatti (1660–1725). Occasionally, Scarlatti added a solo instrument or a second solo singer to the basic group of three performers, but the intimate style remained unchanged.

Stylistic Dualism

The Baroque was a musically dualistic period in many ways. Stylistically, it embraced both the single-line emphasis of monody and the multiple strands of polyphony. Rhythmically, it vacillated between capriciousness and exactitude. Some aspects of a Baroque score were meant to be performed exactly as written, but soloists were expected to add melodic embellishments to their parts, and, in realizing a figured bass, the performance required additions to the printed page. Duality in form existed in the pairing of recitative and aria, and in the combination of improvisational rambling and contrapuntal rigor within the seventeenth-century madrigal. Obvious problems arose when the basically polyphonic medium of the madrigal was combined with monodic goals. On the one hand, the monodic ideal of textual clarity was threatened by the independent melodic lines of the madrigal texture. And on the other, although drama might redeem the single recitative line, nothing could save combined lines if they were devoid of melodic significance. One solution was found in using fewer singers and more linear instruments in the ensemble, so that the instruments could provide contrapuntal interest and variety in color without obscuring the words. Recitative style was reserved for internal solo sections; emotional expressiveness was created primarily through unconventional harmonies, variable tempos, and dynamic contrast. No single madrigal style emerged as typical of the period; instead, there were many styles as a result of ingenious attempts to reconcile the inherent conflict between polyphony and monody.

Instrumental Music

In Italy, intense cultivation of the voice was paralleled in instrumental music by concentration on the violin. It seems natural that an era enamored of beautiful singing should cherish the instrument most closely resembling the human voice. Violin playing emulated the principal voice types—the lyric soprano in warmth and clarity of tone, and the coloratura soprano in wide-ranging flexibility and pyrotechnic displays of virtuosity. The art of violin making reached its climax with the still-coveted instruments created by Amati (1596–1684), Stradivari (1644–1737), and Guarnieri (1698–1744). The vaunted technology of the twentieth century has thus far been unable to produce any violin of a quality comparable to those of this illustrious trio.

As the violin grew in popularity, composers increasingly turned their attention to the creation of music designed to exploit the idiomatic virtues of this instrument. The title *sonata* (meaning "to be played") was loosely applied to both solo and ensemble works, and these sonatas evidenced kinship with the suite in their incorporation of stylized dance forms. Consecutive movements alternated between slow and fast tempos, often being paired in much the same manner as the recitative and aria. The slow movements tended to be short, homophonic, and rhythmically flexible; the fast movements, on the other hand, were strongly metric and often polyphonic in texture.

Three performers were required for the presentation of a "solo" sonata: a violinist and the inevitable basso continuo pair. Early sonatas were written for anywhere from one to eight instruments, but by mid-century the *trio sonata,* for two violins and basso continuo, had become the prototype of the Baroque sonata. The use of two violins rather than one offered greater contrapuntal and textural interest, and the presence of a second instrument provided a safeguard against the kind of interpretive excesses to which a single virtuoso was prone. Trio sonatas were written for both church and secular performance. Dance rhythms were a prominent feature of both, but in deference to the sacred setting, individual movements of church sonatas were prefixed by innocuous tempo markings rather than by dance titles.

Side 4 Band 8

Trio sonatas were usually made up of a series of short movements, all but the first in binary form. In the Trio Sonata in E♭, Op. 2, No. 11, by Arcangelo Corelli (1653–1713), the individual movements average only about one minute each, and are thus even shorter than the norm. The work begins with a nondance movement ("Preludio"), followed by a dance of German descent ("Allemanda") and a dance of English ancestry ("Giga"), but despite this cosmopolitan gesture, the style is thoroughly Italian. The "Preludio" is slow and dignified with a solid, substantial texture. The "Allemanda"—contrary to German traditions of dignity, contrapuntal texture, and moderate tempo—is a fast movement in homophonic style with more than a hint of bounce. The "Giga" follows the English format of fast tempo and triplet subdivisions, but it makes no concession to the imitative style usually associated with this dance. While the bass marches forward in steady strides, the two violins combine in melodic concord, blending harmonically rather than competing contrapuntally.

THE BAROQUE IN FRANCE

While the Italians were concentrating exclusively on their efforts to perfect the violin, the French were directing their energies toward refining a variety of instruments. They used scientific research in the design of instruments, to insure both acoustical impeccability and maximal efficiency. Their primary focus was on winds, and French leadership in the development of these instruments continues to receive acknowledgment. The appellative "French horn" is an obvious example, and the strong preference of present-day oboists for instruments of French construction indicates that French supremacy in this area was by no means confined to the seventeenth century.

The *grand motet* was the popular choral form in France, produced regularly at the "spiritual concerts"—the name of the first permanent public concert series in Europe (founded in 1725). These motets consisted of contrasting movements—instrumental movements, recitatives, arias, duets, trios or quartets (called *petits choeurs,* or "small choruses")—and they always began and ended with full chorus (called *grand choeur*), which consisted of

More than two hundred ballets were produced in France before the accession of Louis XIV in 1643. Many of them featured groups of courtiers dancing with guitars or lutes, as in this illustration.

five parts: soprano, alto, tenor, baritone, and bass. The motet was a setting of a psalm, either penitential, laudatory, or comforting.

Cantate Domino, by Jean-Joseph Cassanéa de Mondonville (1711–1772), is a setting of Psalm 149, a psalm of praise. The opening chorus, to the psalm's first verse ("O sing to the Lord a New Song, for he hath done wondrous things"), begins with an extended instrumental introduction. The sopranos enter first with the basic melodic idea, and the other voices join them all at one time. A simple *da capo* form maintains the mood and the energy roughout.

Side 4 Band 9

The aria "Psallite" is for bass, accompanied by solo bassoon and basso continuo. The opening instrumental section, repeated at the end of the A section, is typical of da capo arias in all countries, but the halt near the end with the slower section following it is characteristic only of the French style.

Musical Theater and Opera

France was reluctant to relinquish Renaissance ideals for those of the Baroque. Italian monody made an appearance at court early in the century, but it met with a cool reception; its unabashed fervency offended French dignity. Further, recitative style was basically inimical to the French language, so there seemed little to recommend it.

Nor was there any stampede to import opera. Frenchmen preferred to savor their music and drama separately, admitting no adulteration of either. French drama of the seventeenth century was a highly developed, much cherished form, and any attempts to tamper with it would have bordered on sacrilege. The French taste for spectacle and musical theater was amply satisfied by ballet, already a well-established tradition. Not until the last quarter of the century did opera make a belated appearance in the French theater, and it entered on the coattails of ballet.

LULLY

It was Italian-born Giovanni Battista Lulli (1632–1687)—Jean-Baptiste Lully to the French—who composed the first French operas. Having come to France as a teenager, he became a French citizen and brought to French music the passionate advocacy of the convert. His operas evidence little of his Italian heritage; they descend, rather, from the French ballet, in which vocal as well as instrumental music had played a part. He succeeded in adapting recitative style to the French language by changing the meter as often as necessary to approximate the natural flow and accent of the language. But recitative in Lully's operas did not differ dramatically in melodic style from the aria, and since it was accompanied by orchestra (rather than basso continuo) it did not stand out in stark contrast.

Italians paid little heed to the opera orchestra, but Lully, in accord with French delight in instrumental tone color, treated his orchestra as a valuable adjunct in the operatic enterprise. Both his overtures and orchestral interludes show his imaginative and innovative use of instruments. For example, he specified dances for oboes and bassoons only, alternated flutes with trumpets, and insisted on unanimous phrasing and bowing in the string section. In form, his overtures were characteristic of Baroque duality. A typical Lully overture began with a slow, homophonic section in an exaggerated "long-short-long" rhythmic pattern, followed by a lively second section in imitative polyphony, and often ending with a brief return to the rhythm and tempo of the beginning (sometimes adding another fast-slow pair). These overtures were both imitated and imported by other countries, where the form was known as the *French overture.*

A 1682 engraving shows Louis XIV at a royal ball.

Instrumental Music

Renaissance ideals continued to dominate both vocal and instrumental chamber music, with five-part polyphonic texture prevailing throughout the first half of the century. The ever-present lute continued in popularity, but was gradually losing ground to the guitar for accompanying and to the harpsichord (*clavecin* in French) as a solo instrument. Harpsichord suites typically consisted of a group of stylized dances. These were related by key, and their embellishments were usually notated rather than left to the discretion of the performer. The Italian sonata and cantata did not gain popularity in France until the end of the century.

THE BAROQUE IN GERMANY

Musical Theater

Musical theater in Germany was almost totally dependent on foreign sources. Italian opera and French ballet productions were imported, and those that did originate locally were composed by Italian or French musicians, who held the important positions in German courts. Indigenous opera did not emerge until the latter part of the century, and even then, only the city of Hamburg saw any significant productions of German opera.

Cantata

Song writing, which had flourished steadily in Germany for so long, began to peter out at mid-century and was supplanted by the cantata. Early cantatas followed Italian models closely—even to the extent of using Italian texts—but by the end of the century a totally different format had developed. In contrast to the Italian type, the German cantata was written for performance in church; it used a sacred rather than secular text, employed orchestral instruments rather than simple continuo to accompany the singers, and focused on ensembles rather than on a soloist. Solo recitatives and arias appeared within the sequence of movements, but duets, trios, and especially choruses had an integral part in the structure. The Lutheran Church claimed the cantata as its own, integrating it into the regular service as the anthem had been integrated into the English service, and creating a demand for cantatas appropriate to each week of the liturgical year.

Organ Music

The Lutheran Church also benefited from a remarkable flowering of German organ music. The organ itself had developed to a high degree of excellence. Many present-day organists regard

Baroque organs as the culmination of organ building, comparable in quality to Italian violins of the same era. Outstanding German composers devoted a large portion of their talents to the composition of organ music, and this literature constitutes Germany's principal contribution to our heritage from the Baroque. *Chorale preludes* were uniquely German in style and specifically Lutheran in function. The basis of each was a single chorale tune, the treatment of which ranged from simple harmonization to polyphonic development of each chorale phrase in turn. This wide variety is indicative of the imaginativeness that the type inspired.

Polyphonic forms continued to thrive in German organ music, but, in true Baroque fashion, they were normally paired with pieces in homophonic, improvisatory style (Prelude and Fugue, Toccata and Fugue, and so on). The modal Renaissance ricercar (page 93) was replaced by the tonal fugue, in which the intensity of imitative development of a single melodic idea was relaxed by the interspersion of less concentrated episodes. Seventeenth-century Germany produced a profusion of gifted composers of organ music, among whom Dietrich Buxtehude (1637–1707) was particularly outstanding. He exerted a strong influence on music in the late Baroque, and his works form part of the basic repertoire of twentieth-century organists.

The burgeoning of Lutheran music during the seventeenth century had no counterpart in the Roman service. While the Protestant churches were devising new musical types, the Roman Catholic Church was fighting to maintain its prestigious Renaissance tradition. Some abortive attempts were made to incorporate monody into the mass, but monodic style was basically incompatible with this medium. The polychoral techniques of the Renaissance were expanded to spectacular proportions, involving six or more choruses, but in the main, the style of Palestrina prevailed.

THE BAROQUE IN ENGLAND

Vocal Music

The Anglican Church received only peripheral attention from English composers during the first half of the century, but following the Restoration (1660), its musical fortunes improved notably. John Blow (1649–1708) and Henry Purcell (c. 1659–1695) held posts in both the Royal Chapel and Westminster Abbey and were,

The organ at Groote Kerke, Haarlem, the Netherlands, a Baroque instrument whose intimate relationship with architecture is clear.

therefore, professionally concerned with the production of sacred music. Their liturgical works consisted of anthems and services, which were basically conservative in style.

British composers ignored monody until the last third of the century, and they never embraced recitative style with enthusiasm. Their experiments with monody were confined to nonliturgical works, and these were far more melodic and rhythmically regular than recitatives. Foreign influence in the early seventeenth century was minimal; England remained a tight little island, musically a nationalistic bastion of the Renaissance until after the Restoration. Charles II, as Pretender, had lived in France, and with his return, French musical practice infiltrated the court. Somewhat later, the invasion of Italian opera resulted in the musical conquest of a nation. Italian opera so dominated British musical theater that not only were the operas themselves imported but so were Italian musicians to produce them and Italian castrati to sing the leading roles.

Home-grown musical theater productions in Great Britain were influenced both by French ballet and by a national partiality for spoken drama. Theatrical productions involving music took the form of *masques,* which incorporated song, dance, and instrumental music, or of standard plays with incidental music. Despite their extravagant admiration for Italian opera, British composers were reluctant to give up the spoken word, and refused to make a firm commitment to musical drama that was sung throughout. There were two notable exceptions—*Venus and Adonis,* by John Blow, and *Dido and Aeneas,* by Henry Purcell—but they were unprecedented and, for a century and a half, unsucceeded. In fact, following the death of these two composers, not only opera but British music in general became dormant and remained so until the end of the nineteenth century, when British-born composers once again assumed an active role in creating new music.

During the Baroque era, it was in the more intimate forms of solo and chamber music that British composers excelled. Monody had little influence on the British art of song writing; English songs were unabashedly melodic, and, fortunately, composers were discriminating in their selection of poems in an era of great poets. Harpsichord music had long been an area of special attention, and British excellence in this medium continued unabated. Suites and sets of variations, particularly those built over an ostinato bass (page 71), were the principal seventeenth-century forms. In vocal chamber music, the madrigal was finally dethroned by a brazen upstart, the *catch,* which was a canonic part song, somewhat rowdy in character and frequently bawdy in text. These impudent songs enjoyed enormous popularity and attracted the attention of Britain's best composers. Instrumental chamber music in the first part of the century centered on Renaissance-type consorts, particularly of viols, and it was only in the eighteenth century that the characteristically Baroque trio sonata became preeminent.

Instrumental Music

Toward the end of the seventeenth century, the flamboyance that characterized the Baroque began to color concepts of instrumental ensembles. Although chamber music in general, and trio sonatas in particular, continued to flourish throughout Europe, there was growing interest in larger groups in which, as in choirs, each line was strengthened by multiple performers. Opera orchestras had demonstrated the fullness of sound that such groups could produce, but purely instrumental music with several performers playing each line was a new concept, one that was open to all kinds of experimentation. Some ensembles resembled expanded consorts in being composed of a single instrument type, usually strings; others, such as wind bands, were related only by the physical means of generating sound, resulting in less homogeneity of tone. Still others incorporated both strings and winds, emphasizing contrast at the expense of blend. At first, in the absence of music composed especially for these larger ensembles, the literature of other media was adapted to suit their needs. Chamber music provided a ready source that required nothing except copying extra parts; and keyboard suites were invaluable, since they existed in profusion and called for only minor modifications in adapting them for ensemble performance.

THE LATER BAROQUE IN ITALY

Concerto Grosso

Italian composers were quick to recognize the potential of an expanded ensemble and to create new music for it. Tentative attempts resulted in the orchestral *concerto,* a work for string ensemble in several movements. The earliest concertos resembled chamber music in concept, and reflected Baroque style in their emphasis on the outer voices and their use of a continuo.

Their sound was resonant but lacking in contrast, so that there was little possibility for creating dramatic effect. Full idiomatic exploitation came with the development of the *concerto grosso,* which proved to be one of the most significant forms to emerge from the Baroque. It was a work that contrasted the sound of a string ensemble having two or three performers on each line with the sound of a small chamber group having only one performer on a line. The term *concerto grosso* (meaning "large consort") was applied to the large group as well as to the composition itself, and the diminutive, *concertino,* was used to denote the small group. Drama was inherent in the juxtaposition of two such contrasting ensembles, and the dramatic element was heightened by the adoption of a fast-slow-fast tempo scheme. A fast first movement ensured audience attention from the outset; a slow second movement offered respite as well as variety; and a fast final movement contributed to the goal of ending in a blaze of glory. The fullness and greater dynamic intensity of the concerto grosso was balanced by the virtuosity and flexibility of the concertino; in performance, contrast between them was emphasized by the polychoral technique of placing the two groups apart from one another. Concerto grosso form acquired definitive shape in the hands of Corelli, a remarkable musician who had also popularized the trio sonata and who contributed substantially to the expansion of violin playing techniques.

Opera

Italian opera had become so popular that, by the turn of the eighteenth century, it constituted an international mania. In Italy, access to opera was no longer a prerogative of nobility and wealth; the entire population was in love with opera, and public opera houses were thriving in several cities. But opera, unfortunately, seems by its very nature to trigger abuses in one form or another. Initially the musical element was slighted in favor of the dramatic; later, drama received short shrift. The new Italian distortions detracted from both. In Venice, opera had deteriorated musically as the grandeur of staging increased. Interest centered so strongly on elaborate stage machinery and the full panoply of spectacle that the quality of the music declined, and the drama became ridiculous. It is paradoxical that the best "Venetian" operas of the time were produced in Germany. The small German

Producers of Baroque opera competed in the display of extravagant sets and effects. This scene from *La Monarchia Latina Trionfante* by Antonio Draghi (1635–1700) includes live elephants.

courts could not afford such lavish mounting, and this austerity had a wholesome effect on the operas of resident Venetian composers. In the absence of elaborate staging, emphasis turned from spectacle to artistry—especially to the musical content. Thus even though drama was used vehicularly, there was redeeming merit in the music.

In Naples, abuses arose from the star system. Public adoration had given supersopranos—both castrati and women (who had returned to the stage in limited numbers)—a preposterous notion of their musical importance. An insatiable appetite for applause led them to indulge in exhibitionistic displays of vocal virtuosity solely for the sake of ego gratification, and the result was artistic mayhem. Drama sank to new depths; melody was distorted through willful alterations and magniloquent additions, and, in pace and timing, entire productions grew more and more ludicrous.

The music merited better treatment—Neapolitan composers were a talented lot, whose well-shaped melodies deserved an

Each of these English playing cards, printed in 1728, includes the words and music of one of the airs from *The Beggar's Opera* by John Gay.

undistorted hearing. Although, like their predecessors, they paid lip service rather than honest tribute to drama, their arias were among the best of the Baroque. Lyric arias were frankly sensuous in appeal, and those for coloratura abounded in cascades of brilliant passage work. The leading composer of Neapolitan opera was Alessandro Scarlatti. In addition to over one hundred operas, he wrote more than a thousand cantatas and a sizable quantity of sacred and instrumental music as well.

STYLE GALANT AND *STYLE BOURGEOIS*

Public performance of opera had begun in Venice in 1637 and had expanded throughout Europe by the end of the century. Instrumental music made its public debut somewhat later; the first concerts for an admission-paying audience originated in England during the last quarter of the century. By the beginning of the eighteenth century, music had developed a following of such proportions that public taste became a force to be reckoned with, precipitating a stylistic schism at the height of the Baroque. Aristocratic taste was represented by *style galant* (also called *rococo*), which appeared primarily in instrumental music. This style was homophonic, transparent in texture, highly ornamented—and, above all, graceful. Rococo music eschewed Baroque grandeur and extravagance in favor of simplicity and grace. *Style bourgeois,* on the other hand, acknowledged the validity of middle-class taste, and this style found its expression in new forms of musical theater. It had always been beautiful singing and expressive melody that had attracted the public to opera; audiences had never been enthusiastic about flimsy plots based on mythological subjects, and they had endured rather than enjoyed recitatives. Bourgeois style gave the people what they wanted—light opera, in which recitatives were replaced by spoken dialogue, the plot had a measure of contemporary relevance, the language was their own rather than the inevitable Italian, and the songs were expressive and simple, without sophisticated ornamentation. The new form found fertile soil in England, where the format was something like that of a Broadway musical. One outstanding hit of the 1720s was *The Beggar's Opera,* by John Gay and John Pepusch, which was the model for Kurt Weill's twentieth-century *Three-Penny Opera.*

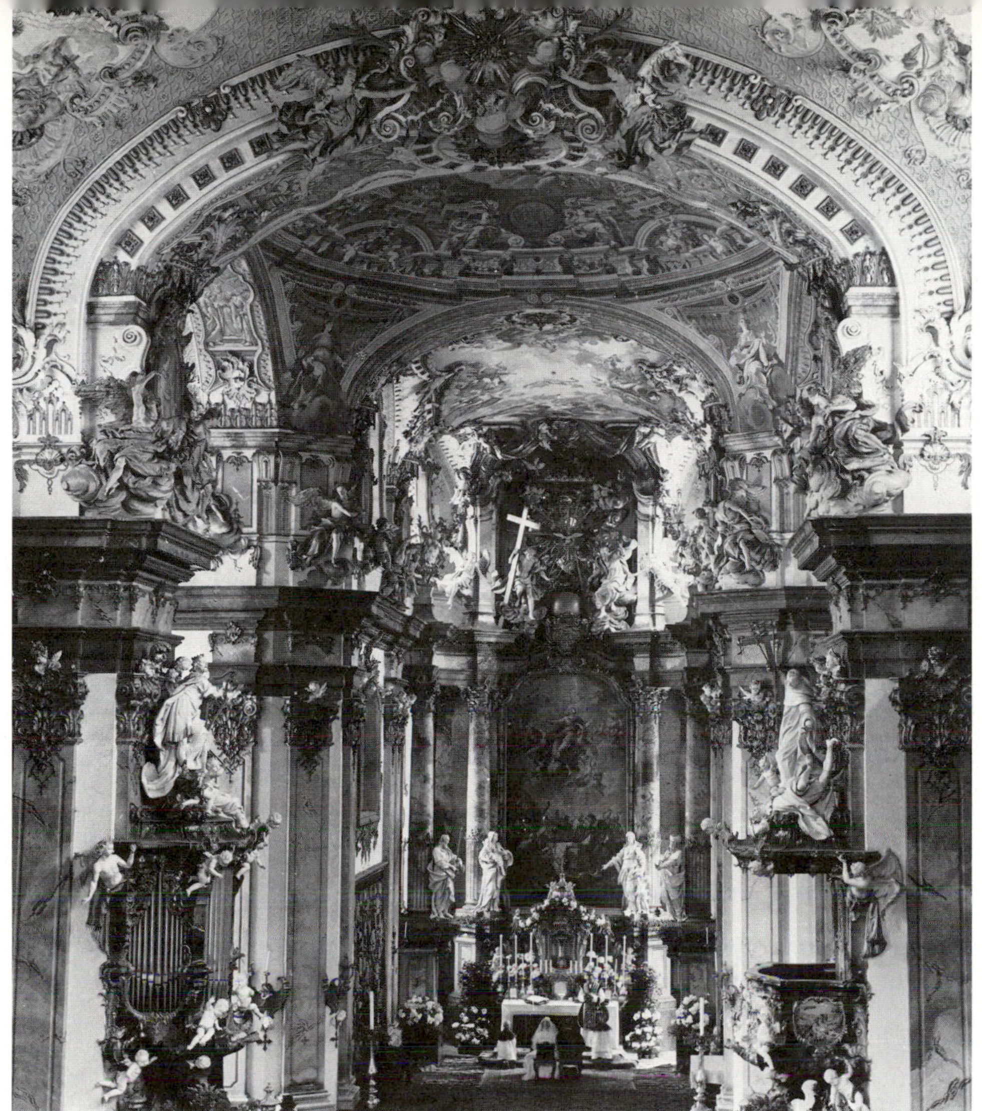

An ornate interior typical of early 18th-century churches. This is the relatively small Collegiate Church of Wilhering (near Linz), Austria. Its many details seem to blend into a gracious whole.

The most popular opera of the 1730s was a comic opera, *La Serva Padrona* ("The Servant Is Mistress") by Giovanni Battista Pergolesi (1710–1736). It calls for only two singers and a dancer, it has no machinery—not even an elaborate stage setting—and it consists of only two short acts. The plot details the clever scheme of a servant girl to get her bachelor master to propose marriage to her. This she accomplishes with the aid of a coservant, a mute, who dresses as a "Turkish" army officer with ideas of marrying her. The master is by no means unwilling and the ruse forces his hand with no difficulty. The recorded example begins with the final recitative, a dialogue between master and maid as they agree to the marriage. Its conversational nature, its harmonic instability, and its rhythmic irregularity are entirely characteristic, as are the interjections and nonverbal elements—recitative often included sighs, sobs, laughter, tongue-clicking, and even an occasional scream.

Side 5 Band 1

The ensuing duet aria by contrast is tonal, strongly metric, and lyrical. The aria (da capo) tells of love, emphasizing that the heart goes pitter-pat, a rhythmic motive repeated in the voice and echoed in the strings, pizzicato. Although a duet aria is generally less usual than a solo aria, it is fairly common in comic opera. So is the bass voice, which was thought to possess the incisive and verbally expressive qualities that would make it particularly suited to humor—an idea that *La Serva Padrona* charmingly supports.

COUPERIN

Style galant is exemplified in the work of the French composer François Couperin (1668–1733), whose harpsichord music represented a culmination of the gallic spirit—that typical French *esprit*—which was cultivated both at court and in private salons. Couperin represents this French ideal at its height, before it received the pungent injection of Italian elements. Crystalline in texture and concise in musical language, his short pieces are characterized by a melodic embroidery of variegated ornaments. Couperin frequently gave his pieces fanciful titles, such as "The Knitters" or "The Cuckoo," and his suites were often composed of pieces related by title as well as by key. His music has a deceptively simple sound that masks the technical difficulties of playing intricate configurations with absolute clarity.

SCARLATTI

Side 5 Band 2

The most remarkable harpsichord music of the late Baroque was written by Domenico Scarlatti (1685–1757; son of Alessandro). His single-movement sonatas were far in advance of their day both in harmonic vocabulary and in the character of their thematic material. In technical demands, they mirrored the virtuosity of their creator, who was probably the greatest harpsichordist of the Baroque. His sonatas continue to enjoy wide popularity with present-day keyboard performers—pianists as well as harpsichordists—and are among the most frequently performed works from the Baroque era. The recorded example, Scarlatti's Sonata in A, L. 345,* is a brilliant, hard-driving piece that offers the performer little respite except at cadences. The opening theme uses several different registers in quick succession, requiring very fast sideways motion of both hands. The lengthy transition that follows this theme is full of intricate finger patterns, syncopation, and, later, a pattern involving quick crossings of the left hand over the

*Scarlatti's 500-odd sonatas were assigned numbers first by Alessandro Longo and more recently by Ralph Kirkpatrick. The sonatas are variously identified by "L" numbers, by "K" numbers, or, among belt-and-suspenders scholars, by both.

right in playing alternate high and low notes. This hand crossing continues in the closing theme, which is characterized by a two-note figure in a low register. The second section begins quietly with no radical changes of register, but as it proceeds, the cross-hands technique reappears, and the music builds to an impressive climax. Only a fraction of the excitement of this sonata can be communicated through a recording. Visual effects—especially the rapid hand crossing—are part of its total concept, so only a live performance can convey the full impact of its sense of danger and bravura.

THE LATE BAROQUE

Early in the eighteenth century, concerto style underwent a radical change: the dramatic impact of opposing forces became even greater as the large group was expanded in numbers and power, and the small group was replaced by a single soloist—usually a violinist—whose brilliant virtuosity assumed heroic proportions. (The concerto grosso continued to be a viable form throughout the Baroque, but the increasing popularity of the solo concerto signaled its eventual decline and demise.) Antonio Vivaldi (1676–1741) was the most persuasive exponent of the new sound in concertos; the simplicity of his orchestral writing, coupled with the virtuoso character of the solo part, placed attention squarely on the soloist, to the same degree as on the singer of an operatic aria. Vivaldi's harmony was clear and predominantly diatonic, and it was completely unequivocal in establishing tonality. Musical interest centered on rhythm, which was straightforward and vital, driving relentlessly toward the final cadence. Solo concertos provided performers with a flattering David-and-Goliath setting for presenting their talents to the public—and there is no doubt that the form hastened the rise of virtuoso solo performance as a career.

VIVALDI

The concerto reached its height in Germany with Georg Philipp Telemann (1681–1767) as it had in Italy with Vivaldi. The recorded example, the first half of Telemann's Concerto for Flute, pairs a graceful slow movement with a rousing fast one, combining musical charm with virtuoso performance demands on the soloist. The opening movement is a long flute solo bracketed by phrases in the large string group. This solo begins as a gently lyric statement over a lilting chordal accompaniment, and gradu-

Side 5 Band 3

ally becomes more ornate. After a passage of quick alternations between registers, the solo culminates in a passage for flute alone. The ensuing fast movement begins with a fugal section for the large group, working out a lively repeated-note theme in all registers; the flute entry brings its own theme. The movement is basically an alternation between large string group and solo flute with minimal accompaniment, between intense imitative sections and airy intricate solos.

Performance techniques in the Baroque placed high priority on clarity, and to that end, attention focused on surface texture (page 37), and phrasing. With the exception of pieces in free, improvisatory style, a steady, propulsive beat was basic, a vital force impelling the music forward. Hemiola (page 67) was used sparingly, as was any other rhythmic device that might reduce the inexorability of the beat. Surface texture was related to tempo: in a fast piece, semidetached consecutive tones enhanced clarity, but in slow movements, the suavity of unbroken connection was used to stress expressive factors. Strings in particular were called upon for a great variety of attacks: short bow strokes, long bow strokes, rapid changes of bow on a single pitch, pizzicato, and even the then-novel harmonics (isolated overtones). Phrasing was crucial for clarity of both melody and form. Melodically, the shaping of subphrases as well as complete phrases was vital to expression, and formally, the articulation of figures and phrases, as related units within larger sections, was imperative for musical coherence.

During the Baroque, a subtle shift in the power balance of the musical community began to take effect, resulting in a redefinition of the traditional roles of composer and performer in shaping the sound of music. Historically, a composer's domain had not extended much beyond indication of pitch and rhythm; in other musical aspects, the performer-producer made crucial decisions. But changing musical ideals needed far more comprehensive directions from the composer. For example, the development of idiomatic writing for instruments inevitably transferred decisions regarding instrumentation from producer to composer. Music designed specifically for strings, incorporating double-stops and pizzicato, could not comfortably wear the all-purpose label "to be played or sung." The communication of drama and emotion meant that the composer must specify appropriate levels of dynamic intensity; to have left such a vital element to chance, as in earlier music, would have been folly. Beat was basic to Baroque music,

Processions, with wagons full of musicians, were an important part of royal pomp.

and since the rate at which beats progress profoundly influences mood, it behooved composers to offer some indication of a suitable tempo. The tempo traditionally determined the appropriate attack, so that composers needed to indicate attack only occasionally, when they wanted an exception from tradition. The performer's sphere of sovereignty had dwindled appreciably, but it still included phrasing and, except in French music, the free addition of ornaments. Improvisation continued as a separate solo art, but its role in the performance of formally composed music was reduced to melodic embellishment by soloists.

Imagination was highly prized during the Baroque, and except in variations and chorale preludes, compositions were usually based on original melodies rather than preexisting sources. The melody was the center of attention, the bass counterbalanced the melody and generated harmony, and the beat impelled the whole structure forward in time. Melodies were shaped to express emotion, so that they often contained large, sometimes awkward leaps to create tension. The soprano range was preferred for its brilliance and poignancy, and it predominated melodically in instrumental as well as vocal music. Important nonpolyphonic techniques of melodic development were the echo phrase and, above all, the melodic *sequence* (at least one repetition of a melodic pattern at a different pitch level, normally a step above or below the original). The musical fecundity of Baroque composers was stimulated by the public's seemingly insatiable demand for new music—a demand very different from the present-day preference for old favorites.

HANDEL

Although Italian influence prevailed throughout the Baroque, historians tend, in retrospect, to see the culmination of the period in the works of two German-born composers, J. S. Bach and George Frideric Handel (1685–1759). The international character of the Baroque was personified in Handel; born and raised in Germany, he spent his impressionable youth in Italy, and then made his career in England. Opera was his first love, and much of his life was devoted to that medium, both as composer and producer. His operas were totally Italianate: not only were his arias Neapolitan in style, they used Italian librettos as well. But if he was Italian in his operas, he was totally English in his oratorios.

The *oratorio* had its origin in Italy during the middle of the seventeenth century. Primarily devotional rather than dramatic in character, it was based on a biblical story, but it was nonliturgical in function. Oratorios were produced by prayer societies in church-associated halls. They were unassuming works of modest proportions, not more than twenty minutes in length, in which polyphonic choruses figured prominently. Not so with Handel. With his flair for the dramatic, oratorios became major works of impressive length, dramatic rather than devotional in character, and designed for presentation in a concert hall rather than a church. Variety pervaded every aspect of Handel's work. Stylistically eclectic, he used recitatives, arias, duets, and both homophonic and polyphonic choruses. And to extend the color range still further, he included some purely instrumental music as well. His oratorios were English in both language and style, and it is with considerable justification that the English claim him as one of their own. In addition to operas and oratorios, Handel wrote a vast quantity of instrumental music for both solo and ensemble. It is primarily on the towering achievement of his oratorios, however, that his fame rests today, and had he written nothing but *Messiah,* history would still number him among the great.

In England and in many parts of America, performances of *Messiah* have become traditional to the Christmas season—although the second half of the text is more appropriate to the celebration of Easter. Many of the choruses from *Messiah* are known and loved throughout the English-speaking world. "And the Glory of the Lord" is a particular favorite—and with good reason, as it embodies the full grandeur of Handel's superb choral writing. Throughout this chorus, the texture fluctuates—varying in density and alternating between homophony and polyphony—while wide ranges in pitch and dynamic intensity give the work strong dramatic impact. Each segment of the text receives distinctive musical treatment: "And the glory of the Lord" has an ascending melodic line that is presented both in unison and in harmony; "shall be revealed" is treated imitatively; "and all flesh" is repeated by each section, then all sections combine to sing "shall see it together"; "for the mouth" is declaimed on a single pitch, and "has spoken it" is fully harmonized to form a majestic cadence.

Side 5 Band 4

BACH

In contrast to the cosmopolitan, renowned Handel, Johann Sebastian Bach (1685–1750) was a little-traveled provincial choirmaster whose modest fame in his own day centered on his remarkable abilities as an organist rather than on his compositions. He lived and worked in the shadow of his friend Telemann, who at the time was Germany's outstanding modernist composer and whose fame was international. And if the Baroque erred in undervaluing Bach, history has compounded the error by neglecting Telemann; his cantatas, sonatas, and concertos deserve more frequent performance than they are accorded today.

Bach's position in relation to the Baroque is comparable to that of Palestrina in the Renaissance. Like Palestrina, Bach was no innovator, nor are his works typical of the period, yet he is the most frequently performed composer of the entire era. Like most church musicians, he was at home with tradition, content with his musical inheritance, and willing to leave pioneering to more venturesome souls. Opera interested him not at all, nor was he greatly attracted by style galant. His natural mode of expression was tonal polyphony, and even his allegedly harmonic writing usually had a degree of linear interest.

Fugue was Bach's specialty, and many of his most important compositions in this form were written for organ. The "Little" Fugue in G minor is one of his most popular works, and its saucy subject effectively contradicts two common misconceptions: that Bach's music is always solemn, and that music in the minor mode is necessarily sad. Following the normal fugal pattern, the "voices" enter one by one, each stating the subject, then continuing with a countermelody as the next voice enters. The episodes, which separate and frame statements of the subject, are comparatively thin in texture, and tend more toward sequential development of a melodic fragment than toward intense contrapuntal activity. This fugue reaches its climax in the final statement of the subject (played on the pedals) and ends with a forthright harmonic cadence of unquestionable finality.

Side 5 Band 5

Bach was a versatile composer who wrote in nearly every medium except opera, and he brought the forms with which he dealt to near-perfection. His cantatas and Passions, conceived as Lutheran liturgical music, have yet to be surpassed. The forty-eight preludes and fugues of his *Well-Tempered Clavier* remain prerequisite to the musical and technical training of every serious pianist, and the heritage he left organists forms a cornerstone of organ literature. His music is infused with an emotional intensity that is deepened by the restraint of order and intellect. His works are frequently serious in mood, but flashes of humor occasionally come through in a piece like his secular *Coffee Cantata*. His position in music history is unique, and if the high estate to which he has risen has been at the expense of his contemporaries, perhaps it might be considered compensatory justice.

COMPARATIVE STYLE CHARACTERISTICS

	MIDDLE AND LATE RENAISSANCE	BAROQUE: Homophonic Music	BAROQUE: Polyphonic Music	EARLY CLASSICAL PERIOD
TEXTURE	five-voice texture equality of harmonic and linear concepts	contrasting densities dramatically juxtaposed	consistent density—only slight variation within a movement	varying in density, tending toward thinness
CADENCES	lines cadencing separately rather than simultaneously, creating a "seamless" effect interval of the third standard in coinciding cadences	sectional cadences—clear-cut and definitive internal cadences—clear-cut but often rendered less decisive by motion in the bass or an inner voice final cadence—emphasized by repetition	except for final (or sectional) cadences each line cadencing separately, creating a "seamless" effect	clear-cut, definitive, and predictable, with all lines cadencing simultaneously occasional overlap of phrase endings and beginnings final cadences emphasized by repetition
POLYPHONY	free imitation, sometimes occurring only briefly	(some polyphonic techniques superimposed on homophonic texture)	imitative polyphony combined melodies	(seldom used)
HARMONY	harmonic passages used in contrasting sections	modal, tonal primarily diatonic occasional use of extreme chromaticism simple modulations to closely related keys	modal, tonal primarily diatonic simple modulations to closely related keys	tonal primarily diatonic simple modulations to closely related keys
RHYTHM	uniformity of pulse uniformity of subdivision	consistent meter consistent tempo consistent subdivisions some use of variable meter and tempo in fantasia-type keyboard works single rhythmic pattern often dominates	consistent meter consistent tempo consistent subdivisions some use of hemiola, especially approaching cadences single rhythmic pattern often dominates	consistent meter consistent tempo subdivisions variable, especially the use of threes within a framework of twos variable rhythmic patterns
DYNAMICS		terraced limited range (except in organ music and oratorio)	terraced limited range (except in organ music and oratorio)	shaded limited range

	MIDDLE AND LATE RENAISSANCE	BAROQUE Homophonic Music	 Polyphonic Music	EARLY CLASSICAL PERIOD
ARTICULATION		semilegato in vocal style detached in instrumental style	variety of attacks, combined to differentiate individual lines	legato in slow tempo detached in fast tempo two-note slurs
VOCAL FORMS	motet chanson mass madrigal lied	solo madrigal solo cantata oratorio	choral cantata single choruses in oratorio mass	oratorio mass
INSTRUMENTAL FORMS	set of variations dance suite	trio sonata concerto grosso suite one-movement sonata set of variations	fugue suite	symphony concerto sonata string quartet divertimento theme and variations
INSTRUMENTAL TONE COLOR	blend homogeneous consorts	brilliance clarity contrast	clarity contrast	clarity blend
ORCHESTRA		very small (12–20) no standard instrumental grouping strings continuo few brasses (possibly one each of trumpet and French horn) few woodwinds (possibly one each of flute, oboe, and bassoon) little or no percussion	very small (12–20) no standard instrumental grouping strings continuo few brasses few woodwinds little or no percussion	small (20–40) no continuo standard ensemble included strings, woodwinds (one flute, two oboes, two bassoons), brasses (two each of trumpets and French horns), timpani
MUSICAL THEATER		opera ballet (France)		opera

8. Performance

MUSIC HAS ACTUALITY only in performance. Notation can project an idea as a blueprint, but that idea does not come alive until it is realized in sound. Musical communication, then, is a triangular process: it begins with a composer's projection; it continues with a performer's probing the score to discover the composer's intent and presenting his or her interpretation of the work to an audience; it ends in the audience's reception of the work. This reception, in turn, should indicate to a composer either that the message has been received or that something is amiss—the interpreter was obtuse, the audience was unenlightened, or the composer's idea was poorly expressed and should be returned to the drawing board. In improvised music, communication is more direct: an idea travels in a straight line from the composer-performer to the audience, with no intermediate person involved. The audience response is transmitted with equal immediacy to the creator.

SOLITARY AND SOCIAL PERFORMANCE

Playing alone—just for oneself, with no audience—is something like talking to oneself, but it is by no means eccentric. A performer must spend long hours in the privacy of the practice room, working out technical problems and polishing an interpretation, to achieve an "effortless" performance. Such solitary labors presuppose an eventual audience and are preparatory to communication. But when the shepherd plays a flute to pass the time in the field, or the lone traveler sings to a sansa as he walks in the bush, or the cowboy plays a harmonica after he has rounded up a stray—all of them are also thinking out loud in musical terms. Most communication is shared, yet all of us think simply within or to ourselves, so it is in no way remarkable that musicians should play for themselves, with or without an anticipated audience.

While private music making is certainly necessary for public performance, it is still true that most musical performance involves an interaction—both among performers and between performers and audience. And at times, all are one—everyone performs. Performance at a sing-in, for example, touches the universal qualities of musical community. There is no audience apart from the performers. Everyone participates, so that there is a blend of musical and social factors. Songs that consist of solo-

and-answer verse followed by unison chorus represent a universal kind of music making. Such songs have a leader, who sounds off to set the pitch and tempo and to select the verse. The group echoes each line of the verse, then all join forces in singing the chorus. Particulars may differ in individual cultures, but this type of call-and-response group singing is found all over the world.

It is interesting that this kind of music making, in which everyone is involved, is limited by its nature to relatively small groups and simple vocal techniques. Even then, a really gifted singer is likely to stand out from the group, attracting admiration for a splendid sound or an improvised addition. Instrumental performance is less likely to be so inclusive—the use of instruments tends to create a separation between performers and audience. Almost any instrument played with consummate artistry will draw an audience to hear it and grant special recognition to the artist who has mastered it.

This cellist is sharing a private musical moment with his cat.

The performance of music for other people, by musicians admired for their special skills, is a matter of "professionalism" in the business world of the West, where certain people make their livings by providing music; but in world terms, it is difficult to sort out such ideas as "professional," "non-professional," "amateur"—or, as we have seen, even "performer" and "audience." Many cultures have no professionals (in music or any other occupation), and a figure comparable to a Western musical professional would simply be a person who is admired as an outstanding performer—like someone with a reputation as a great cook.

VIRTUOSO SOLOISTS

The instrumental virtuoso is found in every culture that emphasizes instrumental music, and, although each instrument presents its own technical difficulties, virtuosity on all instruments hinges in part on sheer speed. The ability to execute complicated maneuvers at, say, ten to twelve notes a second with clarity and accuracy is impressive in itself; the ability to do so with tonal finesse and musical conviction places a performer among the elect. Dynamic control is another common factor; loud, fast playing is certainly part of the picture, but any virtuosos worthy of their salt must be able to make their instruments whisper as well as roar. A special kind of electricity hangs in the air when a performer seems to accomplish the impossible—the suspense felt for the tightrope walker, combined with the appreciation felt for the orator, whose command of the voice is as moving as his shaping of ideas. But comparatively few instruments have figured prominently in such performance—koto, sansa, harmonica, accordion, bagpipes, guitar, harp, lute, zither, orchestral and keyboard instruments—only a tiny fraction of the four-thousand-odd instruments of which we have knowledge.*

The pipe-and-drum player flourishes everywhere. This Yaqui Indian of Arizona sits on a mat and holds the drum against his foot.

"SMALL" MUSIC AND "LARGE" MUSIC

For all its excitement, solo performance remains relatively rare in music. It is more common to find musicians performing in groups, or *ensembles.* Ensembles are generally classified by size: "small" music, in general, is made by a few people in a small place, for themselves or for a few listeners. It is often characterized by spontaneity, variation, embellishment and, in some cases, humor or innovation. "Large" music, in general, is made by a great number of people in a large place for a great number of listeners. Its performance is likely to be characterized by ceremony and formality.

*And even these four thousand, according to Emanuel Winternitz, former curator of instruments at the Metropolitan Museum of Art, New York, "represent only a small and accidental residue of the types that must once have existed." "Images as Records," *Times Literary Supplement,* June 21, 1974, p. 658.

The guitar, a quiet instrument, is well suited to musical cogitation; the player here is the virtuoso Narciso Yepes.

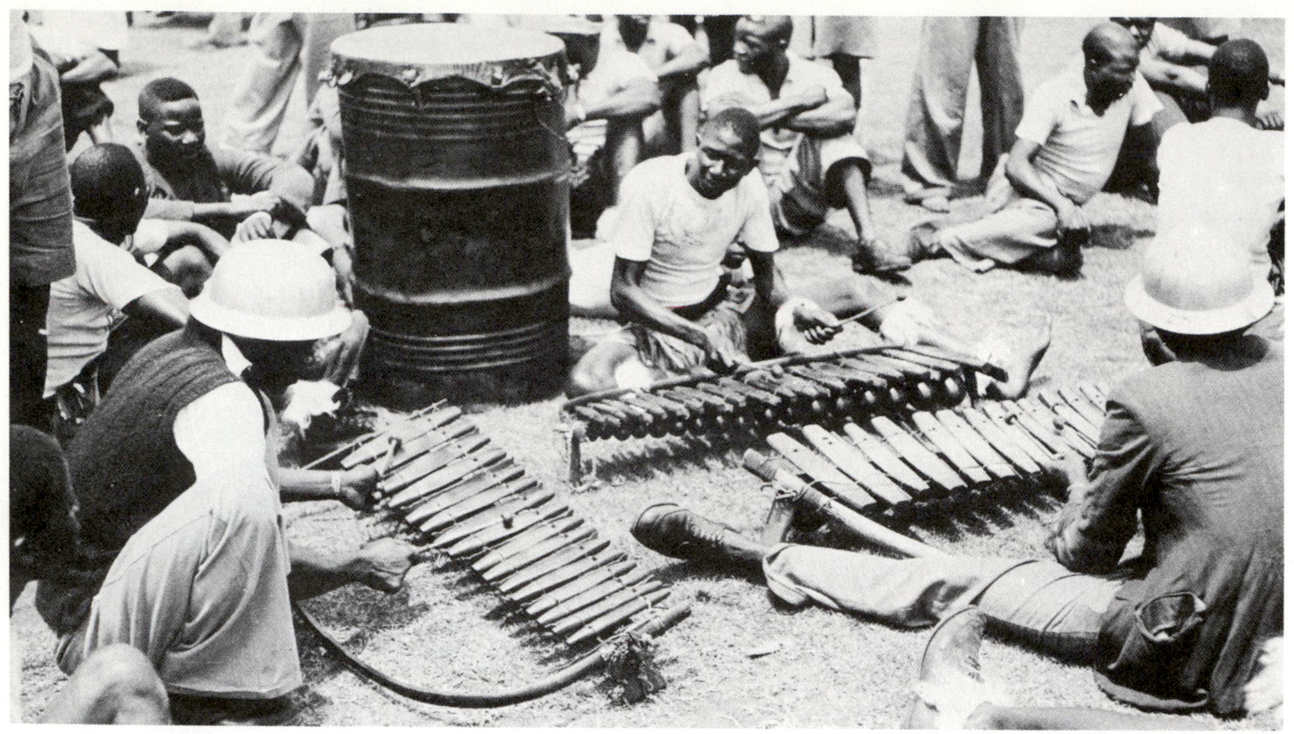

These marimba players are South African miners enjoying a break.

Three, two, or even one piper is enough for an informal Scottish dance such as the Highland fling, but fifty or sixty pipers must signal an occasion of ceremonious importance. And in African groups, numbers are also a clue to solemnity. When the Renaissance explorer Vasco da Gama arrived in East Africa, he was met by a courtly committee of two hundred men with trumpets and flutes—most certainly a state occasion. In contrast, the African marimba game, played by only two people, borders on the frivolous. One player sits on each side of the instrument, and the two of them play a musical game of follow the leader. They switch sides as in a tennis match, which means that they must play the instrument both forward and backward—comparable to a pianist's finding the higher pitches sometimes on the right and sometimes on the left. The brisk musical repartee of this interchange creates its own delight and hilarity.

A soloist, instrumental or vocal, with additional singers or instruments as background support, is the most universal type of performing group. The background most often provides tonal and rhythmic stability against which flights of virtuosity can contrast effectively. This support may be a drone, or one or more drummers providing a constant pattern, or, in the West, it may be a large group providing a harmonic pattern and a steady rhythm.

In non-Western terms, virtuosity and improvisation are indissolubly bound together. Notation, if it is used at all, provides only a framework, making composer and performer equal partners in creativity. Europe, during the past two centuries, has become increasingly note-bound and composer-dominated, but in twentieth-century America, the spirit of improvisation has enjoyed a splendiferous sunburst in the art of jazz.

Throughout the world, improvisation is highly structured, features soloists plus background furnished by other players, and offers variation on materials known to the players and to the audience. Jazz is less typical of universal practice in the equality of its performers within the group. All the musicians are virtuoso soloists in their own right, and no one is perpetually relegated to providing background support. And unlike any other kind of improvisation, jazz performance is unique in its simultaneity of melodic improvisation. Although heterophony exists throughout the world, only rarely do virtuosos combine their talents in its creation.

Most jazz groups are small, but their performance cannot comfortably be classified as "small" music; the volume of sound generated and the size of the audience make any diminutive label incongruous. And the absence of formality or solemnity equally

The joy of jazz lies in its ebullient independence and spontaneity, evident in this session. From left: Lionel Hampton, vibraphone; Illinois Jacquette, saxophone; Benny Goodman, clarinet.

The Pathetic Song, by the 19th-century American painter Thomas Eakins.

precludes the classification of jazz as "large" music. But this difficulty in categorizing jazz is a crisis only for the most determined cataloger.

Small groups are sometimes contained within large ones. Many festival presentations include a group of trumpeters to provide fanfares. And in many cultures, from the pre-Columbian Aztecs to present-day Polynesians, a group of drummers coordinate processions, recitations, and dances—pacing an entire ceremony in a crucial way.

Famous throughout the world is the Indonesian instrumental ensemble known as the *gamelan,* a substantial group with a substantial heritage. It is made up of pitched percussion instruments. Each player has two instruments at right angles; one is tuned to a five-tone scale and the other to a seven-tone scale, both with pitch relationships unfamiliar to Western ears.

Typically, gamelan music can be summarized as stately heterophony. A basic melody, known by performers and audiences alike, is played by one member of the ensemble with very slow, even motion, while the other players present simultaneous variations of this melody. The scales used, the complexity of the basic melody, and the inventiveness of the players determine the intricacy of the result.

A curious kind of performance, universal but always rare, is that in which performers contribute one or two pitches each to a larger musical design in techniques of instrumental hocket (page 69). In the West, this practice is found in jug and bottle bands, in which each player holds one jug (one pitch) or two bottles (two pitches) and supplies the pitch or pitches as needed. The same technique is used by handbell ringers, who work out fairly elaborate arrangements with two bells per player. Unique to the West (and peculiar to Great Britain) is the old tradition of change ringing. This is the playing of a peal of tower bells, one ringer for each bell, in mathematically-derived permutations. A full set of changes is likely to range from five thousand to twenty-five thousand combinations. A set of peals was rung to celebrate the marriage of Princess Anne in London in 1973.

Chamber Music Groups

In the West, "small" music and "large" music have exact parallels in chamber and orchestral music. The original term *chamber* referred to palace halls, but it soon took on connotations of a comfortable living room and the concept became one of intimacy. In France, it was the *salon,* a formal living room, and the Paris salons were the focus of public (and semipublic) performances through the middle of the nineteenth century. Chopin's concert career took place in the salons.

By far the most common form of vocal chamber music is the combination of solo singer and pianist. Professional vocal groups without instrumental support are rare in the modern West—the ideal of the vocal consort and the sociable enterprise of madrigal singing (page 90) was ousted by the relentless instrumentalism of the Baroque, and ever since the Baroque period, the most important chamber groups in the West have been instrumental. The Renaissance consort had begun by playing vocal pieces. Later, works were written for consorts in imitation of vocal style.

But at the height of vogue of the consort, composers did not specify what consort they intended, and the performers chose for themselves.

The Baroque trio sonata (page 152) was by all odds the most popular small performing format in Europe for almost a century. Its instrumentation was in part specified by the composer and in part chosen by the performers. National preferences colored these choices. In Italy, it was taken virtually for granted that the two treble lines would be played by two violins, with the basso continuo most often played by cello and harpsichord. But in Germany, the instrumentation was more variable, with contrasts considered desirable. In Germany, the two treble lines were often played by violin and oboe, oboe and recorder, or flute and violin; in the continuo part, the bass instrument might be cello or bassoon, along with either harpsichord (less often organ), lute, or even guitar, to realize the harmonies. In France, contrast was also prized, but there, where a lively interest in instruments was already a tradition, composers' preferences were often specified in the score.

The *divertimento* was the transitional chamber music type between the Baroque and Classical periods. Divertimenti were composed for specific instruments, but no two seemed to call for the same group. Composers experimented with the way instruments were used, giving melodic material to a horn, for example, or an imitation of recitative to a violin. They included some unusual instruments and sounds, such as a variety of percussions, from timpani and snare drums to children's toys, sleigh bells, and bullwhips. And they developed techniques for other new instruments, notably the clarinet, which was a curiosity at the end of the Baroque but had become a fixture by the end of the Classical period.

The freewheeling instrumentation of the divertimento served as a kind of sieve by sorting out possibilities at a time when composers were searching for clearly defined groups. And although the divertimento died out toward the end of the eighteenth century, a small number of approved types remained, and they defined chamber music through the first half of the twentieth century. These were the string quartet, the piano trio, and the woodwind quintet.

The string quartet as a group was prefigured in many divertimenti for four players and it emerged as a strong type in the

A string quartet rehearsing. The cellist and first violinist are playing, while the violist (second from left) and second violinist count out their measures of rest, bows ready for their next entrance.

1760s. It was one of the first groups to experiment with the coming Classical style; its more complex texture demanded a linear instrument in the middle range—the viola—and made the basso continuo unnecessary. The group was made up of four solo players, each with an individual part:

STRING QUARTET

First Violin
Second Violin
Viola
Cello

Virtually every important Classical composer was interested in the string quartet and contributed to its literature. In the nineteenth century, the string quartet became a rare type of "musician's music," part of the training of musicians, and written only by such form-focused composers as Dvořák and Brahms. But string quartets were not often programed for paying audiences, whose instrumental enthusiasms centered on the piano and on orchestral music. It was not surprising, therefore, that Romantic chamber music almost always included the piano. The internationally popular ensemble was the *piano trio* (piano, violin, and cello). It was rivaled only by sonatas for two instruments in combination, one of them invariably the piano and the other most often a violin (less often a flute, cello, or clarinet). Departures from these norms generally involved either substitution for one instrument (as in the Brahms Trio for Piano, Violin, and Horn) or the expansion of the number of strings (as in the Schumann Quintet for Piano and String Quartet). It might also do both (as in the Saint-Saëns Septet for Piano, String Quartet, Double Bass, and Trumpet). In all these cases, however, the piano remained the indispensable common denominator.

The woodwind quintet was a maverick, popular in France at the start of the nineteenth century, even when the piano and the violin were the most popular instruments. This combination offers evidence of the delight the French have always taken in the colors of woodwind instruments:

WOODWIND QUINTET

Flute
Oboe
Clarinet
Horn
Bassoon

Because of the nature of the woodwind attack, which naturally tends toward clarity and nonlegato lines, the woodwind quintet was a bastion of the Classical style. It continued that style into the Romantic era, maintaining an enclave of high-spirited, sometimes humorous music in a time when music tended to be sobersided, characterized by long legato lines and extended musical statements. The crisp wit of the woodwind quintet declined in popularity toward the end of the nineteenth century, but it has had a rebirth in recent decades, along with a rejuvenated string quartet and a resuscitated Baroque trio.

It has been the large groups, however, that have brought particular glory to Western music in the last two centuries. The standard large group at the middle of the eighteenth century consisted of an orchestra and choir brought together to produce choral works. The famed Handel Commemoration at Westminster

A contemporary view of the Handel Commemoration at Westminster Abbey in London.

Abbey in 1787 was one of the most impressive musical events of the century. It was described by a visitor as:

> magnificent . . . sublime. . . . The band consisted of several hundreds of performers . . . and the chorusses [sic] were collected from all parts of England, amounting to hundreds of voices. The King, Queen, and all the royal family sat opposite the orchestra; the body of the church, the galleries, and every corner crowded with beauty, rank, and fashion: such was the rage to procure seats, that ladies had their hair dressed the night previous, to be ready to get to the Abbey on time.*

Such inflated forces were also common in France, where huge productions were mounted for politically related solemnities such as coronations and state funerals. Elsewhere, this trend led to absurdity: at the World Peace Jubilee of 1872, in Boston, the irrepressible bandmaster Patrick Gilmore combined a chorus of twenty thousand with a band of two thousand and a dividend of cannons, anvils, and bells—perhaps transcending absurdity in pursuit of chaos.

The Symphony Orchestra

Useless size, mercifully, seems to have been confined to political affairs. A musically reasonable size was part of nineteenth-century concert life, and culminated in the marvelous structure of the *symphony orchestra.* At its height, the orchestra was a complex group of four sections, or choirs: strings, woodwinds, brasses, and percussion. The string choir was the basic group—the largest of the four—with its heritage strongly based in the concerto grosso (page 156) but with later influence from the string quartet. In the Classical orchestra, the string section functioned as a large string quartet, played by three or four players to a part plus one or two bass viols doubling the cello part an octave lower. A century later, the orchestra typically included sixteen or eighteen each of first and second violins, twelve or fourteen violas, ten or twelve cellos, and eight or ten double basses—a section of up to seventy players.

The woodwind choir began in the Classical orchestra with pairs of oboes and bassoons, to which a single flute was often

*Michael Kelly, *Reminiscences* (New York: J. and J. Harper, 1826), p. 185.

added. By 1790 another flute had been added, and the section also had acquired a pair of clarinets. As nineteenth-century composers expanded these forces, a piccolo soon became standard, and by the twentieth century a series of optional instruments had become available: English horn, soprano and bass clarinets, contrabassoon, saxophone, and alto flute. Thus from the Classical four the woodwinds expanded to a dozen or so, with options for more.

The brass choir began with two horns and an occasional pair of trumpets, and by 1900 had expanded to include ten or twelve players. The trombones entered early in the nineteenth century and were soon standard as a threesome, joined by the tuba to make a quartet of low brass. The horns doubled their original number to become a sectional quartet; two to four trumpets are found in nineteenth-century scores, as are occasional pairs of cornets. (The cornet was a popular band and solo instrument, and cornet virtuosos were featured as star performers in summer band concerts. It was the trumpet, however—brighter in tone, though less manipulable—that seemed better suited to the orchestral milieu.)

The percussion section of the symphony orchestra began with a single performer playing a pair of *timpani.* In early symphonies, the timpanist was not provided with a written part of his own and was obliged to improvise his contribution, taking his cue from the music of nearby trumpet players. Gradually the timpanist gained stature; his part was specifically notated, he often had three or more drums surrounding him, and, on rare occasions, he was even entrusted with thematic material. And he was no longer alone. Additional percussionists were required for the battery of instruments specified by nineteenth-century composers: triangle, cymbals, chimes—and, later, when exotic color was exploited, celesta, castanets, and Chinese gong. In the twentieth century, piano, xylophone, harp, and wood block (and even a typewriter) have been added—all notated in the percussion section of the score. The timpanist has been a specialist from the start, but the other members of the percussion choir must be more versatile. The number of percussion instruments it is possible for only two or three performers to play is often splendid to behold; and in the twentieth century, the huge range of tone quality and special effects has given the percussion section a new glamor.

View of an orchestra. The timpanist is at the rear; the brass section takes up the two back rows of seats and the woodwinds the next two. The strings are seated in curved rows: violins in front, the violas in the middle, and cellos and basses at right rear.

The symphony orchestra is not an invariable group but one whose ideal has changed from decade to decade, and whose embodiment has varied from orchestra to orchestra and from work to work. It is difficult to specify any definite number of players, but a typical listing might look like this:

STRING CHOIR	
First violins	16
Second violins	14
Violas	12
Cellos	10
Basses	8
	60

WOODWIND CHOIR	
Flutes and piccolo	3
Oboes	2
Clarinets	2
Bassoons	2
English horn	1
Contrabassoon	1
	11

BRASS CHOIR		PERCUSSION CHOIR	
French horns	4	Timpani	1
Trumpets	3	Miscellaneous	2
Trombones	3		
Tuba	1		
	11		3

The total might thus be eighty to ninety players. The symphony orchestra is a magnificently flexible and versatile group, capable of a huge variety of qualities and effects, and it has no serious rival as the most popular concert ensemble in the West today. And of all large groups, it has always been the most purely musical. The marching band is associated with ceremony, the concert band with holidays, and the popular band with dancing and romancing. The opera or ballet pit orchestra must accommodate itself to verbal or choreographic elements that are often more important than the music. But the symphony orchestra in a concert has no such competition. It joins only with an occasional soloist for a display of virtuoso-orchestral interaction in a concerto—but that too is a truly musical display and a truly musical interaction.

The twentieth century has witnessed the expansion of interest in performing groups in many directions: backward in time, as musicology awakens interest in past sounds; forward in time, as composers continue to experiment with new sounds; and laterally into ethnic and social adventures, welcoming and legitimizing instruments, groups, and techniques that prejudice would have locked out of Western musical awareness a century ago.

9. Classical Music

THE CLASSICAL PERIOD, which encompassed the second half of the eighteenth century and the first part of the nineteenth, was perhaps the most cosmopolitan era in the history of Western music. National stylistic differences were minimized, and music was hailed as the universal language—a rather grandiose claim in view of the small proportion of the globe occupied by Western Europe. Philosophers, particularly Jean-Jacques Rousseau (1712–1778), played a major role in formulating aesthetic ideals of Classical music—naturalness, simplicity, and a commitment to the equal importance of head and heart.

It was a propitious time both economically and socially for professional musicians. Public concerts were becoming more and more common, thus providing sources of income other than royal or noble patronage. Service at court had always been a mixed blessing, and musicians must have welcomed this opportunity to live more economically independent lives. And their new social status must have been equally gratifying. At mid-century, a composer had been typically a liveried servant, creating music to fill the demands and please the taste of his patron. But by the end of the century he was a free agent, often composing in whatever medium struck his fancy. He had no guarantee of financial success, but he was aesthetically limited only by self-imposed restrictions.

CLASSICAL STYLE CHARACTERISTICS

In style, Classical music was uncompromisingly homophonic. If the Baroque had been ambivalent toward polyphonic rigor, Classicism was single-minded in rejecting it. Simplicity was the watchword, with melodies presented singly rather than in combination. Tonality was the framework for pitch organization, and tertian chords (page 11) formed the harmonic vocabulary. There was a predominance of diatonic chords (chords using only the tones belonging to the key), but rich chromaticism (tones foreign to the key) provided ready contrast and was often used at climaxes or to underscore passages of emotional intensity. The polarity of treble and bass lost its fascination for composers, and inner voices received the same care given to the outer ones.

Meter was a primary unifying force in Classical music. All other musical elements were variable, but the Classical style depended on consistent meter and steady pulse. Tonality contributed both to unity and to variety: during the course of a composition, the tonal center shifted, often with great frequency, but the eventual return to the original tonality was as predictable as it was satisfying.

As in most harmonic music, four-voice texture was basic, but it was by no means constant. Unlike the relatively consistent textures of previous style periods, a constantly changing texture was characteristic of Classicism. Virtually every aspect of texture was subject to contrast: thickness and thinness were juxtaposed, sometimes in quick alternations; several rhythmic patterns were

The Parthenon, built on a hill above the city of Athens and completed in 438 B.C., was completely symmetrical and gently proportioned. Its plan is opposite.

often combined to create internal textural interest; and contrast was sometimes compounded by a different style of attack for each rhythmic pattern. But surface texture was the chief area of concentration. As in the *style galant,* detached attack was standard in fast movements, but Classical music heightened the detached effect by interjecting two-note slurs (smooth connections). More than any preceding generation, Classical composers used silences as a vital element in the musical fabric; the resulting "air" between sounds gave their music its characteristic lightness and buoyancy.

Melodies were simple, graceful, and expressive, with lyric ideals prevailing in instrumental as well as vocal music. Ornamentation was used sparingly, and performers were discouraged from improvising embellishments. Composers claimed ornamentation as their prerogative, thus making further inroads into the performers' territory.

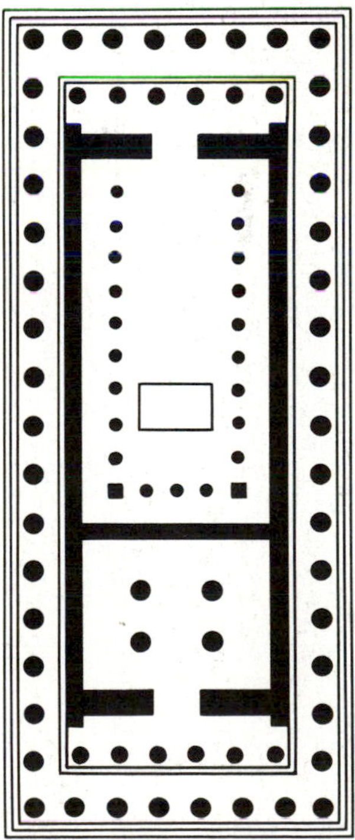

Baroque dynamics had specialized in block contrasts of loud and soft, as exemplified by the echo phrase. But Classicists, finding that the echo phrase had become a cliché, sought subtler effects. They became fascinated with new effects of *crescendo* (gradually increasing volume of sound) and *diminuendo* (gradually decreasing volume). This concept was not totally new, but it had previously been applied primarily to a single tone rather than to a succession of tones. The use of gradational dynamic intensity to build emotional intensity within a phrase was still a novel technique—exciting and ripe for exploitation.

Classical cadences were clear-cut, with all voices cadencing simultaneously. It was standard practice to begin a work with a succession of phrases of identical length, generating a false sense of security, and then jarring the listener out of complacency by using shorter or longer phrases in the continuation. Phrases normally occurred in pairs, the first phrase marked by a light cadence and the second by a more definitive one. Thus each pair was somewhat like a compound sentence in which two clauses are separated by a comma, and the end of the thought is indicated by a period. Balance and proportion were central to Classical music, and phrase structure played a major role in achieving these goals.

Emotional expressiveness in the Baroque had been wedded to the word, and vocal music had aimed at underscoring musically any mood inherent in the text. Only opera was regarded as

The Musician, one of a series of engravings printed in the 18th century that satirized various professions.

capable of conveying the lustier passions. In the Classical era, composers undertook to create emotion through instrumental sound alone, without relying on a text. It was a noble ambition, and if success is measured by the range of responses that their music has inspired, they succeeded admirably. But if success is measured in terms of unanimity of responses, their success is not so certain. For in responding to music, one person's gaiety is another's tranquility, and what gives consolation to one may inspire abject grief in another. The challenge of arousing specific emotion in listeners has never ceased to fascinate composers, and it has become the stock in trade of those who write film music, working with specific words and images.

Humor was particularly attractive to Classical composers. It had long been a part of vocal music, but its entry into the instrumental domain represented an incursion into new territory. Like any language, music has a potential for humor; whether or not this potential is realized depends equally on the composer's imagination and the listener's ability to recognize a musical joke. This ability presupposes familiarity with musical style and vocabulary: only if listeners are aware of what is expected in a piece of music can they possibly hear the humorous *un*expected—incongruity or non sequitur. Classical composers evinced considerable ingenuity and wit in creating both broad and subtle musical jokes. Sudden, violent dynamic changes might be introduced into innocuous passages in which such dramatic procedures were wholly uncalled for; a calm, straightforward first phrase might be answered by one that could only be described as busy; radical changes of register might succeed one another in the same melodic line, often rendered more ungainly by the juxtaposition of unlikely instruments. Mozart's orchestral work *A Musical Joke* features deliberate "wrong" notes, as well as more subtle stylistic witticisms. Beethoven's piano piece *Rage over a Lost Penny* is patently a tempest in a teapot with, as the title suggests, much ado about nothing. And at least once, the visual element was part of the joke: Haydn planned the final movement of his "Farewell" Symphony so that the performers would finish their parts, pick up their instruments, and depart one by one, leaving two lone violinists on stage to end the work. This was Haydn's way of letting his patron know that he and the orchestra needed a vacation. But Classical music has been ill-served by twentieth-century veneration: overly respectful performers sometimes miss the point and turn sparkling musical delight into pedestrian pedantry.

Two of the leading figures in the transition from Baroque to Classical style were, interestingly, sons of that arch-conservative, Johann Sebastian Bach. Carl Philipp Emanuel Bach (1714–1788) was the most famous member of the family. That he succeeded Telemann (his godfather) in the prestigious post at Hamburg is indicative of the esteem in which he was held. Although he composed for a variety of media, C. P. E. Bach is best remembered for his contribution to keyboard music. He was among the first to reject the brilliant harpsichord in favor of a keyboard instrument capable of shaded dynamics. His first love was the clavichord, but its silky, soft, and intimate tone was lost in even a small concert hall or salon. So he turned to the piano, an instrument that had been widely neglected since its invention early in the eighteenth century. His music anticipated Classicism in both style and form and exerted a powerful influence on the younger generation of composers, who brought the Classical style to fruition.

C. P. E. BACH

Johann Christian Bach (1735–1782) went beyond his elder half-brother in rejecting the tenets that had governed their father's life. His music was not only homophonic, it was basically Italian in style—and, worse, opera claimed the lion's share of his attention! He became Italian even in his religion, abandoning the Lutheran faith of his father to become a Roman Catholic. His national origin was repudiated when, like Handel, he became a British citizen. His operas are forgotten today, but his piano music continues to be viewed as important both for itself and for its influence. He was a vigorous partisan of the piano, and he was the first to present a public recital devoted to that instrument alone (in London, in 1768). If his sphere of influence was less wide than that of his illustrious elder brother, it was none the less significant, because it included the young Mozart.

J. C. BACH

Mozart was equally influenced by a type of harpsichord music that he heard in Paris during his first visit there: a multimovement work for harpsichord with added instruments—strings or winds, but without basso continuo. This type of music, popular since the 1730s, began as a combination of the harpsichord with one other instrument. Later, these works included as many as eight other instruments so that they resembled harpsichord concertos.

OPERATIC REFORM

Classical instrumental forms and media were flexible, inviting experimentation and lending themselves readily to changing styles and ideals. Opera, however, represented a problem. The extravagant, spectacular operatic format inherited from the late Baroque was firmly entrenched, but it was totally at odds with mid-century philosophy. Opera was therefore ripe for reform. Naturalism acknowledged drama as paramount, and it spelled doom for the virtuoso castrato, who was clearly on his way out. The clamor for operatic reform was far from universal, and efforts in that direction encountered flinty resistance. Audiences adored spectacle, and singers and stage technicians had vested interests in it, so there was a spirited defense of the status quo. Operatic reform made little headway in Italy, where opera remained basically Baroque. Paris was the scene of the action, and there the battle raged furiously, with Christoph Willibald Gluck (1714–1787) chief among the reformers. Gluck personified Classical cosmopolitanism. Born in Bavaria, he studied music in Italy, traveled widely throughout Europe, lived awhile in Vienna, but his career culminated in Paris. His reforms were directed toward restoring drama to the central place in a theatrical production and at reducing singers from arrogant egotists to interpreters with respect for a composer's intent. Gluck enjoyed the protection of Marie Antoinette and the enthusiastic support of a sizeable number of Parisian operagoers. He was strongly opposed, however, by a large faction of Italian-opera zealots, who did not take kindly to any tampering with their art form.

GLUCK

The conflict was not limited to Paris and the reforms of Gluck. Except for Italy, hostilities were continental in scope. One of the principal issues everywhere was semantics, or what might be called "truth in operatic packaging." Classical reformers believed that every operatic element was open to change, and diehard devotees of the Baroque spectacular refused to dignify any other type with the glorious name "opera." Therefore, every mutation—and there were many—necessitated the coining of a new genre name. Every major country contributed its own terminology, so that in the end the term *opera* rarely appeared without some qualifying adjective. A list of the major types appears on the next page.

OPERAS THAT WERE SUNG THROUGHOUT

GRAND OPERA was a direct descendant of the late Italian Baroque spectacular. The plot (such as it was) centered around noble tragedy, but it was subordinate to singing and lavish staging.

OPERA SERIA (serious opera) also had a tragic theme and a lavish production, but it gave more emphasis to plot and somewhat less to magnificence.

OPERA BUFFA (comic opera) was smaller in scope, involving little or no stage machinery and no mob scenes. The dramatic element was crucial, and characters were contemporary in type and in their humor, which was often bawdy.

DRAMMA GIOCOSO (tragic comedy) was distinguished from opera buffa only by the serious undercurrent in the plot.

OPERA SEMI-SERIA (semi-serious opera) was a term used to describe an unostentatious production dealing with a serious contemporary theme. The staging was not elaborate enough for such a work to qualify as opera seria, and a serious plot removed it from the opera buffa category.

COMÉDIE LARMOYANTE (tearful comedy) was the French equivalent of opera semi-seria.

OPERAS THAT INCLUDED SOME SPEAKING

ENGLISH OPERA, which had first appeared as a manifestation of the style bourgeois (page 134), dealt with both serious and comic subjects. The play was paramount, and music was interpolated at appropriate points in the action. The nineteenth-century term for this format was *operetta*.

SINGSPIEL was a German adaptation of the English opera. Its final shape revealed French and Italian influence as well, but the original impetus came from English sources.

OPÉRA COMIQUE was a catchall term used to describe any French musical production based on a subject that did not qualify as tragedy. Normally it dealt with a comic theme, and its staging was less than magnificent but far from austere.

As the names of the last three types in the list suggest, the categories that incorporated speaking were performed in the vernacular. Italian remained the preferred language for totally sung productions except in France, where both French and Italian librettos were used, and where fierce arguments were waged over the relative merits of French and Italian recitative.

VIENNESE CLASSICISM

Paris was the principal camp of the operatic wars, but the capital of Classicism was Vienna. This lively city was enamored of a new dance, the waltz, which (perhaps because it was considered lascivious) was rapidly replacing the minuet in popularity. The concertgoing public was knowledgeable, enthusiastic, and hospitable to new ideas in music. The exciting musical climate of Vienna was attractive to composers; many outstanding musicians of the period established residence there, giving additional luster to an already musically brilliant city.

HAYDN

Franz Joseph Haydn (1732–1809), the first of the full-fledged Classicists and the last major composer to reap the benefits and suffer the vicissitudes of service at court, was only a sometime resident of Vienna. His musical career began when, at the age of eight, he entered St. Stephen's Cathedral choir school, and Vienna remained his home until 1759, when he accepted a court position outside the city. He was fortunate in securing a patron whose great wealth was equaled by his enthusiasm for music, and who encouraged musical experimentation and innovation. A talented group of singers and orchestral performers were at Haydn's disposal for opera productions and instrumental concerts. Most of his 104 symphonies were written for this private orchestra, which was composed of some two dozen players. (No doubt Haydn would be astounded to see the assembled multitude which participates in performances of his symphonies today.) During his long tenure at court, Haydn made many trips to Vienna to acquaint himself with current developments in the musical capital, and after the death of his patron, Vienna once again became his home.

Instrumental forms were of central concern to Classical composers, and the orchestra was a particularly attractive medium. The size of early Classical orchestras in general ranged from twenty to thirty players, but the orchestras were amazingly diverse and often unbalanced both in distribution of instruments and in

King Frederick the Great of Prussia (1712–1786) playing a flute concerto. Many royal figures were accomplished amateur musicians; Frederick studied with excellent teachers, and he composed as well as performed.

registers of sound. Working for thirty years at the same court, Haydn was able to create a finely balanced group, which became the model for the modern orchestra.

The Symphony and Sonata Form

The orchestra was the medium and the *symphony* was the form that generated the most excitement during the Classical era. This form was a unique manifestation of the period, embodying the ideal of balance and proportion in the organization of varied musical materials. The Classical symphony was typically a four-movement work for orchestra. Each movement was an independent entity, balanced with the other three movements by means of both conspicuous contrast and subtle interrelationships.

The first was a fast movement in *sonata form* (also called *sonata-allegro form*), which, like the symphony itself, was an invention of Classical composers. Sonata form is somewhat like a three-act play: the characters are introduced in Act I, the scene changes and the plot thickens in Act II, and the original setting returns in Act III, revealing the characters in a new light. Translated into musical terms, sonata form begins with an *exposition* (sometimes preceded by a slow introduction), introducing a principal theme or group of themes. This is followed by a modulating *bridge* passage leading to a new key and a new theme or group that both contrasts with and complements the principal theme. Next comes a closing section that rounds off the exposition and cadences with firmness but without finality in the new key (the Act I curtain). Repetition of the entire exposition was standard practice in the eighteenth century, but twentieth-century conductors often disregard the indicated repeat.

Next comes the *development,* which is as unpredictable as the exposition is predictable. The development section is crucial—it is the proving ground for the composer's imagination. A development may be short or long, and may deal with one, two, or all the themes presented in the exposition. Classical composers delighted in viewing various aspects of a theme as separable, and thematic development often involved altering one element while leaving the others intact. If a theme first appeared in a major key, it might reenter in minor; or, if a theme had been presented by the cellos, it might be assigned to the flutes—a change in both color and register. The theme was also subject to dissection, and one of the most characteristic developmental techniques involved intensive treatment of *motives* (short thematic fragments). Harmony, rhythm, attack, dynamics, and texture were other aspects of a theme that could be altered.

Different themes lend themselves to different types of treatment, so that any development section is shaped in large part by the character of the thematic material with which it deals. Only two factors in a development are predictable: it is likely to be tonally unstable, modulating frequently, and it must eventually prepare for a return to the tonic key and lead, without pause, to the recapitulation.

The *recapitulation* (Act III) involves a restatement of the exposition with several crucial modifications. The bridge passage is varied so that it returns to the tonic rather than leading to a new key. And the second theme is presented in the tonic key, with changes of register or mode or both.

If the materials of the closing section do not lead naturally to a convincing final cadence, a *coda* (literally, "tail") is added to bring the movement to a satisfactory conclusion. The dimensions of a coda are unpredictable, ranging all the way from a slight addition of a few chords to a crowning fourth section that indulges in further development of thematic material.

Sonata form might be summarized thus:

(Introduction)

EXPOSITION

First theme (or group) in tonic key.
Bridge passage, modulating to a new key.
Second theme (or group) in the new key.
Closing section, ending in the new key.

DEVELOPMENT

Treatment of one or more themes according to the character of the theme(s) and the inspiration of the composer.

RECAPITULATION

First theme (or group) in tonic key.
Bridge passage, returning to tonic key.
Second theme (or group) in tonic key.
Closing section in tonic key.

(Coda)

Even so generalized a scheme, though vital as a point of departure, was often subject to some exception or other—in fact, it is unusual to find a sonata-form movement that carries the diagram through exactly. Haydn frequently used only one main theme (presenting it in both keys in the exposition); Mozart introduced new themes in development sections or changed keys in the recapitulation. Nevertheless, each symphony maintains most of the format, and the form is clearly recognizable.

Side 6 Band 1

The first movement of Haydn's Symphony No. 88 (one of the "Paris" symphonies) opens with a short, slow introduction. The exposition begins with a sprightly figure that is repeated at a higher pitch, followed by a variant form and then a cadence. This theme is presented in the strings and repeated in the horns. The vital opening figure remains the unifying element throughout the entire movement, featured in the bridge passage to the new key and even in the closing section. A second theme, made up of a syncopated group of chords in a repeated pattern, is secondary in importance, and does not compete with the opening material. In this recording, the exposition is repeated as indicated.

The development section continues the opening figure of the exposition, first sounding it softly in the violins as a falling sequence over a trill, then loudly by the whole orchestra in a minor key, then in a rising sequence. This figure yields finally to a brief sequence using the chords of the second theme, which prepares for the return to the original key.

The recapitulation repeats the opening theme, but with a flute figure added to the strings. It proceeds normally, ending with a slightly extended closing section that features the horns, but the movement has no coda.

The movement's zestful vigor, its highly textured material and imaginative use of it, and the orchestration for strings with two horns, two oboes, and a flute, are all consummately representative of the Classical style in general and of Haydn's style in particular.

The second movement of a Classical symphony was most often a slow movement, contrasting with the first in tempo and tonality as well as thematic material. Occasionally it too was in sonata form, but more frequently it appeared in three-part form (ABA) or as a theme with variations. The Classical bent for concentrating on one aspect of a theme in the development was applied also to variations. It was common practice to include variations featuring change of meter, change of mode, change of texture, or exploitation of different registers as well as the more traditional techniques of melodic embellishment and change of pulse subdivision.

The third movement was a minuet (a vestige of the ancient and honorable dance suite) that appeared in the tonic key and was cast in ABA form. The B section was usually lighter in texture than A and often featured a different section of the orchestra. This movement was usually shorter and less intense than the first two, offering listeners some respite from concentrated emotional involvement.

The fourth movement was most often fast in tempo, brilliant in

The minuet, depicted in a dance text of 1735.

character, and well calculated to serve as a rousing finale. It was unequivocally tonic in key, and in design it was either in sonata form or it was a *rondo.* A rondo is basically an extension of three-part form, including more contrasting sections, each of which is followed by a return to A. Its simplest version is ABACA, but it is sometimes extended to include a third digression (ABACADA) or a return of B (ABACABA). In the Classical rondo, the principal theme was usually lighthearted in nature, and its reappearances frequently revealed an element of jocularity or triumphant exuberance.

In summary, the format of a Classical symphony normally followed this plan:

	I	II	III	IV
TEMPO:	fast	slow	moderately fast	fast
KEY:	tonic	contrasting	tonic	tonic
FORM:	sonata form	theme and variations or ABA or sonata form	ABA	rondo or sonata form

Chamber Music

In the area of chamber music, the trio sonata gave way to larger ensembles, consistent with the new textural emphasis of Classical music. At mid-century, the most popular form was the divertimento (page 152) and divertimenti were as various as they were numerous. The number of movements and the forms of individual movements varied; so did the number and types of instruments for which these works were written. Sometimes the ensemble approached orchestral proportions, but smaller groups were more common.

The string quartet (page 152) was to the Classical era what the trio sonata had been to the Baroque. In form, a string quartet generally followed the same four-movement scheme as the symphony, but music written for the smaller group was more intimate in character than that written for orchestra.

Haydn was always in the forefront of experimentation in chamber music. He contributed about sixty divertimenti and sixty-five trios fairly early in his career, but it is his eighty-odd string quartets that form the core of his later chamber music. During his holidays, Haydn frequently went to Vienna to play quartets with other composers (including Mozart), thus keeping up with new music and having the fun of professional interchange.

The Quartet Op. 64, No. 5, called "The Lark," is a representative work. It has four movements: an opening fast movement, a long and poignant slow movement, a humorous minuet, and a very fast finale. All the movements work out textural interactions among the four players, who are variously singled out, paired, set into brisk four-way conversations, and joined in unanimous melodic or harmonic statements.

Side 6 Band 2

The finale confines itself to two kinds of textural interaction. The opening section, which is repeated, presents the first violin in an extremely rapid, detached line (in the constant rhythm of a "perpetual motion") set off by the three lower instruments playing a few brief, simple chords. After the repetition of this first section, the action spreads to all the players in a fugal section in a minor key. The accumulation of voices is made more exciting by the rising lines, as the instruments proceed into higher and higher registers. Suddenly the action stops. Then the initial section returns, this time thickened by activity in the lower instruments. The movement ends with a brief coda culminating in two pairs of runs in opposite directions. The delicacy, intricacy, and exhilaration of this movement exemplify the flexibility so characteristic of the string quartet.

The Classical sonata was a multimovement work for solo instrument or a duet (two instruments in combination) that followed the same overall formal scheme as the symphony. (The terms *sonata* and *sonata form* should not be confused. The latter refers to the structure of a single movement of a multimovement work—a symphony, a string quartet, or a sonata.) In many sonatas, however, the four-movement design was reduced to three, with the minuet the most likely candidate for omission.

The vital work of the two Bach brothers did much to define the solo piano sonata, both in style and in form. The duet sonata, however, owed its format to the French accompanied harpsichord piece (page 165); early duets and piano trios (page 154) were published with French titles until the early years of the nineteenth century.

But the piano was equally vital in both types—and that instrument had totally eclipsed the harpsichord by the end of the century and was well on its way toward becoming a household fixture. Classical sonatas constituted the first important body of music written specifically for piano, and they continue to serve as a cornerstone of that literature, both in the education of pianists and in recital.

The Solo Concerto

The piano also figured prominently in the *solo concerto,* a form for solo instrument and orchestra that was given definition by Wolf-

Mozart as a young boy, in a scene from a Salzburg Marionette Theater production.

MOZART

gang Amadeus Mozart (1756–1791). In his hands, the Classical concerto became symphonic in form, and although technical difficulties in the solo part were formidable, the soloist's role was primarily musical rather than virtuoso. Three movements were standard, corresponding in tempo and form to the first, second, and fourth movements of a symphony. Sonata form was handled somewhat differently in the first movement: rather than a literal, note-for-note repetition of the exposition, two separate expositions were written out, the first for orchestra alone and the second for soloist and orchestra in combination. The most dramatic moment of the movement came at the end of the recapitulation, when the orchestra built to a huge climax, came to a rest on a suspense-filled chord, and put down their instruments. At this point, the soloist launched into the *cadenza*—a brilliant solo with dazzling displays of virtuosity and at least minimal relationship to thematic material. Excitement was heightened by the audience's awareness that cadenzas were not part of the score, but were improvised by soloists according to their inspiration of the moment. (That element of drama is missing in modern performances, in which precomposed and prelearned cadenzas are used.) After a trill, traditionally inserted to serve as a cue to the orchestra, a rousing coda involving all forces brought the movement to a close.

Side 6 Band 3

The first movement of Mozart's Concerto in A, K. 488,* is graceful and lyrical in style, and in structure embodies a mixture of conformity to and departure from the usual pattern of sonata form as used in the piano concerto. The two expositions follow the model closely, but the development represents a deviation from the norm. A dramatic pause marks the beginning of the development section, and immediately the orchestra introduces a completely new theme. This new theme is somewhat unstable rhythmically, and in the dialogue that ensues, the piano seemingly seeks to reaffirm the rhythmic issue that the new theme, insistently reiterated by the orchestra, has called into doubt. Conformity in formal design reenters with the recapitulation: all themes, including the one introduced in the development, are restated; the cadenza appears right on schedule; and a short orchestral coda brings the movement to a decisive conclusion.

Although his contribution to concerto literature was substantial, Mozart's concertos are only a fraction of his total work. He was a remarkably versatile and prolific composer whose music epitomized the Classical ideal. Mozart had the great advantages of being born just as Classical ideas were taking definitive shape and of having a father (Leopold Mozart) who was well aware of these ideas, who was one of the century's great teachers, and who made sure that the gifted boy was exposed to the best that Europe had to offer a young musician. A native of Austria, Mozart had taken part in musical activities in Italy, France, Germany, and England before he was twelve. His multifaceted education made him one of the most cosmopolitan and musically sophisticated composers in the history of music.

Mozart was the first important composer to live and work as a free agent—not entirely because he wanted to, but because he was unable to secure a position at court. Most of his adult life was spent in Vienna, where he composed by commission, organized

*K or Koechel numbers, which are commonly used to identify Mozart's works, were assigned to his compositions by the scholar Ludwig von Koechel.

and performed in concerts, and taught privately in a vain attempt to patch together an adequate income. Unfortunately, the expansion of public concerts did not culminate during his short lifetime; and although he was famous throughout Europe, he died a pauper.

The predominance of instrumental music in Mozart's total output reflects necessity rather than preference; he was obliged to compose music of whatever type was commissioned or needed to fill the programs he organized. Had he been able to follow his natural bent, he would have concentrated his efforts more on opera, for that was his great love. But despite his financial problems, he managed to create a number of operas that are still in the repertoire of opera companies all over the Western world. Mozart took no part in the battles surrounding opera—he happily created them in every category: opera seria in *Idomeneo;* opera buffa in *Le nozze di Figaro* ("The Marriage of Figaro") and *Cosi fan tutte* (roughly, "They All Do It"); dramma giocoso in *Don Giovanni;* and singspiel in *Die Zauberflöte* ("The Magic Flute") and *Die Entführung aus dem Serail* ("The Abduction from the Seraglio"). In the field of Classical opera, Mozart was without peer; his Italian operas were the best of that genre, and he elevated German singspiel to a new artistic level.

Le nozze di Figaro was an enormous success at its first performance and still plays to packed houses. The opera is essentially a situation comedy in which the ranking nobleman (Count Almaviva) is outwitted by his valet (Figaro), with the help of both leading ladies. As the plot unravels, tangled threads of love, lechery, and deception ensnarl the characters in quandaries and crises, but in the end, all is satisfactorily untangled with a promising prospect of wedded bliss for everyone. The recorded excerpt,

Side 6 Band 4

the aria "Porgi, amor," interjects a tinge of sadness into this musical romp. The Countess laments the inconstancy of her philandering husband and sings of her longing for the return of his love. The melody matches her mood eloquently: many phrases end with a descending "sigh," expressive of yearning, and the entire aria is a model of Classical lyricism and simplicity.

Despite their concern with the communication of the passions, Classical composers never lost touch with the concept of music as organized sound. The graciousness and good manners that characterized the times are reflected in the music; rudeness and gaucherie would have been as unacceptable musically as they

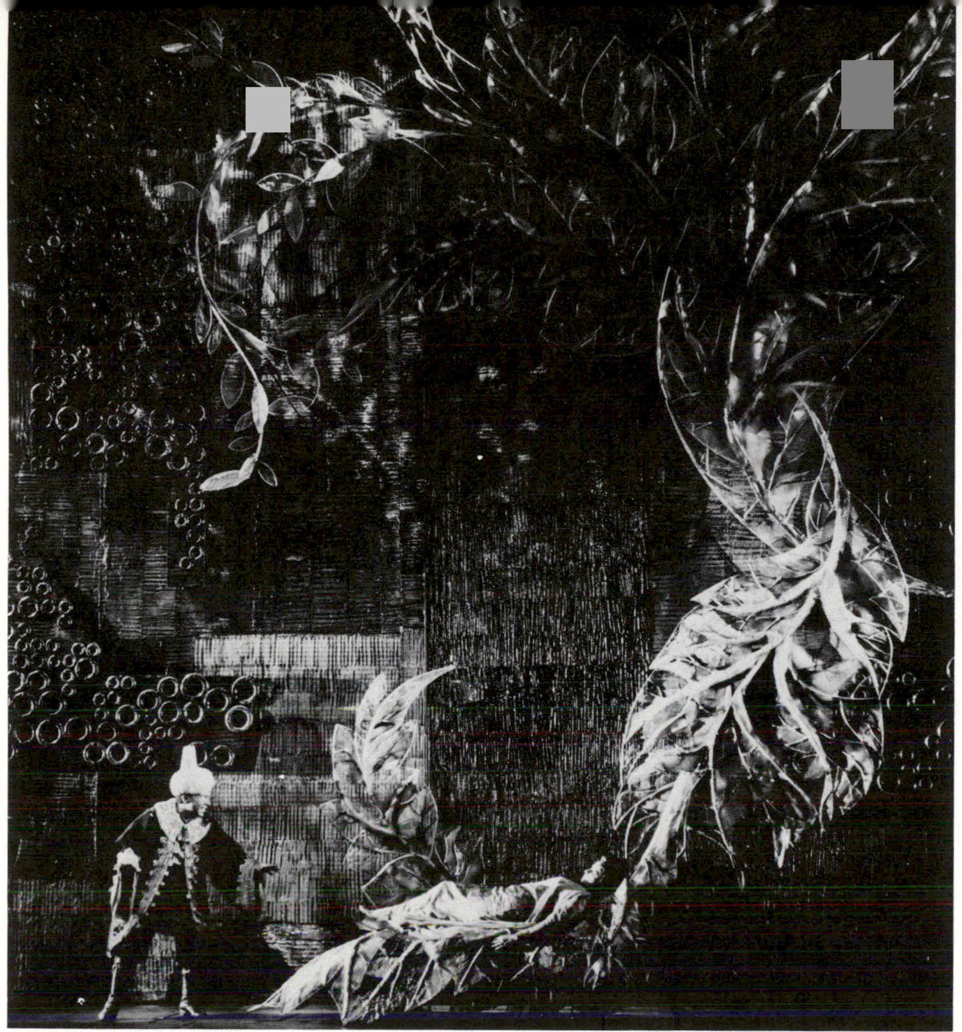

A scene from Mozart's *The Magic Flute,* in a production at the Salzburg Festival, Austria.

were socially. Mozart, in a letter to his father, aptly summarized the Classical creed:

> Passions, whether violent or not, must never be expressed in such a way as to excite disgust, and . . . music, even in the most terrible situations, must never offend the ear, but must please the hearer, or, in other words, must never cease to be music.*

BEETHOVEN

But musical gentility reached the end of the line with Ludwig van Beethoven (1770–1827). Stormy and irascible by nature, Beethoven did not permit proprieties to inhibit him either musically or socially. His policy of deliberately boorish behavior toward the Viennese nobility did not prevent these noblemen from acknowledging his genius by providing him with an income, conditional only on his making Vienna his home. Nor was this unprecedented brand of patronage his only source of income. The

*Quoted in Eric Blom, ed., *Mozart's Letters* (Baltimore: Penguin, 1956), pp. 181–82.

publication of his music, which belonged to him rather than to any patron, and the proceeds from public concerts produced substantial revenues.

Stylistically, Beethoven's music embodies ideals of both Classicism and Romanticism. In mood, it anticipates the Romantic movement with an intensity of passion and the violence with which that passion is sometimes expressed. But in form, Beethoven was a complete Classicist. His organization of musical materials was thoughtful and disciplined, and the forms developed by Haydn and Mozart served to structure his highly personal and emotional style.

But basically, Beethoven marched to a different drummer, and his treatment of Classical forms was no less individual than his style. In general, the four-movement format of the symphony suited his purposes admirably, but the scope of his ideas required modification of certain details. A larger orchestra with full representation of brass and woodwind families was required in the interests of both grandeur and variety of tone color. The minuet seemed anachronistic to him, and he usually discarded it in favor of the *scherzo,* a fast, rowdy movement harboring no hint of courtly elegance. Individual movements were extended in duration and cohesiveness. Development sections became more tightly woven, and a coda frequently took on the character and proportions of a second development. One of Beethoven's favorite techniques of development involved extracting a motive from a theme and treating it as a separate entity. His themes were often motivic in construction and lent themselves naturally to this type of development. A single motive sometimes pervaded an entire movement; the opening four-note motive of his Fifth Symphony is a famous example.

Beethoven's parsimonious Muse granted him relatively brief moments of inspiration. For him the act of composition was a slow, laborious process, involving painstaking effort to shape his materials. As a result, his works accumulated more slowly than those of his predecessors. He produced only nine symphonies, for example, compared with Haydn's 104 and Mozart's 41. His symphonic style, too, developed slowly; his First Symphony was deeply indebted to Haydn, and although the Second took on Beethovenian proportions, it was only with the Third that his full individuality asserted itself. The Ninth Symphony is a giant work, unique in its period for its monumental dimensions—it requires full orchestra, chorus, and vocal soloists, and has been known to consume an entire concert in its presentation.

Beethoven's interest in brass and woodwind instruments extended to chamber music as well as orchestral music. Although string quartets took precedence, many of his chamber compositions combined strings and winds, and a few were written for winds only. Piano figured prominently in much of Beethoven's music; an outstanding pianist himself, he included the piano in a number of chamber works, combined it with orchestra in five concertos, and composed thirty-two sonatas for that instrument alone.

The thirty-two sonatas are a vital component of piano literature; they are basic to the repertoire of every concert pianist. (Schroeder, in the comic strip *Peanuts,* is far from unique in his love of Beethoven.) The best-known of his sonatas are those of a tempestuous or tragic nature, but several lesser-known sonatas are distinctly cheerful in mood, and some are whimsically humorous. His Sonata in G, Op. 14, No. 2, for example, is a musical gambol in which no gravity is allowed to intrude. The Scherzo of this sonata is a jovial rondo that reveals the composer's facetious frame of mind from the beginning. The metric pattern of the opening theme shifts constantly in a technique reminiscent of hemiola, and in subsequent sections, where meter is not in doubt, the effervescence of the music erupts in unexpected dynamic contrasts, erratic register changes, and eccentric accents.

Side 6 Band 5

Deafness, always a misfortune, is disastrous for a musician, and Beethoven's refusal to be defeated by this affliction represents a measure of his indomitable spirit. He had suffered some loss of hearing before he was thirty, and during the last years of his life, he was totally deaf—he could not even hear the tumultuous applause that followed the performances of his music. The music itself he could hear in his imagination, but the excitement of listening to another's interpretation of his works was denied him. Perhaps out of fear that his music would be misinterpreted, he included many precise instructions. Dynamics are meticulously marked, and verbal clues—such as "in a singing style" or "plaintively"—appear frequently in his later scores. But whatever their reason, his incursions into the performer's domain tipped the balance of power and raised the composer to a position of dominance—a trend that was to continue and broaden in scope throughout the nineteenth and twentieth centuries.

10. Music in Context

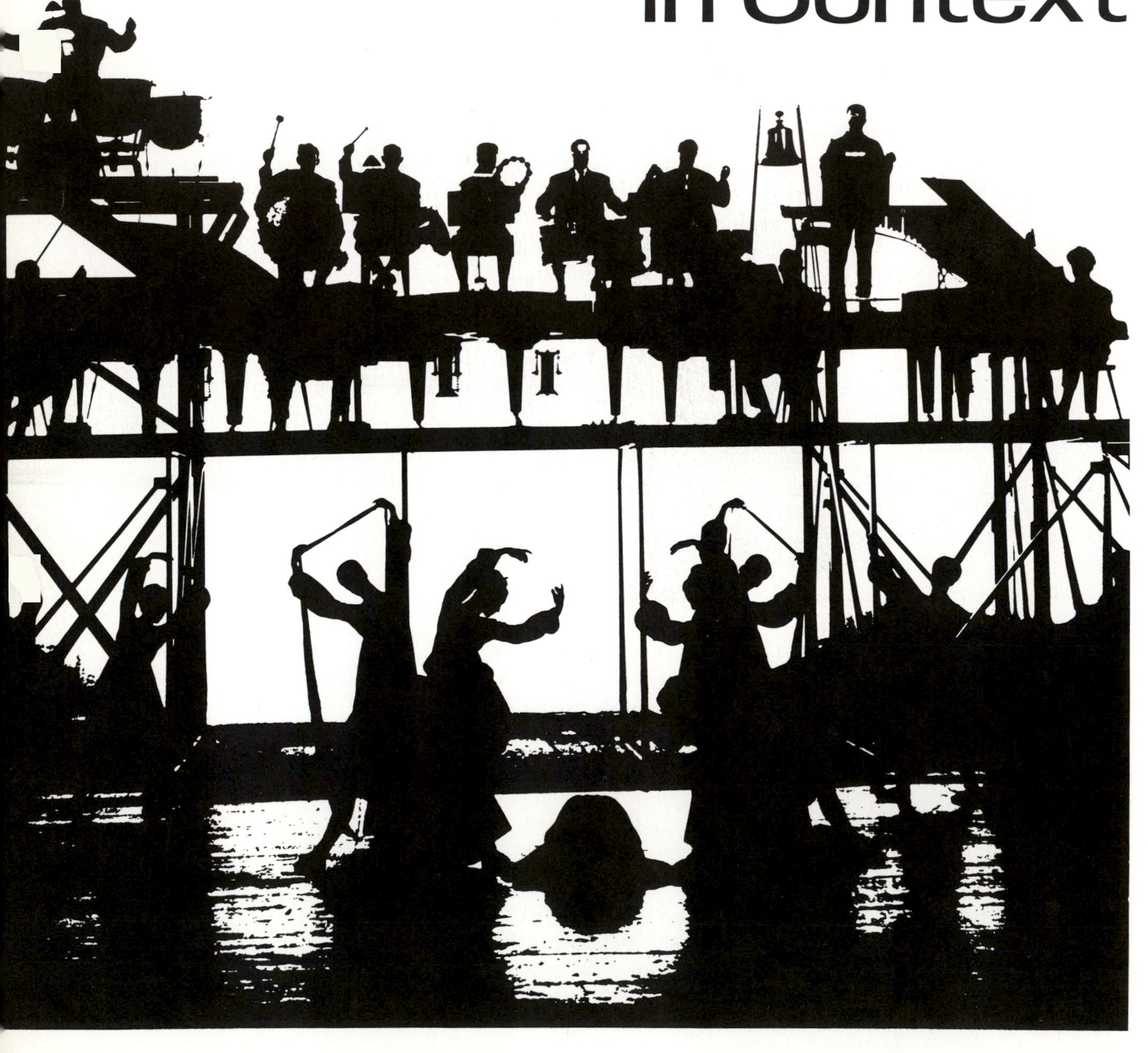

THE EXISTENCE of primary relationships between the various arts is a popular fancy. The idea is intellectually appealing, but it derives more from wishful thinking than from actuality. Marshall McLuhan's contention that the medium is the message may seem overstated, but certainly the medium has strong impact on the degree of precision with which any artistic message is communicated. If, for example, the message involves a mother-child relationship, the meaning can be made explicit through the verbal art of literature, and can gain additional impact when presented through the visual-verbal medium of the theater. A painting or sculpture of a mother and child can be even more poignant, but its meaning is less exact. The painting or sculpture conveys an emotional message with a high nonverbal content that, because the message is colored by individual interpretation, is often more personal than universal. Music, however, has nothing to say on the subject of mothers and children—or, for that matter, on any subject which is verbal or visual in concept. Although musical communication may well be more intensely personal than that of any other artistic medium, it is also the most nebulous.

MUSICAL PARALLELS

Music itself is free of direct meaning, but it can relate to two outside phenomena: sounds (in general—organized or not) and rhythms. The musical concepts "high" and "low," which are visual metaphors, are completely arbitrary—they are, in modern times, actually a reverse of the ancient Greek usage in which our low notes were called "high" and our high notes "low." But "loud" and "soft" are words applicable to any kind of sound, and they are comprehensible to a tone-deaf person. Similarly, ideas of pulse and of relative speed, along with the size and relative energy of melodic gestures, have direct analogy outside of music.

Thus music can parallel quite accurately a number of physical states: for example, it can be passive, soft, and contain a low energy quotient; or it can be active, loud, and contain a high energy quotient. The first set of qualities parallels the body state of a person who is serene or resting; the second parallels the body state of a person who is excited or active. But music cannot differentiate within these or any other general types, and it is utterly powerless to specify any mood with precision.

Two portrayals of mother and child. Above, Study for The MacKintosh Madonna (c. 1512), by Raphael; opposite, *Miserere: "War, Which All Mothers Hate"* (1927), by Georges Rouault.

There is, of course, no reason why it should. A good deal of music in all times and places has been created simply for the delights of sound and of designs in sound—for the sensual and intellectual pleasures of such designs. From the absent-minded strumming of a lone guitarist to the intricate networks of a string quartet, skillfully prepared and offered to a paying public in a concert, such music presents interactions in sound, unencumbered with messages and uncluttered by pictures or words. Musicians have called it *pure* or *absolute* music.

MUSIC AND WORDS

Although in the modern West most absolute music is instrumental, vocal music can be absolute as well. Most cultures practice a nonverbal vocal art; in the West, this is now generally either scat singing in the jazz tradition or nonsense songs, such as "Polly Wolly Doodle" or "Mairzy Doats"—though singing to syllables was popular in the Medieval era, and Renaissance madrigals often fa-la-lahed at great length.

The most universal juxtaposition of words and music lies in the solo song, which is common to all cultural groups past and present. But even lyric song is often virtually dissociated from its text, with a bank of musical phrases put to use for a variety of subjects. All the verses of a song are often sung to the same music, so that one melody serves very different verbal ideas. (That the famous "Amen" chorus in Handel's *Messiah,* for example, had previously served the composer as an operatic drinking song is testimony to the essential neutrality of music.)

It was Baroque recitative that attempted to suit music to a text, but recitative exaggerated the natural inflections of speech and did not create melody. Arias, at the opposite end of the scale, were gorgeously melodic but often had little relation to the text. Baroque composers included occasional thrusts of reference to single words (but not to ideas) that could have specific musical parallel in rhythm or gestures—musical trills for the "warbling" of birds, for example. A few such imitations became conventions: fast repeated notes for the word "tremble" (whether in anger, fear, or awe—in *Messiah,* that convention is used for both "rage" and "glory"), a large melodic leap for "wide," and of course a melodic parallel of words like "fast," "high," or "full." Such conventions also appear in mirroring ideas of ascent and descent—charmingly in Handel's hymn "Joy to the World, the Lord Is Come!," in which the idea of descent from heaven to earth is paralleled in an opening melodic phrase that goes directly down the scale for a full octave.

This word painting in the Baroque period was actually a residue from the Renaissance, when people singing madrigals expected such allusions as part of their pleasure. Like the sometimes intricate interactions of the musical lines, puns were added to the individual parts—much less often to the combined effect—as part of the fun. Some of these puns were very far-fetched, some were outrageous, some uproarious, and some related not to the music *or* to the meaning of the text, but to matters of musical theory or notation. The words "be" ("bee") or "sea" ("see") would use the notes B or C, or the word "pear" would be set for two voices in a pun on the word "pair." Only the imagination of the poet and composer can determine how far such verbal-musical high jinks can be taken.

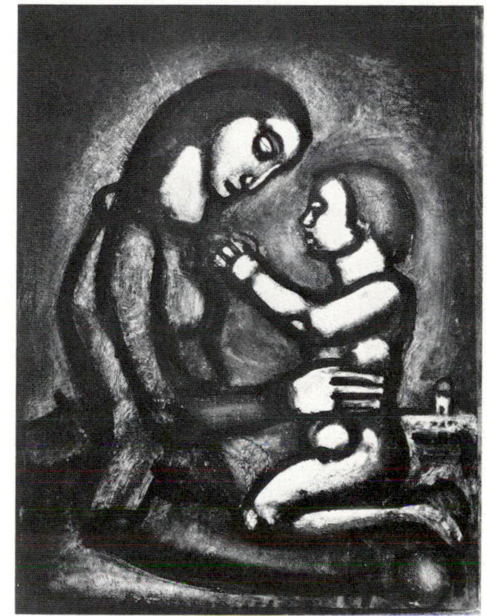

PROGRAM MUSIC

Because the Romantic movement was highly literary, nineteenth-century composers sought means of working more directly with words. The art of the lied (page 199) came to a resplendent height when both vocal line and piano accompaniment were put to work in a line-by-line conjunction of poetic meaning with appropriate musical content. Many Romantic poems were concerned with nature, for example, and the rhythms of brooks or horses' hooves found their way into many song accompaniments; but melodic and harmonic suitability was much more subtle than either word painting or general moods. In Schubert's setting of Goethe's ballad "Der Erlkönig," the music not only underscores the story, with its mood of rising apprehension, but supports extremely fine distinctions in character as well. The father is represented by a stable rhythm and low tessitura, the frightened child by an irregular rhythm and high tessitura, and an enticing melody combines with lightsome rhythm to portray the evilly seductive Erlkönig (Death).

Instrumental music, too, was hoisted into verbal parallels by the Romanticists—an idea that their predecessors would have scorned. Although music can neither portray nor communicate verbal concepts, it can parallel such ideas with appropriate rhythmic and energy content—if the verbal ideas are printed up and given to the audience beforehand. The process is one-way—nobody can derive the verbal ideas from the music. But if listeners are given the ideas and are informed of the intended parallels, they can follow them. Because such information was put into program notes for the audience to read before (and during) performance of such music, the term *program music* was used to describe it.

MUSIC AND DANCE

In the most general terms, music appropriate to nonmusical ideas can be found throughout history and throughout the world. Occasions of pomp have always used music of slow, forthright rhythm and loud commanding sound, which serve to stimulate the blood while inhibiting muscular response. Ceremonies of religious mystery have used soft, mildly active music to help worshipers maintain respectful quiet. Warriors have always been whipped to a need for muscular release by loud, fast, sometimes frantic music—from Aztec invaders charging before the blast of a hundred conchs to Scots Highlanders galvanized into patriotic fervor at the approach of the legendary hundred pipers. And everywhere and always, babies have been put to sleep, the distressed have been comforted, and the restless soothed by slow, soft music that stills the physical and mental functions and reduces tensions.

Greek folk dancers in traditional garb.

The most direct connection between music and anything other than sound is with physical motion, particularly marching and dancing. Because it creates energy, regularly accented music makes people want to move—they unconsciously tap their feet or move their bodies to strongly rhythmic music.

Dance steps are synonymous with rhythmic patterns: the words "waltz," "tango," or "polka" can mean, equally, the rhythms of the music and the patterns of the dancers. Throughout the world, music and the dance are one—or rhythm and the dance are one, for the other elements of music, no matter how compelling, are not really necessary. Melody and harmony add color and detail, but pulse and rhythm are the essence of the dance.

In dance the musical, dramatic, and visual elements are braided together, and when the music that accompanies the dance is integrated with it by being performed by the dancers themselves, these elements become so firmly joined that separation is unthinkable. The distinction between music and dance becomes tenuous indeed when, for example, a Spanish dancer performs a long, rising trill with castanets, describing a wide arc that ends in a snap of dramatic finality.

In addition to social dancing, many cultures, including our own, enjoy dance concerts, virtually all of which are presented with music. Many of these dances are purely decorative—that is, they are concerned entirely with moving designs in space—and many act out stories, often cultural legends known to all and held in great esteem. Such is in fact the basis of formal Oriental dance. It is not always possible to distinguish between such a dance and an opera (if song is included) or a religious ceremony (if the narrative material resides in the realm of sacred tradition). Balinese and Hawaiian dances include narrative elements spelled out eloquently by the dancers' hands; both arts have developed characteristic musical styles.

In the West, Medieval dancing was a miniature summary of world practice. Jongleurs danced while minstrels sang the deeds of valor that enlivened many a castle banquet—and many jongleurs were known for their "hand dancing." Cathedrals included in their services dances depicting certain Christian stories, a practice now limited to a few churches, notably that of Seville. But any village green could turn into a dance floor if a pipe-and-drum player struck up an estampie, or a singer started a dance song.

A Balinese dancer; her intricate hand and arm gestures tell a wordless story.

The Renaissance inaugurated indoor social dancing, a custom that has since remained a lively facet of our culture. From the jig, sarabande, minuet, waltz, cotillion, Virginia reel, cakewalk, maxixe, one-step, Charleston, foxtrot, jitterbug, twist, frug, bump, and hustle, the social dance has virtually defined changing tastes in popular music. And often, a generation later in stylized form, these same dances have entered the mainstream of concert music as well.

The formal dance concert in the West, since the seventeenth century, has centered on *ballet,* and also in the twentieth century, on a hybrid called *modern dance.* Ballet was initiated in the court celebrations of Italy and France, but court ballets used recitation and song; the first production with neither of these was in England early in the eighteenth century. Eighteenth-century ballets were for the most part a mixture of dance and spectacle, a string of songs and dances loosely related by a common subject. In

Swan Lake, Tchaikovsky's first ballet (1876), has become the epitome of the grace and elegance of Classical dance style. This scene is from a Sadlers Wells production at the Royal Opera House, London.

France, ballets were inserted into almost all operas as well. Nineteenth-century ballet introduced the use of plot rather than general subject, the toeshoe, the standard white tulle dress with flared skirt for women, and tights for men. Ballet became a special passion in Russia; a succession of French dancers and choreographers were imported until, at the turn of the century, Russians began to send their ballet companies to Paris. It was there, for the famed Ballets Russes, that Igor Stravinsky wrote the early works that made him famous.

But after the First World War, the United States became a world focus of dance, not only because Russian companies were no longer allowed to leave Russia, but also because a series of remarkable women dancers—notably Isadora Duncan, Martha Graham, Katherine Dunham, and Agnes De Mille—revolutionized the concept of dance in concert and in theater productions. In addition to redefining basic dance motions, these women worked closely with composers and helped to establish new styles in composition for the dance. The height of the American movement in dance came in the 1940s, when Graham produced the choreography for Aaron Copland's *Appalachian Spring* (working with traditional Shaker dances), Dunham for Baldwin Bergersen's *Carib Song* (working with Jamaican anthropological and musical materials, and treating them with a new respect), and De Mille for Richard Rodgers's *Oklahoma!* (seeking the roots of American tradition in western cowboy music and dances). All three were pacesetting works whose influence is still felt in both the dance concert and the Broadway musical.

By the mid-1970s, dance concerts were among the most popular of all art forms, and professional dance companies stood at an all-time high both in number and in quality. Of all the formal arts, dance appears to be the most attractive to young audiences: in American universities, dance concerts outdraw straight music concerts.

MUSIC AND DRAMA

Universally, music is part of the theater. Although in the West it is possible to see a play that has no music, this is exceptional in world terms and by no means standard even where it is found. Musicians are often hired to provide *incidental music:* an overture, intermezzos between acts, sometimes a postlude, and whatever music might be called for in the course of the play itself—perhaps a song, a march, or even a ballroom scene. The most famous is probably Mendelssohn's incidental music to Shakespeare's *A Midsummer Night's Dream.* The Overture is in sonata form, and except for a light, quick opening theme, suitable for the forest milieu and the enchanted goings-on, and an attempt to imitate the sound of a donkey's bray (which occurs in the play), the Overture has no connection with the action. The Wedding March (within the play) was a staple of European and American weddings for a century (along with another incidental wedding march by Richard Wagner, from *Lohengrin*). The Nocturne, heard in the recorded example, is quintessential program music. While having no connection with character or plot, it does mirror the hush of a warm midsummer night and, in the use of the French horn, it exploits the association of that instrument with the countryside. The mood is established by a quiet, long-lined horn melody. A second section continues with parts of the theme, but with enlivened harmonies and frequent modulations, so that this sec-

Side 7 Band 1

A scene from *Oklahoma!,* in a 1949 revival.

One of the traditional gestures of Japanese Kabuki dancing, an intimate blend of dance, music, and drama.

tion contrasts sharply with the first. The return to the opening horn theme features a long sustained tone over which the flutes and violins climb to higher registers, closing the Nocturne in a hush that balances the quiet opening.

Musical theater is a different story. Operas, operettas, and musicals have always been part music, part theater, and part spectacle—and each of these components has dominated productions at one time or another. The overriding importance of music in all of them is shown, however, in the fact that only the music can be isolated and enjoyed as a separate entity: opera arias are sung in song recitals, operas and operettas are enjoyed via radio, and original-cast albums of musicals are among the top sellers.

MUSIC AND CEREMONY

Music has always been a vital element in cultural, civic, and religious ceremonies. Not only are such functions universal, but they are generally well financed, important to their sponsors, and likely to involve an exceptionally large number of musicians.

The installation of officials, the weddings of princes (including princes of industry in the modern world), coronations, celebrations of victory, entrances of royalty, and entertainment of visiting dignitaries all call for ceremonies ranging from quiet elegance to spectacular magnificence, and music is indispensable for such presentations. Marches and choral works are the most common ceremonial music. Unfortunately, the latter often have words of nondescript praise whose lackluster poetic quality forces the composer to ignore the text and write a kind of all-purpose choral music. Musical pomp easily tends to slip into cliché, and the natural desire of established authority to invoke tradition compounds that tendency. Composers who can come up with a fresh, tasteful march or celebration piece that is as effective musically as it is ceremonially are as welcome as they are rare.

Religious ceremony differs only in degree from political ceremony. The high-decibel worldliness of the coronation is designed to convince onlookers of the power and splendor of the monarchy; sacred music may lead the listener to recognition of the glory and omnipotence of God, but the music in most cases is geared to a more inward contemplation of that glory. Most sacred music also prepares the listener for the intimate moments at the center of the sacred mystery: the quieter intenseness of the most solemn portions of a religious service is designed to focus attention on inner and higher things.

Sacred music and music composed to a religious text are not the same: the first is intended to be performed in a sacred service; the second is not. Palestrina's *Missa Ascendo ad Patrem* (page 95) is an example of the first, and Handel's *Messiah* is an example of the second: *Messiah* had its first performance in a concert hall in Dublin. The Palestrina represents excellent sacred music. Its conservative harmonic and rhythmic elements present no musical intrusion to the essential matter of the mass, yet its melodic simplicity and tonal unity lend it an inner intensity that serves as an excellent parallel for religious fervor.

Side 7 Band 2

Mozart's four-part motet *Ave verum corpus* ("Hail, True Body"), for voices with strings, although two centuries later than the Palestrina, accomplishes much the same thing. The motet is stripped of everything but the simplest homophonic texture—it is less active rhythmically than the Palestrina, and it has only one melodic focus, the soprano, to which all other voices are subordinated. After a graceful opening phrase, even that melodic line becomes less active, joining the others in an almost purely harmonic statement. The intensity, harmonically full but vocally restrained, mirrors the active mind and quiet exterior of the devout worshipper.

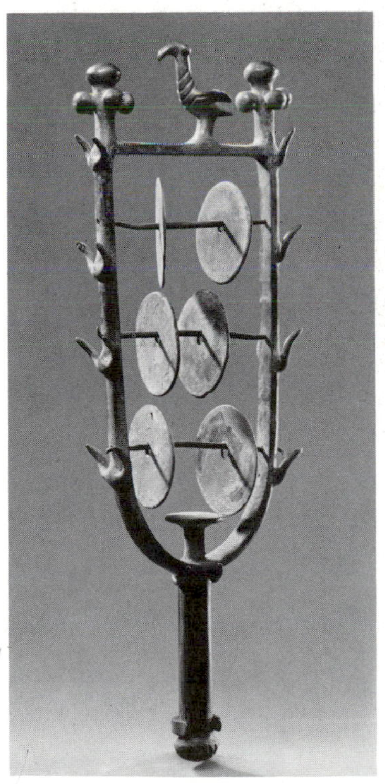

An Egyptian sistrum, a rattle common in the ancient Middle East but sacred to the Egyptians. This one, cast in bronze, dates from around 2500 B.C.; its height is 13 inches.

In many cultures, religion and politics are not separate. The solemn mysteries of religious ritual are often preceded and followed by processions of church officials through the city. Cathedral dedications and the installation of bishops and cardinals, the coronation of popes, call for festivities of a less specifically solemn type.

Small religious ceremonies also require music. The average citizen of the United States is likely to hire musicians directly only for bar mitzvahs, weddings, and funerals. Two hundred years ago most weddings of the affluent used music newly composed for the ceremony, but today it is extremely rare to find payment to a composer for new music on the expense sheet of a wedding.

MUSIC AND THE OTHER ARTS

The more purely visual a work of art is, the less connection it can have to a design in sound; a statue or a painting can have none at all. A very general comparison is possible, however, in terms of energy state and pure size, but to equate size with length or vivid color with loudness is only to acknowledge that all human activity can be perceived as having high or low energy quotients. One might just as well equate a symphony with a cake and a short piece with a cookie (and a tone poem with a gingerbread boy)—fun perhaps, but aesthetically ridiculous.

Common Concepts and Principles

Although the arts share few technical processes (because they use separate materials), they do unite in certain concepts of what is aesthetically effective and in certain general principles for the attainment of aesthetic effects.

All artists create single works—the visual artist creates a painting, a mural, a drawing; the sculptor creates a statue, a mobile; the writer creates a poem, a novel, a play; the choreographer creates a dance; and the composer creates a work of music—vocal or instrumental, for one or more performers, to be heard for its own sake or to be used in connection with something else. In each case, the artist conceives of this single work as having an integrity—a wholeness in and of itself—and in each case this wholeness is achieved through the bringing together of disparate elements in a significant way. These elements may vary only moderately, or they may be strikingly different. Whether gentle or extravagant, this contrast is unique to each art form, even within the same art. Although a sonnet and a limerick are both short poems, they incorporate very different shapes, use words differently, and develop very different contrasts—but both exploit qualities unique in the realm of words.

Art forms overlap in very different ways. Dance shares several things with other arts: it shares time with music; it shares visual elements with sculpture; it shares the motion of bodies on a stage with drama; and often it shares a story element with literary works. But in each case, the dance takes the element it shares and shapes it to its own use, in its own way, and on its own terms. No one type of work shares very much with any other single type, but overlaps in essential elements with two or three others, while maintaining a substantial area of uniqueness to itself. In the case of the dance, for example, one or more bodies move rhythmically in postures and gestures not seen in daily life—a transcendence of ordinary gestures that is the very essence of the art.

Yet the arts have common concerns: in addition to energy and contrast, they share the elements of design and embellishment as well. Each of these elements in turn implies a counterelement: energy seeks rest; contrast seeks reconciliation; design, or coherence, seeks adventure and incoherence; embellishment seeks the bare bones of function.

Musical energy is expressed first and foremost in sound. Of all the arts, music perhaps has the greatest potential of direct energy. Loud tone is more energized than soft; strident tone more energized than dulcet; high tone more energized than low; disjunct tones—whether in pitch or in attack—more energized than sustained; fast tones more energized than slow. A drama shares with music the energy of tones of voice, and also the use of time (both in the timing of a single line and in the pacing of dramatic action), but nothing else—and again, the sharing is on the play's own terms. A painting shares with music the energy of color—although the analogy of tone color and pigment is a tenuous one—in both the vivid (intense) colors versus the pallid (pastel) ones and the warm (red) versus the cool (blue). Loud and soft have been likened to light and dark, but nothing in music is comparable to shadow or to the idea of complementary colors, both of which are vital to painting.

Design in music has an exact analogy in the visual if one limits the concept to a single line of music—in fact, the word "line" is itself an acknowledgment of that analogy. The graphs of single melodies in Chapter 2 assume that the top and bottom of the page are parallel to musical high and low, and also that time runs steadily from left to right. Since melody is a design of musical space in time, such assumptions provide a ready visualization of certain aspects of a single melody—and most modern musical notation in the West makes use of exactly that kind of visualization. In these terms, the shape, range, and pattern of a melody can be "seen," although it is seen all at once, telescoped in time. Accuracy would be much greater if a melodic shape could be projected onto a screen as a single moving dot, creating the graphed line in the rhythm of the music.

Design is in itself a matter of contrast and reconciliation: without contrast, no design can be perceived, and without some sense of relationship, there can be no coherence. In melody, for example, fresh tones and rhythmic patterns are necesssary for interest, but if every pitch or note length in a melody were different, the result would be chaotic. The same is true of comparable elements in the other arts. Although each art (and each work of art) must develop its own meaning, and although nobody has ever successfully defined the relationship between the active and the passive—the varied and static elements in the concept of design—the working out of these counter-elements is central to aesthetic meaning in all the arts. Artistic integrity has been defined as variety achieving unity.

Coherence in music is often associated with some form of repetition, and repetition is also a concept common to all the arts. In a static art, such as painting or architecture, repetition most often is simultaneous and restful; but in the time arts repetition is cumulative and can attain the effect of tension and even of obsession. This kind of repetition could occur in a play in which a character says the same line over and over again (always a sign of trouble in any normal speech). In music, a conspicuous repeated figure is often used to build tension.

In any art focus is important, for unless the artist is able to draw attention where he or she wants it, design is impossible. A painting presents several elements simultaneously; if the viewer's eye is to be drawn to a certain element in a picture, the painter must make that element brighter or bigger or clearer in some way. Musicians—composers and performers—also present more than one idea simultaneously, and they must do the same, but of course in terms of their own materials—making an important idea louder, or setting it off with a solo instrument, or setting it apart in musical space—perhaps letting it soar off in the treble over a less active idea in the bass. In that sense, design is created through relationships between primary (conspicuous) and secondary (inconspicuous) elements.

Music and architecture share the concept of the functional and the decorative in a unique way. All the arts make use of the ideas of function and embellishment, but in music and architecture, the two ideas are not determined by the materials themselves. In addition, their focus may be reversed—that is, composers and architects frequently prefer to hide the functional and focus on the decorative. Bricks that form the walls of a building, for example, might be covered with plaster and paint, but bricks might serve also as a decorative siding for a wall supported with other materials. The same is true of columns and arches. An architect might also take the aesthetic stance that function is beauty, and produce a work that exposes the structural elements—like the George

The Hall of Mirrors at Versailles, a famous site of many musical performances.

Washington Bridge, for example. The structure of a musical work might be a series of harmonic patterns, yet the focus might be on a highly ornate melodic configuration—such, in fact, is the basis of jazz. Or a composition might contain a familiar melody as its structural foundation, subjecting it to harmonic and rhythmic embellishments that are the heart of the aesthetic experience of the work—Medieval organum and the Baroque chorale prelude proceed in that way. But just as functional brick can also be used decoratively, a piece of music can be basically harmonic or melodic or rhythmic in both function and embellishment.

Common Cultural Ideals

General cultural ideals influence aesthetic goals in all the arts. It is undeniable that people living in the same place at the same time share a basic cultural background and are aware of similar fads and fancies, so artists living in the same place at the same time are influenced by the same cultural ideas. The artists who worked for Louis XIV, for example, were filled with the ideal of reflecting the magnificence of that monarch, who styled himself the Sun King and who made himself the center of a strong and newly splendid France. The architects, interior designers, mural

The Brighton Pavilion in England, built for the Prince Regent, later George IV.

painters, landscape gardeners, and silversmiths of Versailles were individually concerned with reflecting that magnificence. The aesthetic particulars were not coordinated—the silversmith and the mural painter received commissions for certain functional objects or for the decoration of certain specified sizes of ceiling or wall space, but they most frequently made their designs without reference even to the central plan of the building. Some of the ceilings were ordered from Italy, for example, before the other visual details were known. Portraits of the king and other works of art were accomplished separately. The theatrical and musical spectacles for court and chapel alike were produced without reference to the other arts. Artistically, all these works shared the general goal of magnificence, although each was independent and each sought on its own terms to reflect the splendor of the royal patron.

Fads too can unify general goals. In the late eighteenth and early nineteenth centuries, for example, Europe was consumed with a mania for Near Eastern customs, which were lumped under the designation "Turkish." Women wore silk pajamas and turbans, munched on Turkish delight, and read *The Arabian Nights* while reclining on newly imported divans. Opera plots featured characters who disguised themselves as Turks—and Mozart wrote music for an opera whose action took place in a harem. Artists, being citizens like everyone else, were swept up in the craze. Painters took to depicting voluptuous harem scenes, architects designed the Brighton Pavilion in England as an imaginary Turkish mosque, poets chose such subjects as the pleasure dome of Kubla Khan, and Beethoven contributed a hugely popular "Turkish March." There was no relationship to unite these works of art in any technical or professional detail, but each had been influenced by the cultural focus of the moment. They served to express that cultural focus and to give it a permanent embodiment.

The same is true in our own time. All the arts separately reflect a cultural focus on the fear of loss of human values in a technological society; on a new view of the world as a finite "Spaceship Earth," to use Buckminister Fuller's words, and a consequent concern for ecological balance; on a new desire for an essential equality of all persons and a hope for mutual acknowledgment and cooperation. Painters since early in the century have turned to mechanistic styles and dispensed with subject matter; poets and playwrights have based a generation of their art on the despair of the human individual; cities have begun to redesign their centers and to include both parks and outdoor statuary as an affirmation of renewal; and popular music, as always, has changed virtually year by year, reflecting even the smallest differences in public concerns, especially those of the young. As usual, mainstream composers expressed the long range view, and also as usual, music has begun a synthesis, a new art of hope. Composers are combining popular and concert styles, using elements of jazz, electronic music, and non-Western sounds in a comfortable unity. And, as always, music stands aside from the other arts; simply because it has no words and no pictures, it can speak the most eloquently of all.

11. Romantic Music

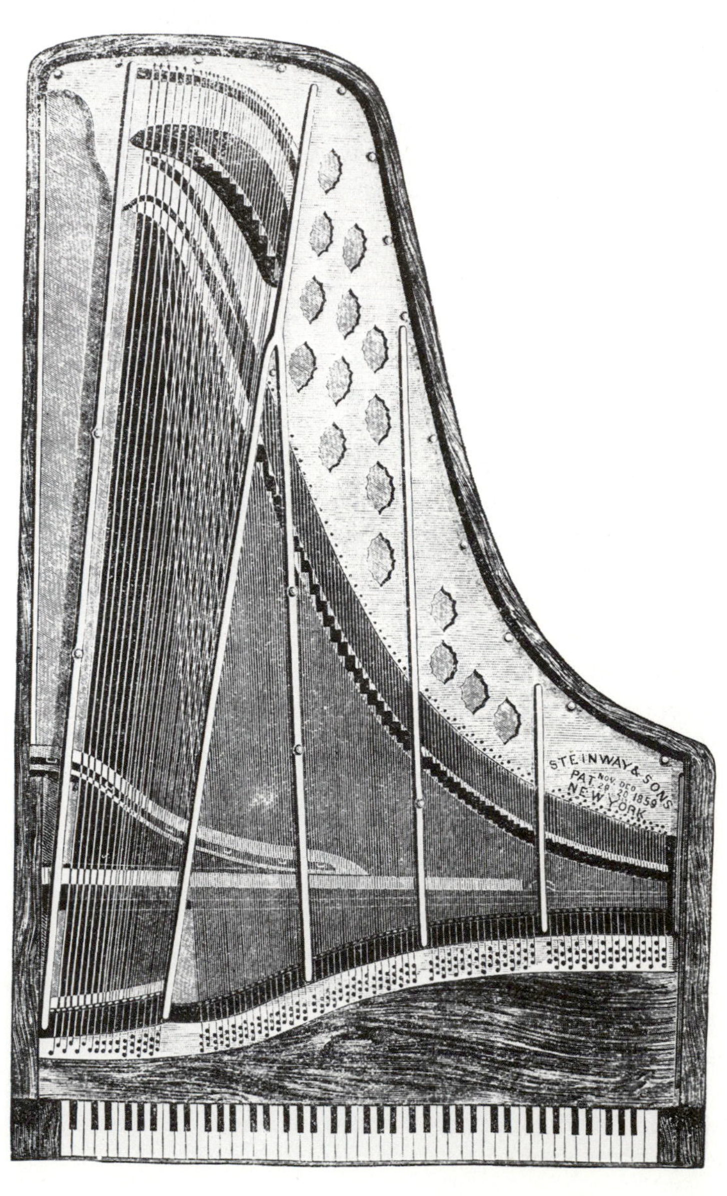

BEETHOVEN'S HEIRS

BEETHOVEN'S MUSICAL PROGENY were numerous—he sired the entire Romantic movement, which accorded him a reverence bordering on deification. Beethoven's heirs were somewhat selective in their inheritance, however. They embraced his individualism and emotional intensity while disregarding his devotion to formal organization. The Romanticists mistrusted reason and placed their faith in feeling—they wore their hearts on their sleeves with pride, and the emotions they strove to communicate were not general sentiments but the personal experiences of an individual human being.

SCHUBERT

The movement began in literature in the late eighteenth century. In music, it started to take shape during the last fifteen years of Beethoven's life. One of its earliest exponents was Franz Schubert (1797–1828), a Viennese freelance composer who was a perfect example of the unappreciated genius starving in his garret. Beethoven was his idol but not his model. Rather than instrumental works of grand design, Schubert's most congenial medium of expression was song, and it was he who gave definition to the German Romantic lied or art song, for solo voice with piano accompaniment. His accompaniments were designed to play a contributory rather than supportive role: their function was sometimes descriptive, they sometimes established, sustained, or changed the prevailing mood, and occasionally they were called upon to create characterization. But Schubert did not allow the piano to compete with the voice. Although his accompaniments went far beyond the level of simple harmonic underpinning, they were innocent of polyphonic intricacy. Mood, character, and form were dictated largely by the poem at hand, and the vocal lines were always endowed with beautiful melodies. Many of his six hundred songs are so basic to the vocal repertoire that they alone make familiarity with the German language prerequisite for an aspiring singer.

Like his idol, Schubert composed nine symphonies, but they resemble Beethoven's only in number. They are far removed from the Classical style, and Schubert's concern for form was, at best, perfunctory. His heart was not in developmental techniques, and the melody of the moment was dearer to him than any concept of balance and proportion. He was above all a melodist, and the vocal conception of his melodies is as evident in his instrumental music as in his songs. Harmony was second only to melody in

Many composers found it amusing to depict cats, mice, and other animals on the keyboard or musical staff; this "score" was penned by Franz Schubert.

Schubert's hierarchy of musical elements, and his colorful harmonic language included an array of vivid chromatic chords as well as basic diatonic harmonies. He was particularly fond of creating an abrupt change of mood by juxtaposing major and minor keys, and to him a dramatic climax demanded a drastic modulation, preferably to a highly unlikely key. Only two of his symphonies—the "Unfinished" Symphony in B minor and the "Great" Symphony in C—have earned established places in the standard orchestral repertoire. Neither is remarkable for cohesive organization, but, as in his piano sonatas, any formal shortcomings are more than atoned for by melodic and harmonic richness.

Schubert's most fortunate ventures into Classical forms were in the field of chamber music. Few Romantic composers were attracted to this intimate medium, and fewer still attained mastery of it. The string quartet is such an intrinsically Classical medium that any composer who elects to write for that combination must subscribe in some measure to Classical ideals. Schubert's early quartets are more Classical than Romantic in style, but Romanticism pervades his later chamber works, which are among the finest of the period.

EARLY ROMANTIC OPERA

WEBER

It seems surprising that, with his superb talent for song-writing, Schubert's operatic works should have been such dismal failures. For the most part they were unperformed during his lifetime, and subsequent generations have not viewed this neglect as a wrong that needed righting. The creation of German Romantic opera must be credited largely to Carl Maria von Weber (1786–1826), who, although less gifted melodically than Schubert, had a thorough understanding of the theater and was highly skilled in the dramatic use of the orchestra. His opera *Der Freischütz* (untranslatable, but originally given in English productions as "The Demon of the Forest") was the prototype of German Romantic opera: its plot involved the supernatural (the hero sells his soul to the devil in return for earthly favors—a recurring theme in German Romantic literature), its melodies were predominantly folklike, and its dramatic effect was accomplished primarily through harmony and orchestral color. Singspiel influence is evident in the use of some spoken dialogue, but the musical organization and

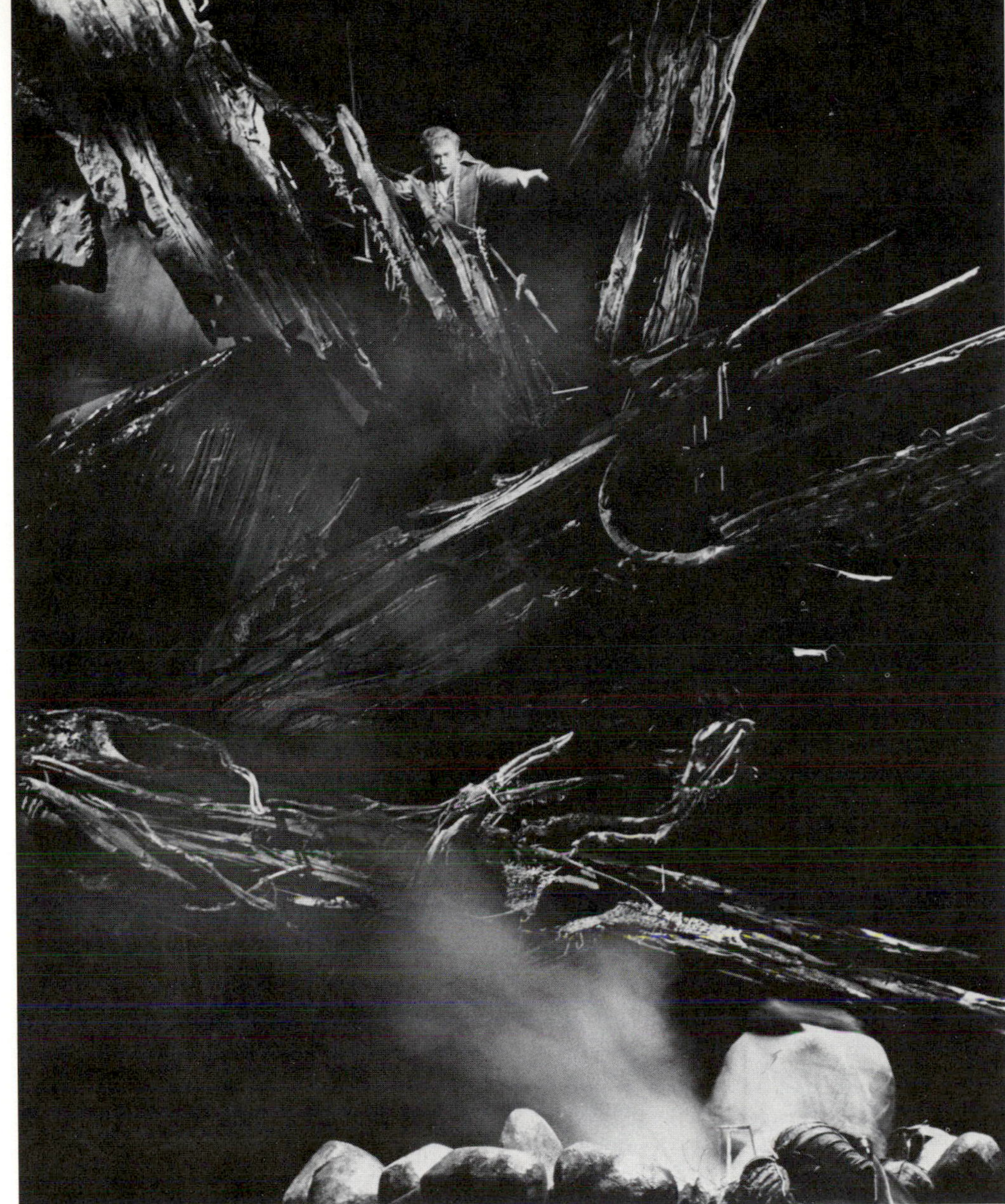

The ominous Wolf's Glen where the magic bullets are forged in Weber's opera *Der Freischütz*. The scene is from the Metropolitan Opera production, 1975.

dramatic intensity of *Der Freischütz* place it firmly in the operatic category. Except for singspiel, Germany had imported opera, either in fact or in style, for almost two centuries, and it was only during the Romantic period that distinctive, indigenous German opera came into being.

French composers were giving their attention primarily to opéra comique in preference to more pretentious forms of musical theater, and in Paris, opera was once again in the hands of foreigners. Italian works were in high favor, and the smash hit was an opera buffa, *Il Barbiere di Siviglia* ("The Barber of Seville") by

ROSSINI

Gioacchino Rossini (1792–1868), an Italian composer of international fame who made Paris his home. The librettos for both Rossini's *Barber* and Mozart's *Figaro* were drawn from the "Figaro" trilogy by the French playwright Beaumarchais, and of course Figaro, the impudent barber, is central to both plots. In Rossini's opera, the romantic interest involves Count Almaviva's love for the beautiful Rosina, and the comic element devolves on the elaborate schemes that Figaro invents to aid the Count in outwitting Rosina's wicked guardian. Figaro makes his initial

Side 7 Band 3

entrance singing the famous aria "Largo al factotum," heard in the recorded example, in which he boastfully tabulates his many talents, enumerates the many demands for his services, and proclaims his indispensability to the community at large. This aria is pure buffa; the humor, although far from subtle, elicits audience delight beyond realm and season.

But it was grand opera that generated the most excitement in Paris, where audiences had been addicted to spectacle even before the days of Lully. Giacomo Meyerbeer (1791–1864), a German-born composer who studied in Italy, was the "Parisian" composer most successful in creating operatic grandeur on a Napoleonic scale. His grand opera *Robert le Diable* ("Robert the Devil") was received with wild enthusiasm in Paris, and foreign demand for the production extended as far as New York (which had also played host to Rossini's *Barber*). Meyerbeer's operas have not stood the test of time and are rarely performed today, probably because their musical merit is considerably less impressive than the grandeur of staging—twentieth century opera-goers tend to find interpolated ballet and mob scenes poor substitutes for beautiful music. Rossini's grand opera *Guillaume Tell* ("William Tell") receives an occasional performance, and its famous overture will live forever in the hearts of all Americans who can remember the *Lone Ranger* radio program of the 1940s, which used that stirring music as its "galloping" theme.

BERLIOZ

France's principal contribution to the new Romantic movement was Hector Berlioz (1803–1869), a radical Romantic whose status in music history continues to be a subject for debate. Seldom a miniaturist, Berlioz sought grandeur in sound through sheer numbers. The formidable difficulties of staging his opera *Les Troyens* ("The Trojans") have made it one of the world's least performed masterpieces. Its highly successful production at the Metropolitan Opera in 1974 was America's first, and it strained the vast resources of that great opera house to the limit. Similarly, his orchestral works were conceived for an ensemble of titanic proportions. His demand for such a huge orchestra was more than a theatrical gesture; he had a genius for orchestration that justified the presence of that vast instrumental assemblage. His treatise on orchestration was a landmark in the nineteenth century, and it continues to command respect today. Length as well as numbers was a factor in his concept of grandeur. He devoted himself primarily to opera, oratorio, and long symphonic works (the *Symphonie Fantastique,* for example) in which he sometimes attempted description or narration through musical sound alone. His musical ideas were revolutionary in their anti-Classical nature, and his musical iconoclasm and passion for the bizarre did little to endear him to his fellow countrymen. Performances of his works frequently met with a cool or even hostile reception, and his influence on the younger generation was much greater in Germany than in his native land.

ROMANTIC STYLE CHARACTERISTICS

The Romantic movement moved into high gear during the fourth and fifth decades of the nineteenth century. Composers born during the vintage years 1809 to 1813 came to maturity in the 1830s and brought the movement to its greatest glory. Paris continued to be a proving ground for new music and performers, but Germany emerged as the new center of creativity and retained its position of leadership well into the twentieth century.

The principal motivating force of full-blown Romanticism was a desire for self-expression, and, in its glorification of the individual, the period was reminiscent of the Renaissance. The Romanticists were a remarkably literary-minded group of composers, frequently deriving inspiration from literature, and always ready to take pen in hand to defend or explain their musical ideas and philosophy. Their writings tended to encourage the public's view of composers as musical geniuses who created in the white heat of inspiration, controlled by some demonic force outside themselves. They stressed inspiration and emotional impact, leaving unacknowledged the perspiration that accompanies any act of creation. They took themselves and their music seriously; their view of Man focused on his tragedy and triumph, his joy and despair. Special stress was placed on sorrow, and Romantic music incorporates every shading of that emotion, from wistful yearning to morbidity. Exuberance and ecstasy were also acceptable, but humor held little attraction for Romantic composers.

Melodically, Romantic music leaned toward *cantabile* (singing) style, long lines, and legato phrasing. Tension-building chromatic harmonies were the rule, and while the music was strongly tonal, it stretched the boundaries of tonality, with modulation occurring even more frequently than in Classical music. Rhythm was metrically consistent, but opposing subdivisions of the beat, particularly two against three and three against four, were combined to create conflict. As in Classical music, phrase structure was normally symmetrical and cadences prominent. Dynamics were constantly in a state of flux, rarely remaining at one level for more than a few seconds, and the dynamic range extended from barely audible to something approaching pandemonium. Textures tended toward density and consistency, in accordance with the ideals of rich harmonic color and legato connections. The light, airy texture that had characterized Classical music had no place in Romantic style; when silence was used, it often took the form of the "pregnant pause"—a dramatic device well calculated to create suspense. In the interests of harmonic sonority and melodic lyricism, the most natural, comfortable tessituras of both instruments and voices were stressed, with extreme ranges reserved for special effects—the very high register for brilliance, excitement, and climax, the very low to express foreboding or gloom. To give tone greater warmth, both singers and string players added the throbbing intensity of *vibrato* (a very slight undulation in pitch). Classicists were horrified, but Romanticists loved it, and the twentieth century, for all its rejection of Romantic ideals, still considers vibrato a normal part of tone quality.

Despite all their rhetorical disclaimers, Romantic composers found the Classical forms of sonata, symphony and concerto irresistible, and occasionally they even succumbed to the seductive intimacy of the string quartet. But they were more at ease and, generally, more successful in dealing with short forms, which require little beyond contrast and repetition to give them satisfactory shape. Only a few composers were at their best in mutlimovement forms, but the careful craftsmanship they brought to such works gives the lie to their anti-intellectual posturing.

The impulse toward self-expression was by no means limited to composers. Performers, too, felt the urge to convey their inner

A Victorian parlor. The upright piano was a standard fixture in the American home—in 1850 there were more pianos than bathtubs in the United States.

feelings, and a new balance of prerogatives and obligations between composers and performers came into being. Pitch was inviolable—whatever composers specified was to be observed scrupulously. But rhythm was flexible and was subject to the whim of each performer, all of whom stretched the beat and varied the tempo according to their inclination and their interpretation of the emotional content of the music. The effect of this rhythmic elasticity, called *rubato* (literally, "robbed"), was highly expressive when used with taste and sympathy for the composer's intention. Unfortunately, however, the practice led to egocentric excesses on the part of some performers, whose passion-at-any-price approach resulted in performances that were more meretricious than meritorious. Most Romanticists—composers and performers alike—possessed a high degree of musical integrity, but the self-indulgent minority so tarnished the movement that today it is an insult to say that a performer "romanticizes."

Consistency was never of great concern to Romanticists, but their contradictory attitudes toward music of the past seem particularly difficult to reconcile. On the one hand, they rejected the music of preceding eras as the naive effort of composers who had wrongheadedly pursued false aesthetic goals; on the other hand, their "discovery" of music history gave them a self-flattering sense of continuity with the past, and they were tireless in arranging performances of works by great composers of former periods. Conservatories were founded as much to preserve and make known the music of the past as to systematize the training of would-be musicians. Most extraordinary of all was the development of a veritable cult devoted to the music of J. S. Bach. Except for the early monodists, no generation had been less concerned with polyphony than the Romanticists, and that they should have so lionized a man who had been interested in little else does seem passing strange.

MENDELSSOHN

Felix Mendelssohn (1809–1847) initiated the back-to-Bach movement. He had loved the preludes and fugues of *The Well-Tempered Clavier* since he was a child, and he remained steadfast in his devotion to Bach's music throughout his life. The story of his discovery of the long-lost manuscript of Bach's *St. Matthew Passion* and his subsequent production of the work reads like Romantic fiction, but the tale is well documented and undeniable. (It has, in fact, been used as the basis for a novel: *Beyond Desire,* by Pierre La Mure.) But this great admiration for Bach influenced the disciple's creative work only slightly. Mendelssohn composed a few preludes and fugues, but for the most part his musical style was Romantic in its melodic emphasis and harmonic vocabulary, and Mozartean in its airy texture. Classical leanings were also revealed in his choice of forms, which included symphonies, sonatas, concertos, and string quartets. His treatment of these multimovement structures was coherent, if not concise—the music flows naturally and logically from idea to idea, but there is no exhaustive exploration of any theme. Perhaps his most successful work was his Violin Concerto in E minor, which is as much a favorite with audiences today as it is with violinists.

Mendelssohn himself was of the Lutheran faith, and his family, although of Jewish descent, had been Christians for three generations. Nevertheless, in Germany he was regarded as a Jew, and his basically successful career was jeopardized on several occasions by encounters with anti-Semitism, particularly in Berlin. But despite these brushes with bigotry, his life was a remarkably happy one, and his music, although sometimes tinged with melancholy, is free from the deep sorrowfulness to be found in the work of many Romantic composers.

SCHUMANN

The city of Leipzig was doubly blessed in numbering both Mendelssohn and his good friend Robert Schumann (1810–1856) among its residents. Vienna continued to be the capital of popular music, waltzing happily to the music of Johann Strauss (1804–1849), but, thanks to the presence of both leading German Romanticists, Leipzig became the new center for nonoperatic concert music. Schumann was the most articulate of all the nineteenth-century composers, supporting himself through his journalistic efforts until the success of his compositions enabled him to devote himself exclusively to composing and teaching. He had no difficulty in obtaining performances of his piano music, for his wife, Clara Wieck Schumann (1819–1896), was one of the leading concert pianists of the day and a dedicated champion of his music. His interest in Classical forms was minimal, and his few symphonies, sonatas, and chamber works do not represent his greatest accomplishment. His finest works are his songs, which rival those of Schubert, and his piano pieces. In his piano works, he experimented with various means of creating long compositions through relating a group of short pieces. He was searching for a Romantic counterpart to the sonata—a work of length and substance, wherein one could expound contrasting musical ideas, but without any necessity for their intensive development. Each set of his pieces seems to be organized on a different principle: for example, *Symphonic Etudes* involves a variation technique verging on metamorphosis of theme, and *Carnaval* consists of a long series of short pieces that are based on the German letter names of four scale tones included in the name of the city where a pre-Clara sweetheart lived.

Piano was Schumann's performing medium, and he was well on his way to a concert career when an injury, resulting from overambitious discipline of the fragile fourth finger, closed that door irrevocably. But his identification with the piano continued in his extensive compositions for solo piano, the Piano Concerto in A minor, and in his songs. The accompaniments in these songs give the piano an extremely important role, often including strong contrapuntal interest and sometimes creating a dialogue between voice and piano. In the recorded example, "Mondnacht" ("Moonlit Night"), from *Liederkreis* ("Wreath of Songs"), Op. 39, the accompaniment is remarkably simple but highly effective in creating that mood of calmness tinged with mystery that is traditionally associated with a moonlit night. The piano begins the song with a

Side 7 Band 4

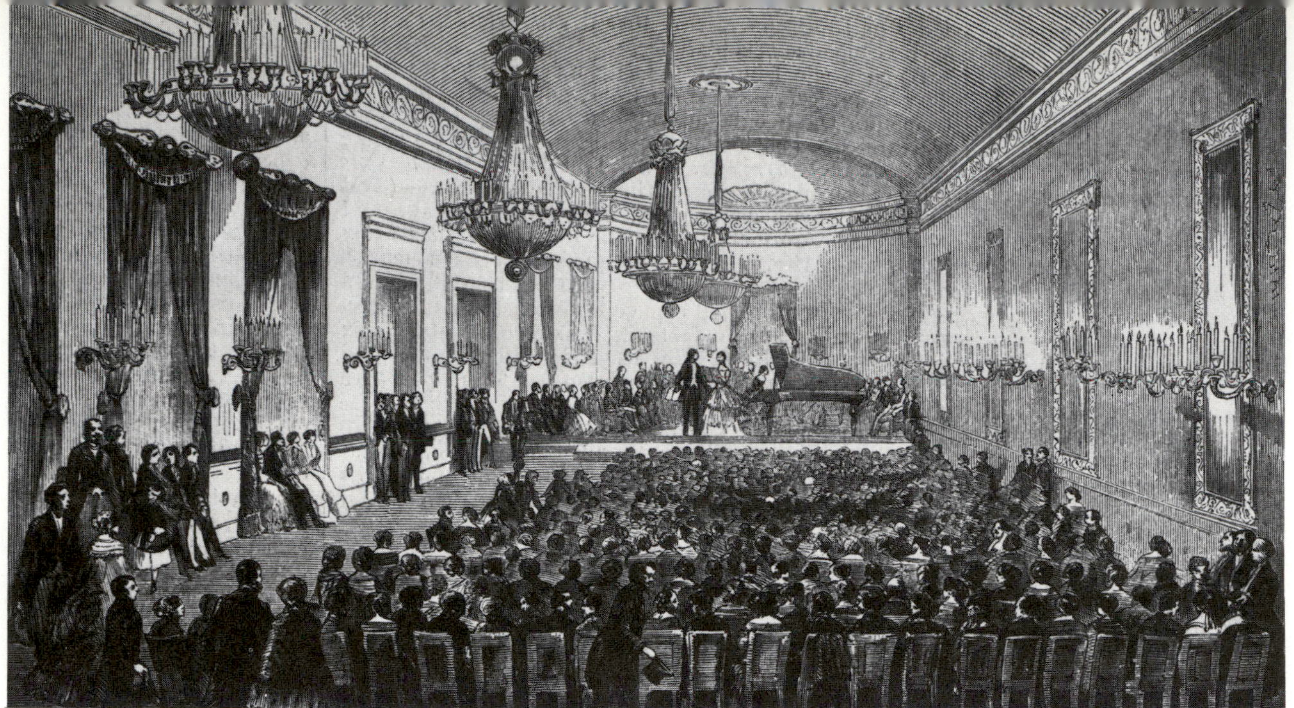

Early concert halls were enlarged salons; this is a 19th-century engraving of the Salle Pleyel in Paris, showing a recital that included the pianist Chopin.

tentative, meandering melody that reappears as an interlude between verses and returns in a low register to conclude the song; but apart from this recurring melody, the role of the piano is primarily atmospheric, consisting of soft repeated tones in muted harmonic colors.

The Classicists' fondness for the piano paled in comparison with the love lavished on it by Romanticists. More than any other, it was the instrument that fired their imagination, and the wealth of music they composed for solo piano constitutes the central core of piano literature today. Nearly all the Romantic composers contributed in greater or lesser degree, but the Polish-born Frédéric Chopin (1810–1849) devoted his entire career exclusively to the piano—as composer, performer, and teacher. Having captivated Paris with his first concert there, Chopin decided to make that city his home, and the French have ever since claimed him as one of their own. (Even in midwinter, his grave in Paris is surrounded by fresh flowers.) His love for the piano was typical of the time, but his intuitive understanding of the instrument was and continues to be unique. Perhaps no other composer has so successfully transformed the piano's inherent defects (such as its inability to sustain a tone at the initial dynamic level) into virtues. Most of his works were short, with semidescriptive titles, such as Polonaise, Ballade, Nocturne, or Impromptu. His style focused on melody, and he favored widely spaced accompanying figures involving embellished harmony. The texture was usually consistent within a very short piece or a section of a longer one, but it varied dramatically from section to section.

CHOPIN

In his *Fantaisie-Impromptu,* Op. 66, heard in the recorded example, the contrast between sections is startling—in mood and style as well as in texture. The A section features restless running figures (ornamented broken chords) that range widely over the keyboard, and the sense of agitation is augmented by a rhythmic pattern of three against four. This section builds to a powerful climax and leads directly into B, in which the mood shifts abruptly from turbulence to wistfulness. The rhythmic pattern changes to a more amiable two against three, and a lyric melody of comparatively limited range dominates the section. A then returns and culminates in a rousing coda that begins violently but ends with a tranquil reference to the wistful melody of B.

Side 7 Band 5

Nineteenth-century audiences were insatiable in their appetite for piano recitals, and virtuoso pianists received tremendous acclaim. Pianistic technique reached unheard-of heights of skill, and the piano itself was developed into an instrument capable of responding to the wide range of moods, colors, and dynamics demanded by Romanticists. The musical world fairly teemed with virtuoso pianists; undisputed master was Hungarian-born Franz Liszt (1811–1886). Judging from contemporary accounts of his playing and from the Herculean difficulty of his own piano compositions, Liszt must have been able to make a piano do anything except leap through a flaming hoop. It is currently modish to disparage Liszt as a composer, and, while it is true that a few of his pieces are merely flashy, his finest works are representative of Romanticism at its best. Among these latter works is the set of six *Transcendental Etudes after Paganini,* which represents a musical Mount Everest. Of these etudes, "La Campanella," the recorded example, is particularly treacherous. Formally, it is a continuous set of variations; its crystal-clear texture offers no place to hide, and the wide leaps must be accomplished with lightning speed and impeccable accuracy. A triumphant performance of this piece constitutes an occasion for bravos, if not a standing ovation.

LISZT

Side 7 Band 6

Unlike Chopin, Liszt's horizons as a composer extended beyond the piano. To the field of orchestral music he contributed a new form—the *symphonic poem.* This form was a one-movement work with an organizing principle of Liszt's own devising, which he called *transformation of theme.* According to this theory, new themes were created out of old ones by means of maintaining pitch relationships while drastically altering the rhythmic scheme.

(The theory harbors a striking parallel to Romantic interpretive technique, in which pitch was considered immutable and rhythm variable.) The following graph outlines several transformations of the opening theme of his symphonic poem, *Les Préludes*. Similar-

Liszt: *Les Préludes*

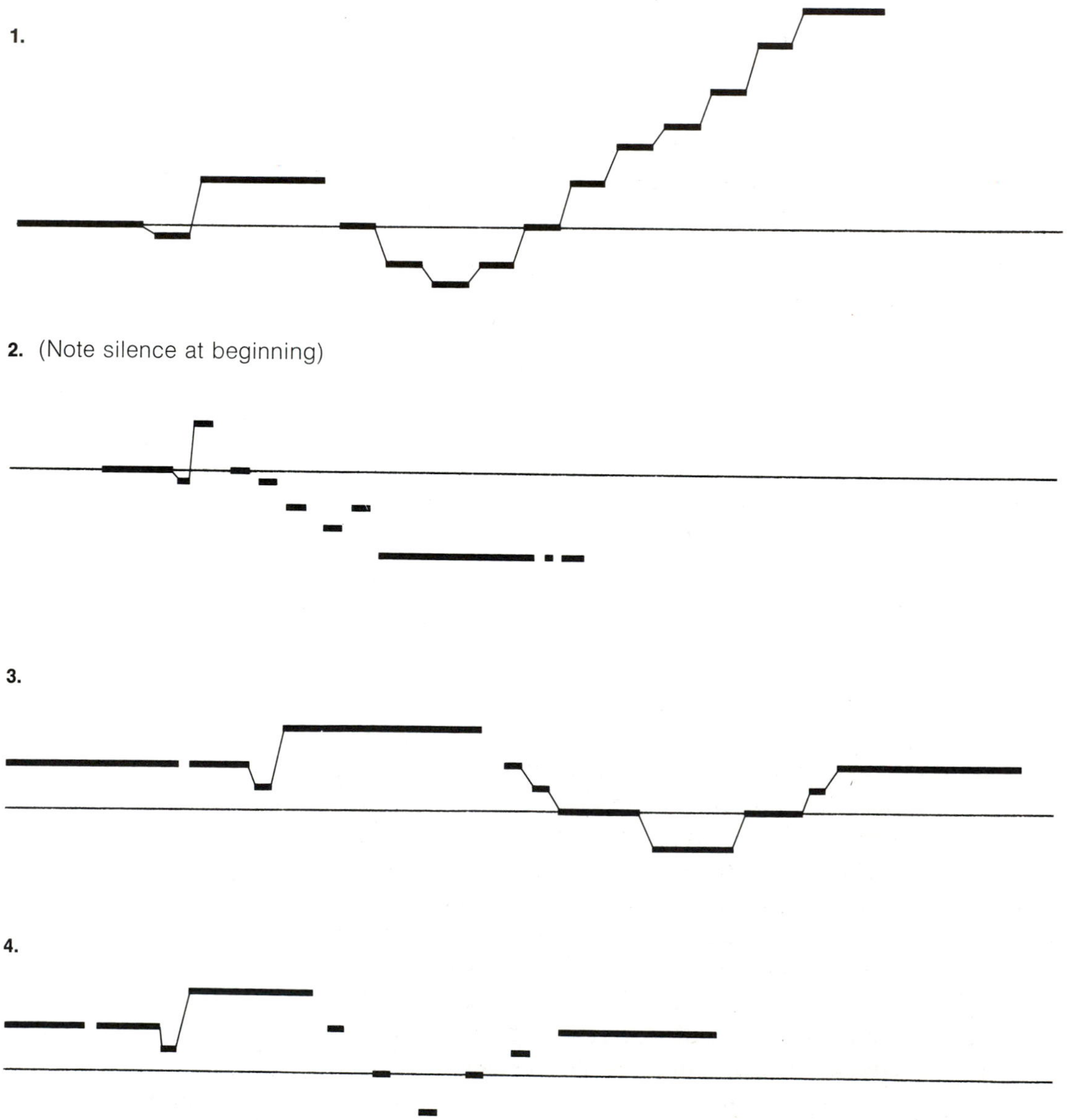

1.

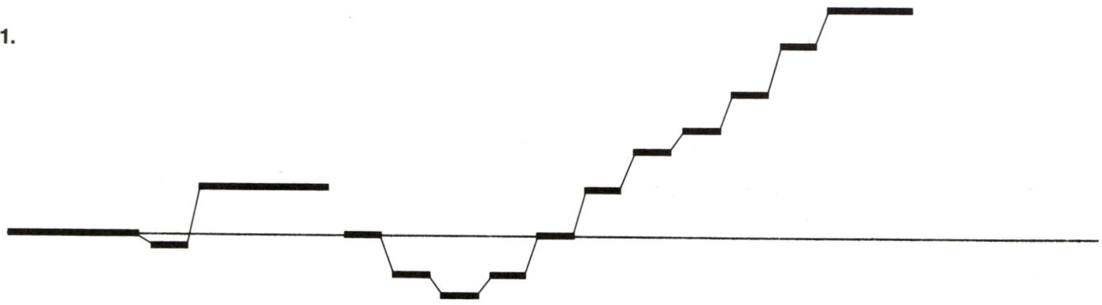

2. (Note silence at beginning)

3.

4.

ities in contour reveal the consistency of pitch relationships, but changes in rhythm and tempo give each transformation a totally different character.

Liszt was never noted for celibacy, and it would be difficult to imagine a less likely candidate for holy orders. Contrary to the laws of probability, however, he became an abbé at the age of fifty-five, and then turned his attention to the composition of church music. He did not withdraw behind cloistered walls, nor did he totally abandon the piano; but in his musical style, the old drama and excitement were replaced by reverence and contemplation, and only the rich, sensual harmonies remained as a reminder of the young firebrand.

Sacred music was of little concern to nineteenth-century composers; the Romantic period was akin to the Renaissance in emphasis on both the secular and the personal. Also, the Catholic Church was in the process of restoring chant to its original purity and reviving Palestrina-style polyphony, none of which fostered the inclination to create new liturgical music in the Romantic idiom. Some requiem masses were written, but these were designed for concert presentation and were unsuitable for devotional use. The most popular choral forms were part songs, cantatas, and oratorios, because they were less austere than the mass and allowed wider dramatic scope and range of sentiment. Of the older generation, Mendelssohn was perhaps the most successful in writing for chorus, and the younger generation was best represented by Brahms.

LATER ROMANTIC OPERA

Italy, of course, continued to produce opera. No radical change was needed to bring Italian opera into line with the ideals of Romanticism; it had been heading in that direction for nearly two centuries. The tradition was upheld and advanced by Giuseppe Verdi (1813–1901) who, in true Italian fashion, gave great thought to drama but consistently subordinated it to beautiful melody. His choice of librettos often tended toward the melodramatic—complicated plots in which mistaken identities, misunderstood motives, and the machinations of Fate figured prominently. In *La Forza del Destino* ("The Force of Destiny") the story is a labyrinth of deception, disguise, thwarted love, and vindicated honor, and although the opera is not often performed by contemporary companies, the Act IV aria "Pace, pace, mio Dio" heard in the

VERDI

Side 8 Band 1

Eltz Castle is a lofty romantic vision above the Moselle River. Such Medieval works were treasured and copied in the 19th century.

recorded example, remains a standard in the soprano repertoire. It is a prayer for inner peace, sung by the distraught heroine whose anxieties include guilt feelings arising from partial responsibility for the untimely death of her father, anguish over the loss of her lover, and fear of a brother who has threatened her life. The plot may be somewhat incredible, but the emotion of this music rings true; Verdi has reconciled conflicting sentiments by blending the serene tone quality of the harp with disquieting chromatic harmony and a poignantly moving melody.

Verdi was a late bloomer—it was not until after mid-century that he hit his stride, but with the appearance in 1853 of both *Il Trovatore* ("The Troubadour") and *La Traviata* ("The Doomed One") his style and his reputation were established. In contrast to German Romantic opera, in which nature, mythology, and the supernatural were basic elements, Verdi's works dealt with lifelike human beings and their response to personal calamities. His arias are among the best loved in the annals of opera, and the popularity of his works shows no sign of diminishing. Like his fellow Romanticists, Verdi had no great interest in humor; of his surviving operas, only the last one, *Falstaff* (1893), falls in the opera buffa category.

WAGNER

During the first part of his career, Richard Wagner (1813–1883) continued the German Romantic opera tradition, but after the production of *Lohengrin,* he turned his back on his early operatic formats and even on the term "opera" itself: henceforth his works were to be called *music dramas.* First he wrote a long explanation and defense of his theories, and then he composed the four music dramas that constitute *Der Ring des Nibelungen* ("The Ring of the Nibelungs"), a cycle based on Norse mythology. According to Wagnerian theory, music and drama were to be unified in his works: the drama would unfold uninterrupted by "set pieces" such as recitatives, arias, or duets. Instead, there would be continuous harmony, like a sea on which melodies would float, and the orchestra would advance the action as well as underscore emotion. Musical symbolism was a crucial feature in Wagner's plan. Every person or object that figured prominently in the plot was represented musically by a short melodic fragment called a *leitmotif* ("leading motive"), which was associated with that person or object throughout the opera. As the drama unfolded, these leitmotifs were modified musically (in a manner similar to transformation of theme) to reflect dramatic developments. Leitmotifs were the key to the orchestra's ability to advance the action, and they also provided a purely musical unity to the work.

Reactions to Wagner and his music were extreme. His supporters could speak only in superlatives, and his detractors found language (any language) inadequate to express their loathing. Even today, people tend to view his music dramas either as the work of a supreme genius or as the long-winded ramblings of an egomaniac—very few respond with indifference. His influence on the development of opera was profound: his concept of continuous music succeeded in slaying the dragon of required recitative, and the leitmotif principle, in assorted mutations, found favor with many of his successors.

THE LATER ROMANTICS

By the mid-1850s, Chopin and Mendelssohn were dead, Schumann had suffered a complete emotional collapse, and Liszt was about to enter the religious life. The nonoperatic field was clear for the younger generation, with Johannes Brahms (1833–1897) as heir apparent. Brahms was the only Romantic composer to accept Beethoven's legacy in its entirety. Thoroughly Romantic in his melodic style, harmonic vocabulary, and emotional intensity, Brahms was a Classicist in his love of form. The symphony, sonata, concerto, string quartet, and theme and variations were all forms with which he was very much at home. Thematic relationships and techniques of development were fascinating to Brahms, and his four symphonies are as tightly woven as those of Beethoven. (Referring to Brahms's First Symphony as "Beethoven's Tenth" is an old joke among musicians.)

BRAHMS

Side 8 Band 2

The third movement of Brahms's Second Symphony, heard in the recorded example, typifies his fusion of Romantic style and Classical economy of means. It has emotional warmth—complete with long-lined, lyric melodies and rich harmonies—but in organization it is Classically compact, with all important thematic material deriving from a single melodic idea. The form is ABABA, and the opening theme of A is the source of the "new" themes of the contrasting section; these themes follow approximately the same melodic outline, whether right-side-up or inverted. Initially, A is performed by woodwinds accompanied by pizzicato strings. In its second appearance, a French horn interjects a countermelody, and the third time around, the theme is played by the strings. Section B introduces changes in both tempo and meter, and in style it is far more aggressive than the amiable A section, which ambles forward with no sense of urgency. In mood, this movement is somewhat atypical of nineteenth-century music: neither dramatic nor heroic, it fairly radiates cheerful good humor.

Brahms's music frequently contains strong contrapuntal interest, both in the combination of different melodies and in the use of canonic or fugal techniques in development. Crossrhythms, involving both pulse and subdivisions, are characteristic of his style, and he alone of the Romanticists made extensive use of hemiola (page 67). His excellence in the fields of chamber music and choral composition is in no way surprising; both demand a disciplined kind of writing which was as natural to him as it was inhibiting to most other Romantic composers.

Nineteenth-century audiences and critics saw Brahms and Wagner as exact opposites, both musically and philosophically. Brahms professed great admiration for Wagner, but Wagner was less charitable. If he had kind words to say in support of Brahms, history does not tell us what they were. Partisanship was so intense that it became impossible to champion the music of both men. From the safe distance of more than a century, it seems incredible that music lovers once felt compelled to view the music of these two men in an either-or light. Since Wagner wrote only operas and Brahms wrote in every medium except opera, they were not in direct competition—and in fact there was no true basis for comparison. One might as well be called on to choose between Wilt Chamberlain and Henry Aaron.

Nationalism

The bumper crop of composers who had been born in the 1830s and 1840s was due in part to an expansion of the geographical base of Western music. Nations which had once imported their composers were beginning to develop their own, and, naturally, these first native composers were acutely conscious of their national origin. Their music reflected a pride in nationality that was more self-conscious that that expressed in Chopin's Polanaises or Liszt's Hungarian Rhapsodies. Nationalism was both the motivating force and the goal, and to ensure a uniquely national flavor in their music, composers used folksongs of their own

The French Ambassadors (1533), by Hans Holbein. The wide interests and sophistication of the two Renaissance men are demonstrated by the presence of globes, books, and both scientific and musical instruments.

(Opposite) *Bahram Gur in the Turquoise Pavilion on Wednesday* (detail); a miniature in a 16th-century Persian manuscript.

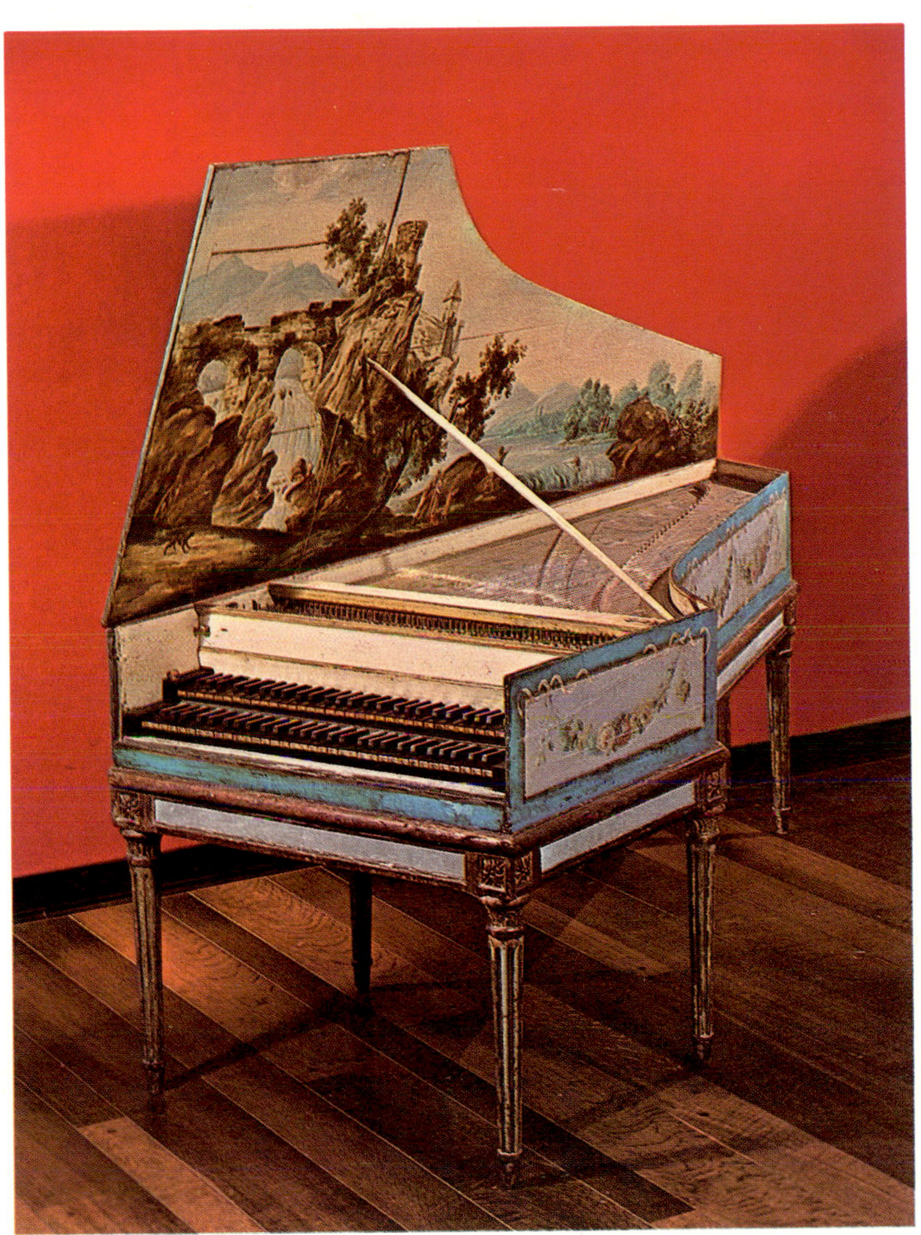

A two-manual harpsichord built in France around 1760; its elaborate decoration is typical of the instruments of that period.

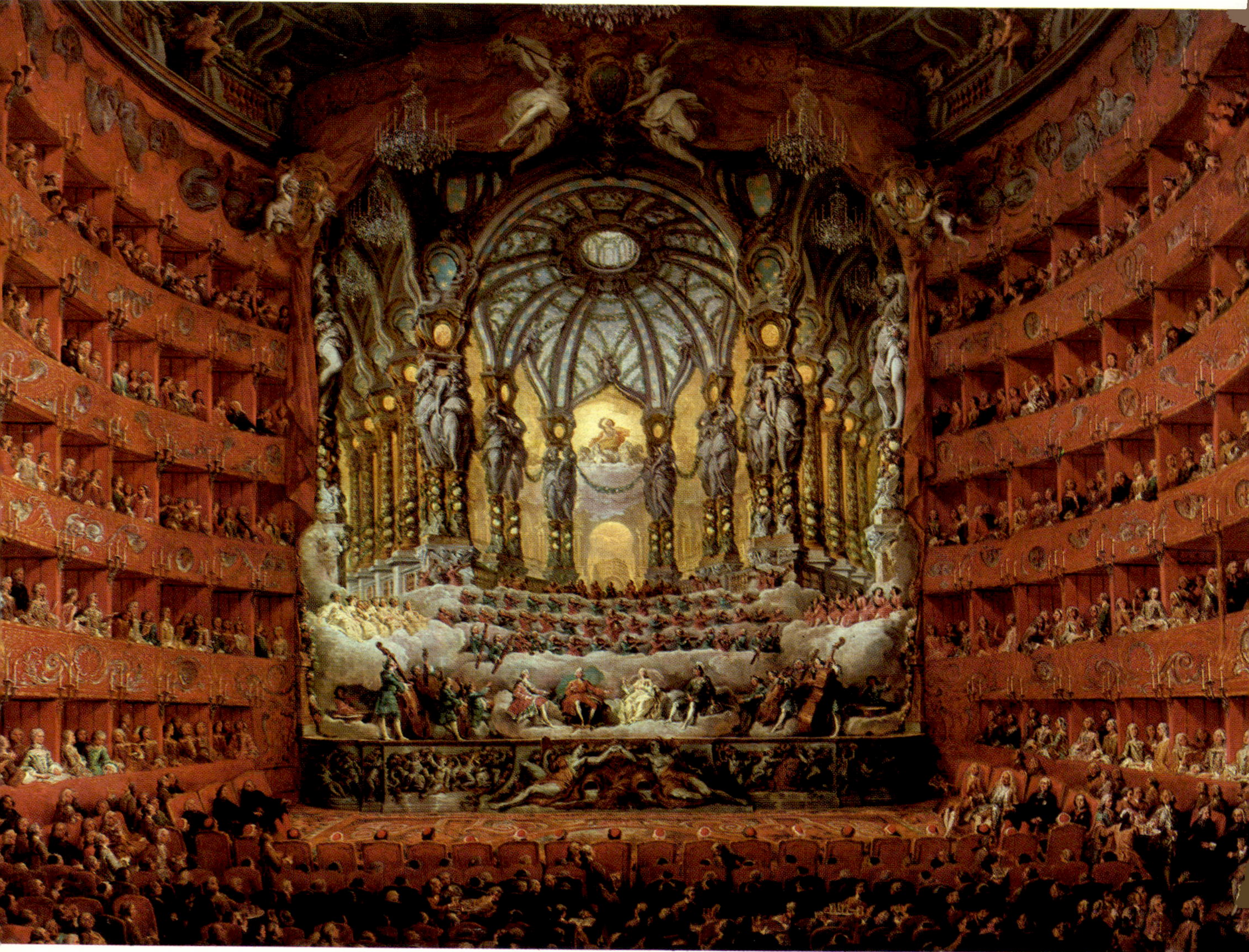

Eighteenth-century opera in Rome, in a painting by Giovanni Paolo Pannini, 1729. The opera house, in the palace of a cardinal, was typically lavish.

(Opposite) *Café-Concert: At Les Ambassadeurs* (1877), by Edgar Degas.

A scene from Georges Bizet's opera *Carmen* (1875) in a 1967 production at the Metropolitan Opera House.

(Opposite) The ceiling of the Paris Opéra, by Marc Chagall, completed in 1964.

Timorese dancers of Indonesia. Both the feather headdresses and the hand drums are found throughout the world.

The Polovetsian Dances from Alexander Borodin's *Prince Igor,* at the New York City Opera, 1969.

country as thematic material and also incorporated characteristic native rhythmic patterns.

THE FIVE

The most successful venture into nationalistic music began in Russia with The Five. They were Mily Balakirev (1837–1910), César Cui (1835–1918), Alexander Borodin (1833–1887), Modest Mussorgsky (1839–1881), and Nicolai Rimsky-Korsakov (1844–1908). All except Balakirev were amateur musicians whose national purity had never been tainted by contact with German conservatories, where most Russian musicians received their training. They were thus able to be uninhibitedly Russian in musical utterance, and they were highly successful in establishing an identifiably nationalistic style. Balakirev and Cui owe their renown more to association with The Five than to any durability of their own music, but the other three created music that has remained in the concert repertoire and continues to be performed with some regularity. In opera, *Prince Igor* by Borodin, *Boris Godunov* by Mussorgsky, and *The Golden Cockerel* by Rimsky-Korsakov have all found favor with twentieth-century opera-goers. Mussorgsky's piano work *Pictures at an Exhibition* is an enduring favorite, and in America, increased interest in the Russian language has stimulated a revival of interest in his songs. Only Borodin contributed significantly to the chamber music literature: his String Quartet No. 2 was the first Russian work in that medium to earn a continuing place in the repertoire. Rimsky-Korsakov's symphonic suite *Scheherezade,* and Borodin's Second Symphony have become orchestral staples, and the many recordings of the former indicate that its popularity with the public exceeds the frequency with which it is programmed in concerts. Borodin's music received the ultimate compliment—the American musical *Kismet* was based on melodies pirated from his compositions.

TCHAIKOVSKY

Less self-conscious in his nationalism but no less unmistakably Russian in style was Peter Ilyich Tchaikovsky (1840–1893). He was less insular than his compatriots: Western music in general was his sphere of interest, and musically, he was primarily a Romanticist and secondarily a Russian. His music is intensely emotional, with a prevailing cast of Slavic gloom. Yearning melodies, rhythmic vitality, and sensual harmonies characterize his style, and a Tchaikovskian trademark is the modulating sequence in which each repetition of the pattern slides into a new key, building to a tremendous climax.

Side 8 Band 3

Tchaikovsky's Sixth Symphony (the "Pathétique") is both a monument to despondency and a model of musical craftsmanship. The recorded example is the second movement, in three-part form. It begins with an A section that bravely attempts gaiety, but pathos is never far from the surface, and in the B section it emerges undisguised. A is characterized by an ambiguous rhythmic scheme in which the beats are theoretically grouped in fives, but 5 + 5 sometimes sounds more like 7 + 3. Long phrases cover a wide melodic range, proceeding primarily in stepwise motion, with strings and woodwinds alternating in presenting the melody. The final string statement brings this section to a climax with the modulating sequence described above, but no pinnacle is reached, because the pattern descends with each repetition, robbing the climax of any sense of triumph. Throughout the B section, an ominous ostinato in the timpani casts a pall of foreboding, and the melody is hesitant, fragmented, and rather narrow in range. After an antiphonal exchange between motives of B (strings) and a motive of A (woodwinds), a somewhat abridged version of A returns, and in the short coda that follows, the underlying sadness of this movement is confirmed.

Two of Tchaikovsky's operas, *Eugene Onegin* and *The Queen of Spades,* have survived, but his best-loved works are orchestral. The last three of his six symphonies have become concert fixtures and are probably programmed more frequently than those of any other Romanticist except Brahms. Tchaikovsky's concern for formal organization, while far from Classic, was considerable, and gives his symphonies cohesion. Like Schubert, however, his love for beautiful melody, spun out in long lines, is always evident. His Piano Concerto in B♭ minor and his Violin Concerto in D remain popular, and orchestral suites based on his ballet music for *Swan Lake* and *The Nutcracker* rival the symphonies in audience attraction.

Of all the would-be nationalists, only The Five stayed clear of German influence. So great was the musical dominance of nineteenth-century Germany that aspiring musicians from other nations did not feel qualified to compose or perform until they had made the pilgrimage to Leipzig, Berlin, or Frankfurt. After this indoctrination, the nationalistic elements in their music—the folk material of their own country—became fused with a musical language that was primarily Germanic. The range of German influence was wide, and the roster of nationalistic composers who came under that influence is a distinguished one: Antonin Dvořák (1841–1904) from Bohemia (now Czechoslovakia); Edvard Grieg (1843–1907) from Norway; Sir Arthur Sullivan (1842–1900) from England; and, later, Isaac Albéniz (1860–1909) from Spain; Edward MacDowell (1861–1908) from the United States; and Jean Sibelius (1865–1957) from Finland.

Music in France

France, however, stood aloof, refusing to acknowledge Germany—or, for that matter, any place outside Paris—as the musical Mecca. In the eyes of the French, their own Paris Conservatory was the finest in the world, and there was no need to send their young musicians to any foreign cultural center for training. Nationalism as a doctrine held little attraction for French composers, but during the last half of the century, they developed a brand of Romanticism that, if not self-consciously French, was at least different from Germanic style.

FRANCK

César Franck (1822–1890), a Belgian-born French composer, was unique among Romanticists in his taste for contrapuntal textures and techniques. Canonic writing was frequently encountered in his music, and the combination of melodies previously presented singly was his favorite climactic procedure. He was Romantic in his highly chromatic harmonic language, but the fragmented, motivic structure of his melodies was totally at odds with the prevailing preference for long, unbroken phrases. Franck was perhaps the latest-blooming composer of all time, reaching his stride only after the age of sixty. His finest works include his one symphony (in D minor), a sonata for violin and piano, the *Variations Symphoniques* for piano and orchestra, and a large body of organ music.

SAINT-SAËNS

Camille Saint-Saëns (1835–1921) was another composer who contributed to the resurgence of French instrumental music. Saint-Saëns combined a Classical sense of form with a French interest in instrumental technique and tone color. He was Romantic in melodic and harmonic style, but on the emotional plane, he was more French than Romantic. His music is characteristically brilliant and exciting; it may, on occasion, be wistful, but never lugubrious. His Classical leanings are clearly revealed in his three symphonies and five piano concertos, while the Romantic side of his nature is more readily apparent in his symphonic poems, particularly the famous *Danse Macabre.*

Side 8 Band 4

Saint-Saëns had little sympathy for the expression of personal emotion as a musical goal; to him such self-indulgence bordered on decadence and led inevitably to corruption of the art. He was a purist, for whom ideal beauty was the only appropriate aesthetic goal, and the cultivation of form was the means of achieving it. The third movement of his Piano Concerto in G minor, heard in the recorded example, illustrates his concern for form and his scorn for sentimentality. This music delights the ear and engages the mind but elicits no overpowering emotional response except exhilaration. The movement is in sonata form with an introduction. The first theme is debonair and bouncy and the second theme, with insistent trills, is more assertive. The introductory theme, which seems altogether prefatory at the time, features a three-note descending motive that assumes great importance as the movement unfolds; it repeatedly invades thematic territory and eventually infiltrates both themes, tightening the structure through thematic interrelationships.

Opposite: the Grand Staircase of the Opéra, Paris.

Opera in France, unmoved by Wagnerian theory, continued in the grand manner. But it was gradually moving away from specta-

AMPHITHEATRE
FICHOT

cle toward lyricism, and the chasm that had divided opéra from opéra comique (page 167) yawned less wide. Saint-Saën's *Samson et Dalila* came close to the old grand-opera tradition and qualified unequivocally as opéra, but other musical theater productions proved less easy to categorize. Both *Faust* by Charles Gounod (1818–1893) and *Carmen* by Georges Bizet (1838–1875) began life as opéras comiques, and both, after spoken dialogue was legitimized as recitative, were later accepted as lyric operas. In the pure, unambiguous opéra comique category were the genuinely comic operas of Jacques Offenbach (1819–1880), whose *Orphée aux Enfers* ("Orpheus in Hades") and *La vie parisienne* ("Parisian Life") have never lost their appeal.

Offenbach's English counterpart was Sir Arthur Sullivan who, in collaboration with the poet William S. Gilbert, wrote a series of operettas that rank among the most widely and frequently performed works in musical theater. *The Mikado, H.M.S. Pinafore,* and *The Pirates of Penzance,* to name a few, were box office bonanzas in their day, and today, nearly a century later, they still play to enthusiastic audiences. One invariable feature of a Gilbert and Sullivan operetta is the *patter song,* which demands a singer with impeccable enunciation. The words come forth at breakneck speed, and audiences are inclined to hold their breath lest they miss a pun or a witty rhyme.

LATE ITALIAN OPERA

Verdi remained the dominant force in Italian opera until nearly the end of the century. The changing of the guard did not occur until 1893—a year that witnessed Verdi's last opera *(Falstaff)* and the first international triumph *(Manon Lescaut)* of his successor, Giacomo Puccini (1858–1924). Puccini was typically Italian in his love for beautiful melody, and he had a gift for creating melodies that continue to haunt the listener long after the final curtain. He was particularly fond of beginning an aria on a poignant high note, then descending by degrees, either directly or with a series of decorative arabesques. His arias with this trademark are among the most passionate in all opera. In the recorded example, "Che gelida manina" from *La Bohème,* this trademark appears not at the beginning but at the climax of the aria. To set the scene, Mimi and Rodolfo have just met, and it is clearly a case of love at first sight. Rodolfo's first words, freely translated, are "Your

PUCCINI

Side 8 Band 5

A scene from *The Mikado* by Gilbert and Sullivan, perhaps the most popular operetta of all time.

hand is cold! Let me warm it for you!" Having captured her hand, he sings lyrically about her charms, then launches into a passionate declaration of love.

Puccini was altogether un-Italian in the degree of attention he devoted to dramatic elements. His characters inspire empathy; the action of his operas progresses at a credible pace; and his plots, even if they verge on sentimentality, carry a sense of conviction. Puccini's place in the operatic repertoire seems secure, and if frequency of performance can predict longevity, *La Bohème, Tosca,* and *Madam Butterfly* bid fair to live forever.

MUSIC IN THE UNITED STATES

Nineteenth-century America, having long since established its political independence, was still a far cry from achieving artistic self-sufficiency. Americans imported European productions and deferred to any country on the far side of the Atlantic in musical matters. An invidious sense of cultural inadequacy permeated the national subconscious, manifesting itself in the unvoiced assumption that any musician of consequence must perforce speak English with a pronounced accent. Home-grown talent was suspect—not even training in a European conservatory could eradicate the stigma of native birth, and American musicians were sometimes obliged to carve out careers in Europe, where acceptance on musical merit came more easily.

GOTTSCHALK

New Orleans-born Louis Moreau Gottschalk (1829–1869) won fame and fortune as a virtuoso pianist-composer in Europe, where his piano pieces employing Creole tunes and rhythms achieved great popularity. In America, it was the old story of the prophet receiving no honor in his native land—Gottschalk's piano music was scarcely known until its revival in 1969 in commemoration of the hundredth anniversary of his death.

MACDOWELL

Composer-pianist Edward MacDowell was more fortunate in attracting the support of his fellow countrymen—but only after extended study in Germany and, even then, only after the Germans had paid him the ultimate tribute of inviting him to teach in their conservatories. Despite his German saturation, MacDowell recognized the stultifying effect of European domination on the development of music in America. He called for "absolute freedom from the restraint that an almost unlimited deference to European thought and prejudice has imposed on us."*

American deference to European music and musicians affected all facets of serious music, but in productions of opera, it scaled the height of the ridiculous. In Europe, foreign operas were often translated into the vernacular, but American audiences felt compelled to import a foreign language along with the music—not necessarily the original language, but something less readily understandable than English:

> In grand opera, America was caught in a new "war of the tongues," basically a battle between the German and Italian traditions with the French somewhere between. When the Metropolitan Opera opened in New York in 1883, its first performance was Gounod's *Faust*. As a French opera based on a German drama and performed in Italian, it provided a satisfactory compromise of international interests. But the "war" continued. In the 1880s, the Metropolitan was a Wagnerian bastion, whereas the Chicago Opera remained under Italian control and the American Opera Company (New York) tried opera in English, a solution that seems to have pleased nobody. This new language conflict produced strange turnabouts. In 1889 Wagner's *Lohengrin* was produced in Italian in Chicago and Verdi's *Un Ballo in Maschera* was done in German at the Metropolitan in New York.*

*Quoted in Gilbert Chase, *America's Music* (New York: McGraw-Hill, 1955), p. 355.
*Edith Borroff, *Music in Europe and the United States* (Englewood Cliffs, N.J.: Prentice-Hall, 1971), p. 543.

LATE ROMANTICISM IN GERMANY

STRAUSS

In Germany, the feuding of the Brahmsians and the Wagnerites continued well into the final decade of the century. When reconciliation finally came, it was in the person of Richard Strauss (1864–1949). Strauss's lucidity of form and occasional polyphonic textures pleased the Brahmsians, his descriptive tone poems based on literature and legend pleased the Wagnerites, and his treatment of the orchestra pleased everyone. The orchestra was his personal medium of expression; his experience as a conductor gave him an intimate acquaintance with instrumental possibilities, so that his writing for orchestra was both imaginative and adroit. His handling of instruments represented a departure from Romantic ideals. Rather than the comfortable, normal tessituras favored by his predecessors, he frequently used extreme registers to obtain fresh, distinctive tone colors. But in other respects, he was a direct descendant of the Romanticists: the harmonic language of his early works has a Wagnerian ring, and the influence of Liszt is apparent not only in his choice of the one-movement symphonic poem form (which Strauss called "tone poem") but also in his use of a developmental technique resembling transformation of theme. The most popular of all his tone poems is *Till Eulenspiegel,* which purports to narrate several episodes in the life of the legendary rogue of that name. Humor is the central issue, ranging from the subtlety of Till's pompous conversation with the pedants to the gallows humor of his death by hanging.

After the turn of the century, Strauss's interest shifted to opera. He did not refer to his works as music dramas, but his use of leitmotifs and an unbroken flow of music, together with the prominent role he gave the orchestra, were signs of the considerable influence of Wagner. *Salome* and *Elektra* were profoundly shocking to early audiences; polite society was not prepared for their Freudian implications, and in New York, *Salome* closed after one performance. *Der Rosenkavalier,* however, was an immediate success, and it is still Strauss's best-loved opera.

Around 1900, Strauss's harmonic writing became less richly chromatic and more austere. Dissonances were left unresolved, consecutive chords were unrelated by key, and occasionally, opposing chords or keys were combined. Although he never completely rejected nineteenth-century ideals, Strauss was beginning to look beyond Romanticism toward the future.

COMPARATIVE STYLE CHARACTERISTICS

	LATE CLASSICAL PERIOD	EARLY ROMANTIC PERIOD	MIDDLE AND LATE ROMANTIC PERIOD
TEXTURE	varying in density	consistent in density, tending toward medium thickness	consistent in density, tending toward thickness and solidity
CADENCES	clear-cut, definitive, and predictable all lines cadencing simultaneously	clear-cut, definitive, and predictable all lines cadencing simultaneously	sectional cadences—clear-cut and definitive internal cadences—less decisive and somewhat unpredictable
POLYPHONY	seldom used, except for brief passages of imitation within a development section	seldom used, except for occasional use of a countermelody	occasionally used, but only within a harmonic context both combined melodies and imitative techniques
HARMONY	tonal primarily diatonic—some chromaticism simple modulations to closely related keys	tonal chromatic harmony modulations, to both related and remote keys	tonal intensely chromatic harmony complex modulations, frequently to remote keys frequent use of tonally ambiguous passages
RHYTHM	consistent meter consistent tempo subdivisions variable, especially the use of threes within a framework of twos	consistent meter within a section tempo changes from section to section elasticity of tempo within a section (rubato) subdivisions variable in any framework subdivisions combined	primarily consistent meter; occasional meter change within a section tempo changes from section to section elasticity of tempo within a section subdivisions variable, including uncommon ones (fives, sevens) subdivisions combined

	LATE CLASSICAL PERIOD	EARLY ROMANTIC PERIOD	MIDDLE AND LATE ROMANTIC PERIOD
DYNAMICS	shaded moderate range	shaded wide range	shaded very wide range
ARTICULATION	variety of attacks, separately and combined clarity of articulation	primarily legato	primarily legato
VOCAL FORMS	mass	solo song part song	solo song oratorio
INSTRUMENTAL FORMS	symphony concerto sonata string quartet theme and variations	short piano piece symphony concerto sonata piano trio	short piano piece symphony symphonic (tone) poem concerto sonata
INSTRUMENTAL TONE COLOR	brilliance blend	richness blend	rich, dark color; sometimes brilliant blend and contrast
ORCHESTRA	medium-sized (40–60) strings woodwinds (clarinet rare) addition to brasses: trombones timpani	medium-large (60–80) strings addition to woodwinds: clarinets brasses percussion section enlarged slightly	large (80–110) strings additions to woodwinds: piccolo, English horn, bass clarinet, contrabassoon addition to brasses: tuba percussion section greatly enlarged
MUSICAL THEATER	opera opéra comique singspiel	opera	opera, music drama operetta ballet

12. Music in the Marketplace

ALTHOUGH THE ART OF MUSIC has occupied a place of honor in every culture throughout history, society has always been somewhat ambivalent in its attitude toward practitioners of that art. The ancient Aztecs were unusual, if not unique, in according musicians high social standing and granting them exemption from taxation in recognition of their contribution to the common good. But the "common good" demanded perfection in performance, and any hapless performer who erred in the execution of ritual music paid for his wrong note with his life.* Taxpaying musicians in other cultures have found social acceptance more difficult but professional activity less hazardous. Society seems to have difficulty in accepting musicians as ordinary human beings pursuing the profession of their choice. According to the usual pattern, outstanding talent has been recognized, sought after, and sometimes rewarded financially, but traditionally, the possessor of that talent has not been granted a correspondingly high social status.

MUSIC AS A PROFESSION

During the Middle Ages, social stigma attached not to being a musician, but to being a *professional* musician. The jongleurs were veritable pariahs, without recourse to law or access to the sacraments of the church.* But troubadours of noble birth, whose music making was divorced from financial gain, suffered no diminution of social standing. Subsequent centuries witnessed some improvement in the professional musicians' lot; they could no longer be beaten or robbed with impunity, they were welcomed in churches, and by the eighteenth century, some had reached the dizzying heights of a social position roughly equivalent to that of head butler. But their standing in the intellectual community failed to make comparable gains; they continued to be regarded as persons of little wit—clever, but incapable of profundity. Only during the nineteenth century could musicians enjoy being accepted as equals in literary, philosophical, and social circles.

*Robert Stevenson, *Music in Aztec and Inca Territory* (Berkeley and Los Angeles: University of California Press, 1968), p. 89.
*Donald Grout, *A History of Western Music* (New York: W. W. Norton, 1960), p. 59.

The twentieth century, heralded as a century of progress, has not included the social status of musicians in its forward march. Professionally, the twentieth-century musician is far from being an outcast: concert artists are regarded with awe by adoring audiences, and rock stars have become musical idols as well as sex symbols to their enthusiastic fans. But musicians are not trusted in either intellectual or fiscal matters. Music professors desiring to establish a line of credit would be well advised to list their occupation as "professor" rather than "musician." Nor is listing one's occupation as "musician" any guarantee of welcome outside the business world. Shortly after the Second World War, a renowned musician initiated proceedings to become a French citizen; his request was refused and his application was returned, stamped "Profession socialement inutile" (profession not socially useful).*

On a purely professional plane, evaluation is usually based on musical criteria, resulting in justifiable, if implacable, discrimination against the untalented. But aesthetic judgments, alas, have not always been entirely unclouded by extraneous considerations. There is no sheltering cloak of anonymity for those who occupy the stage; their extreme visibility leaves them vulnerable to cultural mores and biases relating to physical attributes, particularly skin color and gender.

Blacks in Music

The biggest blot on America's musical escutcheon resulted from prolonged refusal to acknowledge outstanding talent in the black community. Jim Crow stereotyping decreed that although black people possessed a remarkable sense of rhythm, their musical endeavors were primitive at best, at worst conducive to orgy—and in any event were not to be taken seriously. During the years of slavery, music making was actively encouraged; it was considered a harmless emotional outlet, and, further, the ability to play a musical instrument increased a slave's market value. After emancipation, black musicians tried to earn a living with their talents, but the only performing outlets open to them were jobs in honky-tonks that were neither prestigious nor lucrative. For a more rewarding musical career, blacks first had to hurdle the barriers

*Michel Briguet, *50 millions de Français devant la musique* (Paris: Les Editions Ouvrières, 1965), p. 11.

Some of the 75,000 people who attended Marian Anderson's 1939 recital at the Lincoln Memorial in Washington, D.C. (The singer's back is to the camera.)

that denied them access to a first-rate musical education. And once this was accomplished, there still remained the unreasoning assumption of the white community that people with darker skins were necessarily inferior in all areas of human endeavor.

Formal training in music widened the scope of career opportunities, but entry into the European-dominated concert field was difficult for any American-born musician and all but impossible for blacks. That bastion of white supremacy yielded slowly and only to talent of towering proportions; it was not until the early 1940s that blacks were numbered among America's ten most highly paid concert musicians.

Paul Robeson (1898–1976) was an actor-singer who first won fame in the theater and later added the concert field to his list of triumphs. His recital repertoire was drawn primarily from black folk songs, with particular emphasis on spirituals, and it was he who immortalized the song "Ol' Man River" in Jerome Kern's musical, *Show Boat*.

Marian Anderson (b. 1902) was first, last, and always a musician, and her magnificent voice had the power to open closed minds as well as closed doors. But not all closed minds. She was already an established artist of international repute when, in 1939, her scheduled concert in Washington, D.C. was jeopardized by the refusal of the Daughters of the American Revolution to permit a

Negro to sing in Constitution Hall. This demonstration of witless bigotry became headline news, and the entire nation was outraged. The concert itself took place on schedule but in a different locale: through White House intervention, Miss Anderson was invited to sing at the Lincoln Memorial, and more than seventy-five thousand people assembled to pay tribute to the great contralto. In 1955, she demolished another color barrier in music by becoming the first black to be granted inclusion as a permanent member of New York's Metropolitan Opera Company.

There was discrimination in the field of jazz, too, but it was directed primarily at the white man. Jazz buffs were firm in their conviction that the purity of the art depended on improvisation by black performers; written notation and white musicians represented adulteration and were not to be tolerated. Black leadership has been undeniable, but blanket exclusion of whites from the inner circle of jazz is indefensible. The famous jazz trumpeter Roy Eldridge claimed that he could identify a performer's color by listening alone. But when he agreed to a blindfold test, he was right by less than fifty percent—a fact that would indicate that the differences between outstanding black and white jazz performers are more apparent to the eye than to the ear.*

The musicians themselves were blissfully colorblind. Integrated jazz bands and ensembles appeared as early as the 1920s, but public preference leaned toward all-black or all-white groups. Only established leaders, such as Duke Ellington and Benny Goodman, could afford to defy this convention without fear of financial reprisal. Less gifted musicians were more hesitant to risk audience disapproval, and as late as the 1950s, many local chapters of the American Federation of Musicians remained segregated.* The entire color issue became irrelevant when recordings replaced live performances as the principal way of listening to jazz. Today, fans know the names and the sounds of the top performers, but their race, if known, is immaterial.

Women in Music

The participation of women in music making has always been circumscribed by whatever artificial limitations were imposed on

*Leonard Feather, *The Book of Jazz* (New York: Paperback Library, 1961), pp. 51–52.
*Ibid., p.45.

them by the culture in which they lived. Restrictions have varied from one culture to another and from century to century, but their essential arbitrariness has been universal. There have often been unwarranted assumptions concerning what women *could* not do, and society's preconceptions about what they *should* not do have frequently limited the options of women musicians still further. In Nepal, for example, it is not considered proper for a woman to appear on the concert stage. Women musicians may be heard but not seen, and thus professional performance is restricted to the recording studio.

One curious quirk common to a number of cultures is the tendency to invest a musical instrument with either masculine or feminine connotations and to limit its performance to the appropriate gender. Apparently, most instruments have been found to be masculine, since proscriptions against playing them have been directed primarily toward women. Only rarely has a musical instrument become the exclusive province of the female sex. The actual sound of an instrument has had little if anything to do with this type of classification; the Inca civilization permitted a woman to play a transverse flute, but the sexually symbolic vertical flute was reserved for male performers.* Let the reader beware of dismissing this practice as antediluvian—vestiges linger on, in contemporary attitudes toward performers who play certain instruments. Society continues to view the trombone, for example, as a man's instrument, and women are not welcome in that section of the orchestra. There is no aesthetic or biological reason why the harp should be a woman's instrument, but the fact remains that male harpists are as rare as whooping cranes. As for the podium, a young woman will have difficulty in finding a school that will encourage her to major in conducting.

During the past two centuries, career opportunities have become increasingly open to women in both concert and opera, and today outstanding soloists are rarely touched by sex discrimination. Orchestral doors, however, open reluctantly to women, particularly in America. When Fritz Reiner assumed direction of the Chicago Symphony in 1955, he immediately fired all the women in the orchestra. He did not find it necessary to listen to them first—being female constituted sufficient grounds for removal. (Membership in the musicians' union is necessary to get

*Stevenson, *Music in Aztec and Inca Territory*, p. 254.

work, but it offers scant protection against summary dismissal.) Since 1970, the picture has improved, but to this day, relatively few women are included as full-time personnel in major orchestras (harpists are usually hired on a part-time basis).

In jazz, the role of women has been vocal. Ma Rainey and Bessie Smith staked a claim on the blues from the beginning, to be followed by Billie Holiday, Ella Fitzgerald, Lena Horne, and Pearl Bailey, to name but a few of the great jazz singers. A comparable list of female instrumentalists would be impossible to compile, as the instrumental side of jazz has been and continues to be almost exclusively male. One can mention the pianists Dorothy Donegan, Hazel Scott, and Marion McPartland as exceptions to that male monopoly, but their names are hardly household words, and the non-pianists are even less well known.

Discrimination against blacks and women in music has closely paralleled contemporary social practice, but for some reason, there has been no corresponding history of anti-Semitism. On the contrary, Jewish instrumentalists so dominate the field, both in numbers and in renown, that gentiles often constitute a minority in the upper ranks of recitalists and orchestra members. This is not the case with singers, where the distribution of blacks and whites, Jews and gentiles, men and women, bears some resemblance to population ratios.

Only in the field of pre–twentieth-century composition were Jews conspicuously absent—but so, for that matter, were blacks and women. The small number of blacks might be explained by their late entrance into the mainstream of Western music and their difficulties in obtaining formal education, but no such obvious explanation can be found to account for the nearly total absence of women and Jewish composers. Women's entry into the field was retarded by social and pseudopsychological factors: society had long regarded composition as an inappropriate activity for women, and early psychological theory assumed that women lacked the creative impulse, basing that theory on the notion that the ability to give birth precluded other creative talent. Jewish creativity has never been called into question, but Western music derived little benefit from it until Western civilization stopped its active persecution of the Jewish people. The rise in Jewish representation among first-rank composers seems directly related to the decline in pogroms, and only in the twentieth century has that representation assumed a proportion comparable to that in the

Billie Holiday.

field of performance. Jewish composers have arrived, blacks are beginning to receive a measure of belated recognition, but the musical community is only beginning to give serious consideration to the works of women composers.

SOME ECONOMIC ASPECTS OF MUSIC

Composers' Livelihoods

Historically, the composition of music seems to have been undertaken more as a matter of inner necessity than as a means of gainful employment. Only in the nineteenth century was composition sufficiently profitable for composers to regard themselves as self-employed. Before then, composers in the West depended largely on church and noble patronage to support composition, and since then, governments, foundations, and universities have sometimes subsidized composers' work. Few composers have

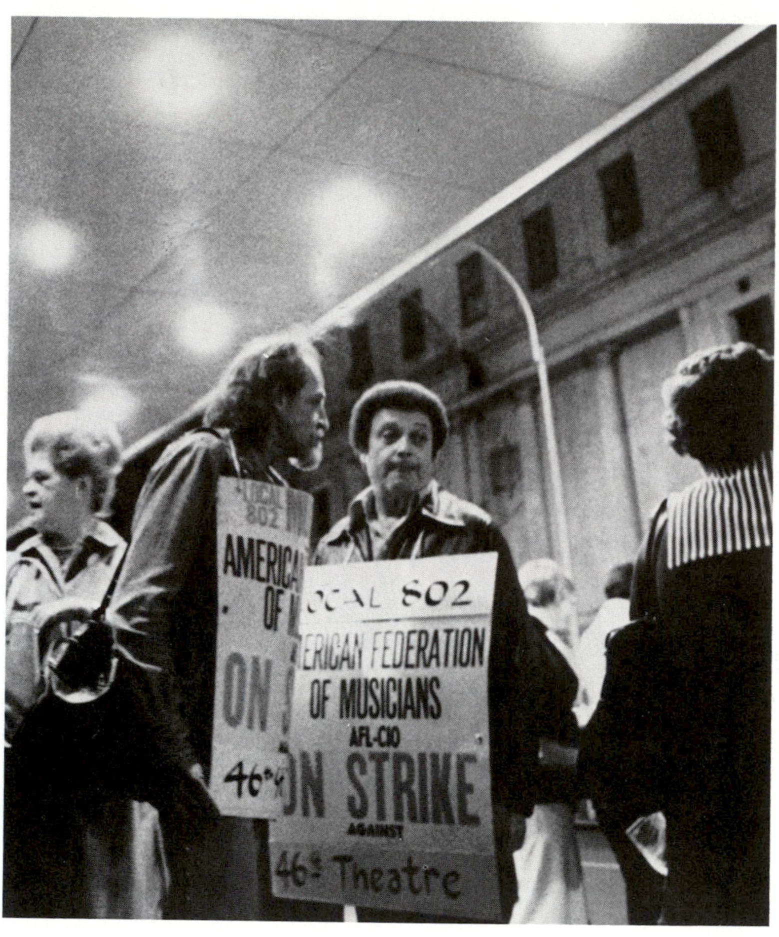

A scene from the 1975 theater musicians' strike, which shut down nine Broadway musicals for more than a month.

been able to devote their undivided attention to creating music. Commissions and royalties combined would not lift many present-day composers above the poverty line, and most, like their predecessors, are obliged to exercise other talents to supplement that slender income. Some perform, others lecture, and almost all of them engage in teaching in one form or another.

East of the Iron Curtain, music is relatively untouched by the law of supply and demand, and composers are free of basic financial worries since the government pays their salaries. These salaries, however, do not come without strings attached; teaching duties are invariably part of the package, and artistic restraints are far from unknown. Polish composers are granted wide creative latitude, and they enjoy enthusiastic public as well as official government support. In Russia, however, composers are kept on a tight artistic rein, and public enthusiasm for new works prudently awaits the sanction of the official Communist Party newspaper, *Pravda*.

Communist China deals with composers in a very different way. In its determination to glorify The People rather than individuals, China has come up with a new approach to musical composition: according to official decree, music must be created by committee. Music *for* the people is written *by* the people, and a composition is identified by title only, since its composers must remain anonymous. Recent examples have placed Chinese music squarely in the mainstream of the nineteenth century.

Composers of popular music have no cushion of subsidy from any quarter. They must either strike a chord of public response, or find some other line of work. But for them, success yields tangible rewards of some magnitude—fame, if and when it arrives, is usually accompanied by fortune. There are not many popular composers with incomes of six figures, but those whose popularity endures for a decade or more have little need to offer piano lessons on the side.

Performers' Livelihoods

Most financially successful musicians—and there are all too few of them—are interpreters rather than creators of music. Monetary rewards for outstanding performers are considerable, but those who reach the top represent only a fraction of the qualified talent. For most of the others, performance is a precarious means of livelihood that must either be supplemented by another job or abandoned in the interest of regular meals. America is particularly chary in its reception of performers; this nation, which buys more records and attends concerts in greater numbers than any other country in the Western world, suffers from the big-name syndrome and is basically unwilling to give unknown artists a hearing. Young pianists determined to storm the concert citadel must, first of all, win an international competition, and follow this triumph with a concert tour of Europe, where audiences are more inclined to appreciate musicians' accomplishments than to damn their imperfections. Then, armed with favorable press clippings, they may attempt to crash the American circuit, but that is a chancy gambit. Groups that sponsor concert series are reluctant to include newcomers, and self-sponsorship—involving high-priced hall rental and publicity—is prohibitively expensive. For most, capitulation is inevitable. Capitulation leaves them the choice between returning to Europe and continuing a concert career or accepting a university teaching position in the United States and watching performance shrink to a minimal part of professional life.

SOME LEGAL ASPECTS OF MUSIC

In addition to problems of audience acceptance and financial uncertainties, musicians have also encountered difficulties in securing professional protection under the law. Prevailing practice under the patronage system gave proprietary control of music created during a term of service to the patron, not the composer. The creative work of composers, as well as their time and talent, belonged to the person who paid their salaries. Free-lance composition was not a viable alternative prior to the nineteenth century; early legal rights pertaining to printed matter profited publishers, not writers. And because of the vested interests of publishers, copyright laws that strengthened the hand of a creator evolved slowly. Tentative efforts in that direction gained some protection for authors, but no provision was made to protect ideas expressed in media other than language. The Constitution of the United States illustrates late-eighteenth-century thinking in regard to ownership of ideas. It empowers Congress to "promote the progress of science and useful arts by securing for limited times to authors and inventors the exclusive rights to their respective writings and discoveries." Congress interpreted this mandate quite literally in its first copyright act (1790); "authors" was interpreted as applying only to writers of books, and "useful arts" did not include music.

During the nineteenth century, ownership and protection of musical compositions became firmly established, and whatever music composers wrote was unquestionably their own property. Upon publication, however, they relinquished all claim to their music, granting publishing rights in one or more countries in exchange for an agreed-upon sum of money. Publishers were not above driving hard bargains, and even so shrewd a businessman as Beethoven could be persuaded to surrender his works cheaply. Muzio Clementi, a publisher and himself a composer, gloated over a transaction with Beethoven in a letter to a member of his staff:

Vienna, April 22, 1807

Dear Collard,

By a little management and without committing myself, I have at last made a complete conquest of that *haughty beauty,* Beethoven. . . .

In short, I agreed with him to take in MS. three Quartets, a Symphony, an Overture, a Concerto for Violin, which is beautiful, and which, at my request he will adapt for the pianoforte, with and without additional keys; and a Concerto for the Pianoforte, for *all* which we are to pay him only two hundred pounds sterling. . . . I have likewise engaged him to compose two sonatas and a fantasia for the pianoforte, which he is to deliver to our house for sixty pounds sterling (mind I have treated for Pounds, not Guineas). In short he has promised to treat with no one but me for the British Dominions.*

Procedures did not alter greatly as the century progressed, but the price of music went up as composers became more wary in dealing with publishers. Further, a growing public for music created a seller's market in which composers could name their prices in take-it-or-leave-it fashion, and compositions were offered singly rather than in job lots. The following excerpt from a letter Chopin wrote to Camille Pleyel is representative of Romantic composers' dealings with publishers:

Valldemosa near Palma. 22 January 1839

Dear friend,

I am sending you the Preludes. . . . I am asking 1,500 francs for the French and English rights. Probst, as you know, has bought the German rights for Breitkopf for 1,000. . . . Since it was your idea, my very dear friend, to undertake the burden of being my publisher, I must notify you that there are other manuscripts awaiting your instructions: 1. The Ballade—which forms part of my German contract with Probst. For this Ballade I am asking 1,000 for the French and English rights. 2. Two Polonaises (you already know the one in A major)—I ask 1,500 for all the countries in the world. 3. A third Scherzo—same price as the Polonaises for the whole of Europe.*

*Quoted in Gertrude Norman and Miriam Shrifte, eds., *Letters of Composers* (New York: Grosset & Dunlap, The Universal Library, n.d.), pp. 65–66.

*Quoted in Arthur Hedley, ed., *Selected Correspondence of Fryderyk Chopin* (London: McGraw-Hill, 1963), p. 168.

By equating one British pound or twenty-five French francs with five U.S. dollars, we can see that Chopin was receiving $1,300 for slightly over one hour's worth of music for solo instrument, whereas Clementi's package purchase from Beethoven for $1,300 represented four or five hours of music, most of which was scored for ensemble, large or small.

Royalty rights, being based on the assumption of continuing ownership after publication, were resisted by publishers, and recording companies fought the royalty concept with a vengeance:

> Before the enactment of the law of 1909 American courts had decided that composers did not enjoy any legal protection against the making of any form of record by means of which their compositions could be mechanically reproduced.*

The rapacity of recording companies was effectively curbed by the new law, and performers as well as composers came under the shelter of the royalty umbrella. Protection for performers, however, was limited to recordings made specifically for record companies; any recording of a live performance was unprotected and could be reproduced without permission. Lack of protection in this area posed no problem until tape technology made the recording of concerts a simple matter. Since the law provided no safeguard against this form of plunder, the musicians' union was obliged to enact its own legislation prohibiting the recording of live performance without prior financial arrangements.

In most European countries, obtaining a copyright is a simple matter—almost automatic—but in the United States, the process is so full of pitfalls that the services of a lawyer are advisable, if not imperative, to guard against inadvertent loss of ownership. From time to time, Congress considers bills to review and revise copyright laws, but their deliberations have rarely resulted in simplification—on the contrary, they have often added to the complexities.

Copyright law, being based on capitalistic concepts of private ownership, posed certain ideological problems for the Soviet Union, and until 1975 their ingenious solution was characteristically unilateral: the music of Russian composers was carefully

*Willi Apel, *The Harvard Dictionary of Music* (Cambridge: Harvard University Press, 1946), p. 185.

guarded, both at home and abroad, but no protection was extended to foreign publications, which were freely used without either consent or payment. Soviet composers receive royalty payments, but they are not permitted to bargain for a higher percentage or to enter into negotiations with foreign publishers; they must assent to state-determined rates, which relate more closely to the size and weight of a manuscript than to its musical worth.

In the United States, the struggle for legal protection is by no means a dead issue. American copyright law is sufficiently archaic that new means for disseminating music seem to be technically exempt from accountability, and court battles are required to establish legal ownership even in areas where proprietary rights are morally self-evident. Manufacturers of tape recordings, for example, initially declared that the copyright law relating to "mechanical reproductions" did not apply to their product, because on tape, music is reproduced electronically. And as recently as 1972, the American Guild of Composers and Lyricists brought suit against the major motion picture and television studios to secure composers' ownership of music written for films and television programs. Prior to this court action, studios had assumed a position comparable to that of an eighteenth-century patron: all rights to music composed under contract belonged to the studio, not the composer. Ownership extended beyond royalty rights to include disposition of the score itself—as composer Maurice Jarre learned to his sorrow:

> When [Jarre] was asked by one of the major symphony orchestras to conduct his music for *Dr. Zhivago,* he called MGM for the score. He was told the music had been destroyed. It seems MGM was short of storage space.*

MUSIC AND BIG BUSINESS

Quite apart from musicians and viewed purely as a commercial enterprise music has become big business indeed. Growth in nearly every segment of the industry has outstripped population growth proportionally, and although the demand for musicians remains small, the market for music is brisk. Through the services of relatively few performers, the recording industry is able to

*Gene Lees, "When the Music Stopped," *High Fidelity Magazine,* Vol. 22, No. 7 (July 1972), p. 20.

A relaxed moment during a Gil Evans recording session in a New York studio.

supply millions with the music of their choice at moderate cost, and in recent years, records have replaced movies as the leading entertainment medium in America, as measured in dollars.* In 1971, the Western world sold approximately 1,716,000,000 discs, the geographic distribution of which is summarized in the following chart.*

USA	719,000,000
Balance of North America	64,000,000
USSR	140,000,000
West Germany	127,000,000
Great Britain	120,000,000
France	95,000,000
Balance of Europe	174,000,000
Japan	150,000,000
Balance of the world	127,000,000
	1,716,000,000

America's position as the world's best customer for recorded music fairly leaps from the page. These figures indicate that numerically America buys over forty percent of the Western world's record output. Considered from a per capita viewpoint,

**Time,* February 12, 1973, p. 60.

*Based on statistics compiled by the Centre d'Information et de Documentation du Disque, Paris, 1971.

the United States holds its lead with an average of something over three records for every man, woman, and child, and in terms of dollar volume, American purchases account for nearly sixty percent of the total.*

The discrepancy between numerical and dollar percentages suggests that American record buyers did not limit themselves to "45s" and bargain-basement reissues; a considerable number of high-priced (and presumably high-quality) albums must have been included in the dollar total. Quantitatively, American consumption of recorded music has been amply documented, but the detailed breakdown, listing percentages for types of music, has not. A study of the Schwann Catalog of recorded music (a recent issue of which devoted 163 pages to listings of concert music, 4 pages to musical shows, 30 to current popular music, and 20 to jazz) must suggest, from sheer quantity of offerings, that concert music dominated the market, but such page-weight evidence would be misleading in the extreme. Concert music's share of local record markets varies from four to fifty percent, and it is probably in the neighborhood of fifteen percent of dollar volume nationally.

Concert Music

Schwann's overwhelming preponderance of concert music listings cannot be explained either in terms of commercial expectation or as quixotic philanthropy on the part of record companies. Record manufacturers are strongly profit-oriented and unlikely to misjudge the market grossly or indulge in unprofitable musical altruism. A recording of popular music is a short-term investment, requiring quick turnover in large volume, because of the brief life span of a popular song. Musical shows and jazz albums have a longer shelf life, and recordings of concert music go on forever—or until revolutionary improvements in sound reproduction render them less desirable acoustically. Recording the standard concert repertoire offers many advantages: it represents a stable, long-term investment unaffected by passing fads; union scale for concert musicians in recording sessions is less than that paid to performers in the popular field; and—except for twentieth-century works—there is no obligation to pay royalties to composers.

**Time,* February 12, 1973, p. 60.

An orchestral recording session.

Performers' royalties pose no problem; a producer is not obligated to pay royalties until he has recouped recording costs from record sales.

The market for avant-garde music is limited, and record companies are understandably reluctant to embark on projects that are certain to lose money. Now that composers from the first half of the twentieth century are included along with Beethoven in *Billboard*'s chart of "classical" best sellers, their music is regarded as a good gamble and their listings in Schwann have expanded; but avant-garde representation remains minimal. For many European companies it is a matter of prestige to record works of the avant-garde, but their American counterparts see little glory in red-ink enterprises. They cannot ignore music of recent years, but in order to hold losses to a minimum, they make recording costs a prime consideration. Large-scale works are bypassed in favor of compositions for one performer or small ensemble, and electronic music, being the least expensive to record, is preferred to music that relies on live performers:

> In this regard Martin Mayer made a noteworthy prediction at the 1968 IMC [International Music Council] Congress. After pointing out that recordings will become increasingly important for composers' earnings and reputations, he said that there would be a strong trend towards issuing university-produced electronic music, which relieves the record company of studio costs, rehearsals, musicians fees, etc. The record company simply transfers the finished tape to records. Mr. Mayer predicted that because economic factors favor composers of electronic music, "some sort of counter-force is going to have to be mounted, or we are going to have a very limited musical life in the years ahead."*

Popular Music

Popular music commands a vast market, but it provides no panacea for the woes of record companies. Styles and tastes change so rapidly that producers dare not limit themselves to established tunes and artists, yet issuing discs that feature new songs or unknown performers is so speculative that it should be prohibited in states where gambling is illegal. The majority of such recordings fail abysmally at the cash register, but when one strikes the public fancy in the grand manner, it generates revenues sufficient to eradicate the losses of a fistful of failures.

No sure-fire formula for creating a best-selling record has yet been found. Producers have great faith in concert appearances by the artist and in massive publicity campaigns, but these ploys have proved to be neither infallible nor indispensable. Highly touted albums collect dust on dealers' shelves, while those of, for example, Carole King, who almost never concertizes and actively avoids publicity, disappear from stock with gratifying rapidity. Her album *Tapestry* averaged three million discs in annual sales for four straight years, making it the best-selling album since the advent of rock.

The most productive promotional device has become illegal. In the 1950s, a nationwide "payola" scandal erupted, revealing that disc jockeys had accepted secret payments from record companies to plug certain songs, thereby creating an illusion of

*Everett Helm, *Composer, Performer, Public* (Florence: Leo S. Olschki, 1970), p. 68.

popular demand. Payola paid off handsomely; a duped public dutifully went forth and bought these spurious "hits," transforming fiction into fact. But once the public realized that it was being hoodwinked, outrage reached such proportions that Congress enacted legislation limiting cash payments to a pittance and gifts of merchandise to a level that would not tempt anyone to compromise his or her integrity. It would be naive to assume that disc jockeys and record companies obey this law to the letter; payola still continues, but now outside the law.

Basically, the music profession does not lend itself to crimes other than plagiarism. During the Prohibition era, jazz musicians were employed in gangster-run speakeasies, but their only contribution to the bootlegging business lay in luring more customers to the illegal liquor. Real crime—and big money—bypassed them altogether. As recording and related enterprises became conspicuously lucrative, the Mafia moved in, starting with jukeboxes. On the face of it, leasing jukeboxes would seem to be totally legitimate, but in practice, installations were accomplished through coercion, and maintainance involved "protection" and frighteningly efficient collection procedures.

Counterfeiting records has swelled the coffers even more. Duplicating records is a simple process that requires only minimal investment, and with neither recording costs nor royalties to pay, that investment yields a high return. Initially, these bootleg recordings were peddled in relatively safe foreign markets, but the lure of the lucrative American trade proved too great to resist, and avarice inevitably triumphed over caution. Duplication is a hazardous operation in America; legitimate companies are protected by laws prohibiting both the reproduction of recordings for profit and the counterfeiting of labels. But despite the risks, this form of piracy is likely to persist; counterfeiters' share of the market in 1972 has been estimated at nearly two hundred million dollars.*

Despite the obvious economic hazards, the profession of music in America continues to attract more fine talent than it can absorb, and for performers, the future holds little promise of any expansion of career opportunities. The proliferation of recorded music has reduced the demand for live performance, and inevitably the ranks of performers have dwindled. The disproportionate

**Time,* February 12, 1973, p. 62.

ratio of listeners to performers that sustains the recording industry is duplicated in rock festivals; the teeming multitudes of fans who assemble to hear their favorites of the moment enrich the few, but create no increase in the market for performers. Concertgoers continue to value the excitement of live performance, and the demand for concert artists, if not increasing, is stable; at least for established performers. But for jazz musicians, employment opportunities are diminishing with frightening rapidity. There is a growing public for jazz, but recordings, many of which now feature electronic effects that cannot be duplicated in live performance, seem to satisfy the hunger. We have not yet reached the point where performers can be declared an endangered species, but if the demand for live performance continues to diminish, business executives will hold the awesome power to determine whom and what we hear.

13. Music from 1900 to 1945

DURING THE LATTER PART of the nineteenth century, there were some isolated rumblings of discontent with Romanticism, but not until the early 1900s did the disenchantment become widespread. The Romantic attitude of emotional openness seemed embarrassingly naive to twentieth-century sophisticates, who were more comfortable with emotional restraint than with unbridled passion. Nor could they share the nineteenth-century view of man as a splendid creature who loved, suffered, struggled, triumphed gloriously over adversity, and retained his nobility even in defeat. Sigmund Freud had changed all that. According to Freud's psychological theory, the "splendid creature" was helpless in the clutch of his anxieties and subservient to the animalistic demands of his id. Shorn of dignity and nobility, man was but a species of animal, with only the saving grace of intellect to recommend him. Small wonder that the twentieth century has so prized mental prowess, trusting only in objective evidence weighed by dispassionate reason. Subjectivity received short shrift in the new regime, and it was evident that to enter the mainstream of the Century of Progress, music must renounce Romantic ideals. That much was clear, but the precise direction of departure was less readily apparent.

ROADS AWAY FROM ROMANTICISM

As the century opened, Western music was so fragmented stylistically that it defied descriptive generalization. Musical tangents were shooting off in all directions, related only by motion away from Romanticism.

DEBUSSY

The French composer Claude Debussy (1862–1918) was the first to repudiate Romanticism and devise an alternative. His rejection of Romanticism came at the height of that movement and was based purely on aesthetic considerations, without the Freudian overtones. He was repelled by the cloying sweetness of thick, chromatic harmonies and luscious, legato melodies, and to him Germanic emotional intensity was a blot on the musical landscape. Tone color, always dear to the French ear, was his primary interest, and to achieve subtlety of shading he treated chords as pure color—vertical sonorities without linear implications. (In traditional tonality, the most colorful harmonies are perceived as active dissonances that require resolution to specific tones, thus giving horizontal obligations to each note of a chord.) This was a radical departure, not only from Romanticism but also from the tonal system that had served for centuries as the basis for pitch organization. Debussy weakened tonality, but he did not destroy it. In most of his music, the listener has at least occasional key orientation, and the final cadence most often confirms an underlying tonal center. Debussy's treatment of tonality in the first movement of his Violin Sonata, the recorded example, is typically vague. The tonal center remains indistinct throughout most of the movement, coming into clear focus only at important cadences. Rhythm provides the principal element of stability. Except for a few brief polymetric effects, the piano and violin maintain consistent rhythmic agreement. Contrast is achieved through the variety of textures, registers, dynamics, and degrees of harmonic activity.

Side 9 Band 1

Impressionism

Debussy's musical language was eclectic, taking inspiration from a variety of sources both musical and nonmusical. Mussorgsky's music aroused his admiration, and some exotic elements of Far Eastern music made their way into his vocabulary; but perhaps the most crucial influence in shaping his aesthetic was the work of the Impressionist painters. The play of light and shadow, the blurring of linear distinctions through the mingling of colors, and the concept of suggestion rather than depiction appealed to his imagination, and he was remarkably successful in adapting these techniques to the medium of sound. Like the Impressionist artists, he strove to capture the evanescence of a fleeting moment and its mood. He had no desire to portray a scene or arouse strong feelings in his listeners; he dealt in color for its own sake and sought to evoke ephemeral emotions.

Pianistically, he was heir to the mantle of Chopin. Few composers have understood the piano so well, and only Chopin ranks as Debussy's equal in idiomatic writing for that instrument. Debussy's piano music requires a sensitive touch and a keen awareness of color and tone quality. It also demands fleetness of foot, for his exploitation of pedal effects involves the use of both feet and all three pedals.

In orchestral writing, Debussy used a large orchestra, not so much for a big sound as for variety in tone color. He used his resources sparingly and selectively to create subtly sensuous rather than sensual effects; in his music, kaleidoscopic changes of orchestral color delight the ear without building tension to fever pitch. His tone poem *Prélude à l'après-midi d'un faune* ("Prelude to the Afternoon of a Faun") and the three symphonic sketches that make up *La Mer* ("The Sea") have become standard repertoire, but at their initial presentations, they created something of a furor because of their radically different sound. The Boston premiere of *La Mer* was greeted with what was considerably less than enthusiasm. One critic suggested sourly that the title must be in error:

> It is possible that Debussy did not intend to call it *La Mer,* but *Le Mal de Mer,* which would at once make the tone-picture as clear as day. It is a series of symphonic pictures of sea-sickness. The first movement is *Headache.* The second is *Doubt,* picturing moments of dread suspense, whether or no! The third movement, with its explosions and rumblings, has now a self-evident purpose. The hero is endeavoring to throw up his boot-heels!*

Vaslav Nijinsky as the Faun, in a poster by Léon Bakst for the 1912 Ballets Russes production of *Afternoon of a Faun*.

Imitators of Impressionism were legion, but few could successfully manage the delicacy, finesse, imagination, and solid craftsmanship that the style demanded. Impressionism might well have remained a one-man show had it not been for Maurice Ravel (1875–1937). His early works emulated Debussy's in style, but as he matured he moved away from Impressionist vagueness toward a style that featured sharp, biting dissonance, tonal brilliance and clarity, and driving rhythm. In the recorded example, the Toccata from his piano suite *Le Tombeau de Couperin* ("Tribute to Couperin") there is no vagueness in the treatment of tonality; Ravel used major keys, minor keys, and modes, and although modulations come thick and fast, the tonal orientation is never in doubt. The perpetual-motion character of the rhythm and the crisp texture of the resolute main theme dominate the movement, overpowering tentative efforts of the more lyric second theme to check the forward momentum until just before the towering final climax. In this work, Ravel focused on each register of the piano individually, moving from one to another in successive phrases or phrase fragments. Individual phrases are often quite limited in range, but during its course, the piece sweeps from one end of the keyboard to the other, leaving very few keys untouched.

RAVEL

Side 9 Band 2

*Louis Elson, quoted in Nicolas Slonimsky, *Lexicon of Musical Invective* (New York: Coleman-Ross, 1953), pp. 94–95.

The roster of first-rank Impressionist composers was limited to two: Debussy and Ravel. The English composer Ralph Vaughan Williams (1872–1958), who studied with Ravel, and the Spanish composer Manuel de Falla (1876–1946), who studied with Debussy, were influenced by the styles of their teachers, but neither can properly be described as an Impressionist.

Debussy's influence was incalculable. He broke new ground in his revolt against Romanticism, and he anticipated most of the vocabulary and techniques of composition that attracted composers during the first half of the twentieth century.

Seen in retrospect, Debussy's departure from tradition was a modest one, but his example opened the way for less temperate, even hostile attitudes toward the established order. Most merciless of all the new iconoclasts was the Viennese composer Arnold Schoenberg (1874–1951). His early career gave little hint of latent musical nihilism. For a time, he was content to follow the precepts of Wagner and Richard Strauss, but when he broke with tradition, it was cataclysmic. He precipitated a major upheaval, and when the ground had settled, the only surviving element appeared to be the musical alphabet itself.

SCHOENBERG

Atonality and Expressionism

Schoenberg felt that Romanticism was diseased, and that only radical surgery could save music from utter degradation; what remained when he finished carving was totally unfamiliar. Late Romanticism stretched tonality, Debussy weakened it, but Schoenberg annihilated it. And with tonality went all the familiar chords and melodic idioms of tertian harmony. Through atonality (page 31), Schoenberg attempted to establish a new organization of pitch materials, in which no single tone could be heard as a focal point, melodies were to be antilyrical and angular, and vertical sonorities were to be selected with the peculiar intention of avoiding consonance, which Schoenberg declared to be beside the point. But rhythm received no drastic modification. Pulse remained basic to rhythmic progression, and meter, whether constant or variable, remained an organizing factor. The most noteworthy rhythmic elements in Schoenberg's music were unusual subdivisions, and the occasional interpolation of a rhythmic figure that sounded incongruous within the prevailing rhythm. His style was uncompromisingly severe, and the passage of time has not noticeably mellowed the austere sound of his music.

Early in the twentieth century, Schoenberg founded *Expressionism,* a musical movement that had its philosophical basis in the Freudian view of man. Expression of inner feeling was the primary goal of this movement but it was nonetheless anti-Romantic, for the emotions with which it dealt were those that people normally prefer not to experience—tension, fear, and neurotic anxiety. He achieved spectacular success in realizing this goal, but in gaining his objective he lost his audience. Schoenberg's music precipitated a crisis of audience alienation that has plagued new music throughout the twentieth century.

Sustained by his convictions and undaunted by his unpopularity, Schoenberg continued to seek the salvation of music through atonality. He was convinced of the validity of his new style, but problems of organizing pitch materials without benefit of the structuring effects of tonality remained to be solved. In his initial efforts he had sidestepped the issue by using very short forms or by relying on a text to unify his compositions. When he finally came to grips with the problem, he gave it his undivided attention for a number of years, during which time he evolved his theory of *twelve-tone* composition. In the beginning, atonal philosophy had been negative and anarchic, dedicated to overthrowing tonality by avoiding emphasis on any one tone. Schoenberg's new technique was positive: it established order by applying the principles of utopian communism to the realm of music.

The system specified that all tones were to receive equal treatment: a series of twelve different pitches called the *row* would be introduced in a fixed order. That order, subject to assorted permutations, would be maintained throughout, and each tone would appear an equal number of times during the course of a composition. After its initial presentation, a row might be repeated in its original form, upside down, backward, or upside down and backward; but in any event, the ordered relationships of the original series were to remain intact. Pitch was rigidly systematized, but rhythm could change freely. These techniques were reminiscent of Medieval canonic procedures, and the variation of rhythm suggested Liszt's transformation of theme, but the resulting music bore no resemblance to either.

Textures were predominantly contrapuntal and melodies were fragmented, with many wide leaps and radical register changes.

Vertical sonorities were even more austere than those of Expressionism, and audiences liked them even less. The intelligentsia, however, were delighted, seeing the new method as a means whereby music might cleanse itself of Romantic impurities and regain its long-lost academic respectability. Despite critical acclaim for Schoenberg, the concertgoing public refused to be convinced and regarded twelve-tone composition as the musical equivalent of the emperor's new clothes. Schoenberg's reputation was made, however, for his supporters included both critics and historians. Thus Schoenberg became the first "Great Composer" who had no substantial following among those who buy the tickets.

Schoenberg's influence on contemporary music was not immediate. Two fellow Viennese composers, Alban Berg (1885–1935) and Anton Webern (1883–1945), were his devoted disciples, but the majority of composers preferred to travel other roads away from Romanticism. The full impact of his theories on the future of music was not felt until after the Second World War, when most of the younger generation embraced the twelve-tone concept as the principal organizing factor in their music, and when many older composers, who had rejected the concept earlier, also entered the fold.

Barbarism

Far removed from the intellectual austerity of twelve-tone atonality but equally consistent with Freudian thought was *barbarism.* Philosophically, it was based on an animalistic view of man, dehumanized and intrinsically primitive, and in sound it was savage, brutal, and, in Freudian terms, virile. Listeners were battered with irregular rhythms, rude dissonances, and, at climaxes, an almost unbearable volume of sound; and they responded with either shocked delight or furious outrage. The leading composer in this style of expression was Igor Stravinsky (1882–1971), a Russian-born student of Rimsky-Korsakov who burst to prominence through three early ballets: *L'Oiseau de feu* ("The Firebird"), *Petrouchka,* and *Le Sacre du printemps* ("The Rite of Spring"). Commissioned and produced by Sergei Diaghilev, these ballets electrified Paris, and *Le Sacre* precipitated a riot at its premiere at the Théâtre des Champs-Elysées in 1913. Gertrude Stein was there and recorded her eyewitness account of the fracas:

STRAVINSKY

A scene from Stravinsky's "Le Sacre du Printemps" in a Mary Wigman production, Berlin.

> No sooner did the music begin and the dancing than they began to hiss. The defenders began to applaud. We could hear nothing, as a matter of fact I never did hear any of the music of the *Sacre du printemps* because it was the only time I ever saw it and one literally could not, throughout the whole performance, hear the sound of music. The dancing was very fine and that we could see although our attention was constantly distracted by a man in the box next to us flourishing his cane, and finally in a violent altercation with an enthusiast in the box next to him, his cane came down and smashed the opera hat the other had just put on in defiance. It was all incredibly fierce.*

Claude Debussy was also present at this debacle, and he angrily demanded that the audience shut up and listen to a work of genius, but his words, if heard, did nothing to quell the turmoil.

Petrouchka, which had its first performance two years earlier, created no such uproar. It was, in fact, an instantaneous success, establishing Stravinsky as a major talent. When Diaghilev brought the production to America in 1916, the consensus among critics was that although the music was completely appropriate to the action it accompanied, it was much too strange and harshly dissonant to stand alone. The critics were wrong—today *Petrouchka* survives primarily as an orchestral suite and is more often heard than seen. It is scored for a mammoth orchestra of sixteen woodwinds, twelve brasses, ten percussion instruments in addition to timpani, two harps, piano, celesta, and the usual strings. The "Russian Dance" heard in the recorded example occurs in the First Tableau, just after the Magician brings the

Side 9 Band 3

*Quoted in Eric Blom, *The Music Lover's Miscellany* (London: Gollancz, 1935), p. 52.

puppets to life by touching them with his flute. It is a straightforward dance with none of the metric complexities that characterize other scenes and that so confounded dancers in the first production. Emotionally, the music runs the gamut, ranging from the opening mood of exuberant joy to the despair the puppets feel when they realize that their fleeting animate existence holds no promise of a tomorrow.

Unlike Schoenberg, Stravinsky enjoyed a measure of popular support from the beginning; half the audience may have hated his ballets, but the other half found his music stimulating and exciting and were passionate in its defense.

Neo-Classicism

Stravinsky was a man of many styles. Within a decade, he moved from the opulence of big orchestral sound and the freewheeling impulsiveness of barbarism to the restrained medium of the chamber ensemble and the discipline of concise formal organization. This new style, called *neo-Classicism,* dominated his attention during the years between the two world wars and was adopted by so many other composers that it almost became a movement. It did, in fact, bring a degree of stylistic unity to twentieth-century Western music. Actually the term "neo-Classical" was used to describe techniques and styles that might more accurately have been labeled "neo-Baroque" or "neo-Renaissance." Although Stravinsky himself used the dry, air-leavened surface texture and clear homophony of Classical style, other composers revisited the Baroque for rhythmic momentum and melodic variation, or turned to Renaissance dances for inspiration.

Twelve-tone composition had little appeal for Stravinsky; he experimented with atonality, but he was more at home with distortions of tonality than with its destruction. In the early ballets, he had frequently used *polychords* consisting of clashing tertian harmonies, and later he extended this principle to include the simultaneous use of two or more keys, a technique called *polytonality.* Polychords and polytonality provided ample dissonace, and the presence of two or more competing keys reduced the solidity of each, thereby undermining the authority of the traditional tonal system without doing away with it altogether. Another technique well calculated to tweak the nose of tonality was *pandiatonicism,* in which the seven tones of a traditional scale formed the foundation of pitch organization but were used without reference to familiar tertian harmony. Neither polytonal nor pandiatonic techniques cut listeners totally adrift from their past experience. The vertical sonorities were new and strange, but the traditional pitch materials gave something to cling to in an unfamiliar sea.

Stravinsky's departure from tradition was more radical than Debussy's, but more conservative than Schoenberg's. A hallmark of Stravinsky's style was an unsettling rhythmic organization that incorporated both polymeter (page 43) and changing meter, while retaining the time-honored concepts of melody and harmonic structure. His influence on his contemporaries and the coming generation was immediate and enduring. Audience acceptance was minimal at first, but by the time of his death, he was one of the most widely respected and frequently performed composers of the post-Impressionist years.

Neomodality

BARTÓK

Another giant of the same generation was Hungarian-born Béla Bartók (1881–1945). His musical style was comparable to Stravinsky's in its degree of departure from Romantic tradition, but it took a different direction. One way in which Bartók evaded tonality was through *neomodality*—a modern use of Medieval modal patterns which, after centuries of neglect, offered a fresh, new basis for pitch organization. This style of expression arose naturally out of his consuming interest in Hungarian folk songs, many of which are modal or pentatonic (page 28). Tertian harmony, with extraneous tones added for dissonance, formed the foundation of Bartók's harmonic vocabulary, but its boundaries extended to include clusters (page 13) and quartal chords (page 12) as well. Rhythmic vitality is characteristic of his style; much of his music is metrically consistent, with strong use of accent and syncopation, although changing meter is by no means uncommon. His melodies are sometimes lyric, sometimes angular, and are often made up of phrases of unequal length.

Bartók's music for piano represented a new and different concept of the instrument. Throughout the nineteenth century, composers and pianists alike had seen the piano as a stringed instrument, and had concentrated on making it sing. Bartók looked past the strings to the hammers and treated the piano as a percussion instrument. Pounding repetition, disjointed attack, and harsh tone were characteristic of his demands, and to Romantically-oriented listeners of the early twentieth century, such treatment of the piano must have seemed nothing short of sacrilege.

Like Stravinsky, Bartók commanded a growing following throughout his career, but he was concerned about the increasing alienation of the wider audience. With composers and concertgoers speaking different languages, an inevitable communication gap had opened, and rather than simply deploring the problem, he attempted to do something about it. *Mikrokosmos,* his six-volume set of piano pieces that were graduated in difficulty, was designed to expose young pianists to the styles, idioms, and vocabulary of twentieth-century music, and these short pieces have contributed significantly to the education of both performers and listeners. Attractive in their own right, they have advanced the cause as much through their appeal as through instruction.

Bartók's quarrel with Romanticism was one of means rather than ends. Emotional communication was of paramount importance to him, but he felt that the basic vocabulary of chromatic tonality had become a collection of clichés that needed expansion and revitalization. In retrospect, his approach seems somewhat conservative, but audiences in the first quarter of the century would not have agreed. To them his music seemed ultramodern, violent, and revolutionary. Only with the perspective of half a century has his link with the past been made manifest.

Bartók's most significant contribution may well prove to have been his six string quartets. They explore the sound possibilities of string instruments in a way similar to that in which he explored new tone colors for the piano. His novel techniques of bowed and pizzicato playing are now standard, and the quartets have become twentieth-century classics.

Side 9 Band 4

The Scherzo in the recorded example from Bartók's fifth quartet calls for nothing remarkable by way of tone production, but the rhythmic organization is anything but conventional. In form, the movement is a simple ABA, with contrast between sections depending as much on rhythm as on melodic material. Meter is consistent in A; each measure contains nine subdivisions that are divided into 4+2+3, creating a pattern of three unequal beats. This pattern is heard first in the cello and is maintained throughout the section. Melodic interest is distributed evenly among the four instruments in A, but in B a disproportionate share of activity falls to the first violin, which plays running notes constantly, while the other three instruments busy themselves in finding different ways to divide ten subdivisions into four beats: 3+2+2+3, 2+3+2+3, and 2 + 3 + 3 + 2. With the return of A, one might reasonably expect a return to rhythmic stability, but the former solidity fails to materialize—subdivisions are regrouped, miscellaneous meters appear, and rhythmic surprises are the order of the day. All in all, this scherzo is a joyous jumble of rhythmic irregularity, with more than a subtle hint of humor.

Other New Sounds

In addition to revolutionizing the sound of traditional ensembles, composers of chamber music sought new sounds through unaccustomed combinations of instruments, frequently including the human voice. Occasionally the voice was treated simply as one of several instruments, but more often the singer or reciter was the nucleus of the group, commanding the lion's share of attention, as in *Façade* by the English composer William Walton (b. 1902). Based on poems by Edith Sitwell, the work is scored for reader and six instruments, which consistently serve as an accompaniment to the recitation. Dance rhythms are integrated into the poetry, and a highly rhythmic recitation is vital to any performance of the work. In the recorded version of "Polka," the voice is that of Edith Sitwell herself, and the polka rhythm in her declamation is unmistakable. The music is simple and unobtrusive, supporting the voice without competing for attention. The instruments reinforce the text in the obvious areas of rhythm and mood, and add a subtle underscoring of certain words from time to time. The words "hurdy-gurdy," for example, are given special emphasis by instrumental imitation of the hurdy-gurdy's characteristic sound, and the words "the sea" take on greater significance with the fleeting reference to a traditional sailor's hornpipe tune.

WALTON

Side 9 Band 5

MUSIC IN THE UNITED STATES

Musically, the twentieth century caught the United States unaware. This most Romantic of nations continued to wax Romantic long after the movement had waned in Europe. A New England insurance man named Charles Ives (1874–1954), who indulged in composition as a hobby, was a one-man American avant-garde.

IVES

His music, written mostly during the first two decades of the century, received little attention at the time; recognition did not come until after the Second World War, when a climate more congenial to eccentric music began to develop. His style was a mixed bag, juxtaposing old-fashioned tonality and radical twentieth-century techniques, often with wry humor but sometimes in earnest. Opinion remains divided as to whether Ives should be regarded as a genius or a curiosity, but the enthusiasm with which young people of the early 1970s have embraced his music suggests that his audience may only just have arrived. "The Cage," heard in the recorded example, is one of his early songs. It is philosophical in mood and remarkably innovative in technique. The rhythm is completely ungoverned by meter, and the monotonously even motion of the vocal line is countered by the seemingly erratic rhythm in the accompaniment. The harmony is based on quartal sonorities that, in the first decade of the century, were as yet an unnamed novelty.

Side 9 Band 6

Jazz

America's most significant and original contribution to early twentieth-century music was found not in the concert hall but in the dance hall. They called it *ragtime,* and it was just the beginning of what would take the Western world by storm under the name of *jazz.* Ragtime was a national mania during the years prior to the First World War, matched only by the parallel dance craze that had given rise to it. The music was played by a small ensemble featuring a few diverse melodic instruments and a harmony-rhythm section that relied heavily on banjo and piano. There was no attempt to blend the sounds. Each line was distinct and independent in a heterophonic kind of way, and it was all held together by a firm harmonic underpinning and an insistent beat. The rhythmic motivation was African in origin, and the harmony derived from Western tonality. It was melting-pot music, and it could have happened only in America.

Paralleling the development of ragtime was a soulful ballad style called the *blues.* It was a vocal art, in which a meandering melody created complex syncopations over an inexorable pulse. The tempo was slow, the mood mournful, and the effect compelling. Improvisation was basic: the singer (usually a woman) often created her own lyrics and always added the intensity of embel-

King Oliver's Creole Jazz Band, photographed in Chicago in 1923. The trumpeter at center is Louis Armstrong.

lishment to the melody. Certain tones of the scale, especially the third, were variable in pitch, and mutations of these tones produced the so-called blue notes. Blues songs followed a structural pattern based on an asymmetrical three-phrase unit, resulting from the repetition of the first of each two lines of text. "Lost Your Head Blues," the recorded example, by Bessie Smith (1894–1937), is typical in structure, in style, and in the "my man done me wrong" sentiment of the lyrics. Less usual is the prominence given the solo cornet, which maintains continuous dialogue with the singer on near-equal terms. The heritage of the blues was pure black. The origin of this ballad style has been traced back to the sufferings of slavery, with both words and music expressing the deep despondency of rejection and loneliness.

Side 9 Band 7

Jazz was the sophisticated offspring of ragtime. It first appeared about 1917, and reached its golden age during the Roaring Twenties. Almost from the beginning, jazz was a creature of many faces, and the term has become progressively more inclusive with the passage of time and the development of a multiplicity of styles. The first jazz bands played Dixieland—

rugged individualists playing simultaneous variations on a tune. Almost immediately, however, a contrasting style began to develop, in which band members soloed in creating their variations. Different styles flourished in different localities and were sometimes identified by city names:

> Memphis style is sometimes called "take your turn," and New Orleans has everybody in at the same time. In Memphis the theme is established in the first chorus, and then each man takes a separate crack at a variation on it. . . .
>
> But the way they did Memphis was just child's play compared to the way they did New Orleans. Here they were all in on it from start to finish. Each man went his separate and uncharted way, and first thing you know you had two and two equaling at least five. They achieved, you could never say how, a highly involved counterpoint. No accident, either, because they did it on tune after tune, and never the same way twice. Seek out the separate voices and you'd find each one doing nicely, thanks, and then let your ear out to take in the whole, and there it was.*

Side 9 Band 8

"Grandpa's Spells," the recorded example played by Jelly Roll Morton (1885–1942) and his Red Hot Peppers, is primarily New Orleans style, but there is a hint of Memphis style in the frequent use of solos. Morton specialized in a semiorganized free-for-all known as the "head arrangement": any given piece had a known structure, and there was agreement among the players as to who would take precedence in specific sections. But the agreement, undetailed, provided a tenuous framework that issued an open invitation to exuberant pandemonium.

Picasso's title page for Stravinsky's *Ragtime* (1918).

It was jazz that put the United States on the musical map. Europeans were fascinated, and quickly became avid importers of both American recordings and touring jazz bands, thus creating the first substantial West-to-East flow of transatlantic traffic in music. In Europe jazz was taken seriously, and it was not long before elements of the style were incorporated into concert music. Stravinsky had anticipated the vogue by using aspects of ragtime in his chamber work *L'Histoire du soldat* ("The Soldier's Story") and in his *Piano Rag Music,* and during the early twenties, jazz insinuated itself into French ballet in *La Création du monde* ("The Creation of the World") by Darius Milhaud (1892–1974). But widespread exploitation of jazz elements came on the heels of an

*Dorothy Baker, *Young Man with a Horn* (Boston: Houghton Mifflin, Sentry Edition, 1961), p. 43.

A scene from *Gold Diggers of 1933,* a musical comedy film spectacular with dance direction by Busby Berkeley.

American work for piano and jazz band, later transcribed for piano and orchestra—*Rhapsody in Blue,* by George Gershwin (1898–1937):

> After the *Rhapsody in Blue* came the deluge: Krenek's *Jonny spielt auf* [opera], Hindemith's *Neues vom Tage* [opera], Kurt Weill's *Mahagonny* and *Die Dreigroschenoper* [opera], Ravel's *"Blues" Sonata* and *Concerto for the Left Hand,* Constant Lambert's *Rio Grande* [for contralto, chorus, orchestra, and piano], Aaron Copland's *Concerto for Piano and Orchestra,* and John Alden Carpenter's ballet, *Skyscrapers.**

Musical Comedy

In the area of musical theater, another uniquely American art form was developing. The Viennese-style operettas of Victor Herbert (1859–1924) had held the stage during the first part of the century, but by the 1920s, the trend was away from Romantic sweetness and light toward a more realistic style. The new type was called

*David Ewen, *A Journey to Greatness* (New York: Henry Holt, 1956), p. 27.

A scene from *Show Boat,* in a 1946 revival.

musical comedy—not altogether appropriately, since the subject matter was sometimes serious. In time the term *comedy* was dropped, leaving the adjective *musical* (often prefixed by *Broadway*) to function as a noun in identifying the form. *Show Boat* (1927) by Jerome Kern (1885–1945) was something of a landmark, establishing a new standard for musicals in its combination of compelling drama and some immortal melodies. George Gershwin brought the rhythms of jazz and the spirit of the blues into the medium, and the shows written in collaboration with his brother Ira made musical and theatrical history. Their *Of Thee I Sing,* which satirizes political conventions and presidential campaigns, was awarded a Pulitzer Prize; far from being a period piece, its relevance seems to resurface every four years. Songs from American musicals were sung and played all over Europe, and in England, where language was no barrier, entire productions were imported. Gershwin musicals were particularly popular, and apparently the fondness lingers on: as recently as 1974, the London theater season included a production of *Oh, Kay!*—a show that had its New York premiere in 1926.

MUSIC IN FRANCE

LES SIX

A variety of popular styles were incorporated in the music of a group of young French composers known as *Les Six.* This group, which included Francis Poulenc (1889–1963), Arthur Honegger

(1892–1955), Darius Milhaud, Louis Durey (b. 1888), Germaine Tailleferre (b. 1892), and Georges Auric (b. 1899), rejected Impressionism as effete, barbarism as crude, and twelve-tone techniques as hypercerebral. They felt that music was rapidly becoming too intellectual, too cacophonous, and too complex. Simplicity and audience accessibility were the watchwords, and for leadership they turned to Erik Satie (1866–1925), a little-known, nonprofessional composer who had been preaching the gospel of simplicity for some time. Satie saw his mission as stripping away or satirizing musical pretentiousness—especially that of Romantic music. In this cause, he often unleashed his irreverent sense of humor, giving his pieces such titles as *Dried Embryos* and *Three Pieces in the Form of a Pear.* Humor was much less important in the music of Les Six; what most influenced their early efforts was Satie's uncluttered approach. Lyric melody was indispensable in their music, and cabaret style—unpretentious and direct in appeal—was their model. Harmonically, their music was clearly twentieth century, but it was by no means radical. Neomodality, quartal harmony, and tertian chords with added dissonances were the mainstays of their vocabulary. Milhaud and, to a lesser extent, Honegger indulged in polytonality, but none of the six was attracted to atonality, which was basically inimical to their creed.

In early 20th-century art, a movement called Dada thumbed its nose at all conventions. Here is one version of Marcel Duchamp's irreverent addition to a reproduction of the *Mona Lisa*.

The association of Les Six as a group was loose-knit and of brief duration. As they matured, differences in their styles, ideals, and degrees of talent became apparent, and each went his or her separate way. Poulenc successfully continued in the original vein and was at his best in short forms, particularly piano pieces and songs. For Poulenc, music was melody and melody was lyric. Whether he was writing vocal or instrumental music, his love of the human voice shaped his melodic line. The lyricism in the recorded example, "Tu vois le feu du soir" ("You See the Flaming Evening Sky") is typical of his ideal. The melody fits the voice comfortably, with gracefully curved rather than angular contours. His treatment of tonality in this song is equally easygoing: the tonal center changes frequently, but some form of key orientation is always present.

Side 10 Band 1

Honegger moved toward a more dissonant instrumental style but maintained a conservative, sympathetic approach in writing for voices. For him, oratorio—a form widely ignored early in the twentieth century—was an especially congenial medium, and his dramatic *Le Roi David* ("King David") catapulted him into international prominence. Milhaud, the most prolific and best known of the six, became a staunch neo-classicist and wrote primarily in traditional forms. His melodic style remained essentially lyric and his harmony dissonant. Many of his works were more contrapuntal than harmonic in texture, and he sometimes used polytonality to emphasize the linear nature of his music.

The tonal and melodic moderation of Les Six was not representative of all French music. Other, more revolutionary movements were underway, one of them headed by the ultraradical of

VARÈSE

the 1920s, Edgard Varèse (1885–1965). Squabbles concerning degrees of departure from tonality and designs for structuring dissonance were of little concern to him, since he regarded pitch itself as dispensable. Perhaps his best-known work is *Ionisation,* which was written for a large group of percussion instruments (with sirens), and which emphasized rhythm, dynamics, tone color, and texture rather than pitch. There was some doubt as to whether or not *Ionisation* could be called music, but it did attract attention. Supporters of Varèse's music were not numerous, nor was the intellectual community greatly interested in his ventures. Varèse exerted no appreciable influence on the shape of music until after mid-century, when his star rose and he found kindred souls among the younger generation, who were inclined to lionize—if not actually canonize—him.

Despite attacks from all quarters, Romanticism proved to be a pervasive and resilient element in Western music. As late as the 1930s, it was alive and well and living in England, through the music of Edward Elgar (1857–1934); in Finland, through the music of Jean Sibelius (1865–1957); and in America, through the music of an expatriate Russian, Sergei Rachmaninoff (1873–1943). In popular music, it continues to flourish unassailed and undiminished, and it seems probable that so long as humanity inclines toward sentimentality, some form of musical Romanticism is bound to survive.

MUSIC IN RUSSIA

PROKOFIEV

It was not always an either-or, for-or-against proposition in regard to Romanticism. The Russian composer Sergei Prokofiev (1891–1953) managed to combine modern techniques of composition with Romantic goals, producing works full of nineteenth-century emotionalism but with a twentieth-century sound. His melodic style was alternately angular and lyric, and although he employed bitingly dissonant harmonies, his harmonic idiom usually hovered near tonality. Sometimes Prokofiev's style inclined toward barbarism. In the recorded example, his Toccata in D minor, Op. 11, the rhythmic thrust is relentless to the point of brutality. Driving rhythm, strong dissonance, and percussive attack make listeners feel as though a locomotive were bearing down on them. Ravel's Toccata (Side 9 Band 2) and this one are similar only in the use of repeated notes and driving rhythm. Both are exciting virtuoso pieces, but Ravel's is characterized by refinement and Prokofiev's by ferocity.

Side 10 Band 2

Prokofiev was a versatile composer who worked in a wide variety of media. His piano sonatas have become staples in the pianist's repertoire, and his symphonies, concertos, and symphonic suites appear regularly on orchestral programs. On this side of the Iron Curtain, his popularity has steadily increased, but within the Soviet Union, his career suffered several setbacks. On a number of occasions during his lifetime, he was sternly reprimanded by high party authorities for having allowed "Western decadence" to creep into his music, which, by official decree, was supposed to reflect communist ideology. It must be very difficult to write music which adheres to the party line when only *Pravda* is able to define the terms, and then only after the fact.

SHOSTAKOVICH

Dmitri Shostakovich (1906–1975) received even harsher and more incomprehensible treatment from the Soviet high command. His opera *Lady Macbeth of Mtzensk* had run successfully for two years when *Pravda* pronounced it unacceptable, and critics who had originally praised the work were obliged to recant. His music, although different in style from Prokofiev's, frequently reveals a blend of Romantic aims and contemporary vocabulary similar to that of his compatriot. If, as *Pravda* charged, Shostakovich was occasionally beguiled by "formalism" and "Western decadence," his sins were inadvertent. He was a loyal party member, and many of his works—the "May Day" and "Leningrad" symphonies for example—have commemorative significance or ideological annotations.

MUSIC IN GERMANY

The break with Romanticism was most extreme in the German-speaking countries, which had cradled the movement so tenderly a century earlier. The repudiation was a tortuous one, and for older composers, new modes of expression were arrived at only after painful eradication of Romantic remnants, which were engrained in their very being. But for Paul Hindemith (1895–1963), no such agonizing transition was necessary. His style derived not from Romanticism, but from twentieth-century sounds. Expressionism exerted a strong influence on his early works, but he declined to follow Schoenberg into twelve-tone atonality, moving instead toward a style that was less austere and more personal.

HINDEMITH

Like many of his contemporaries, Hindemith was alarmed by the crisis of audience estrangement, but unlike most of his fellow composers, he did not attribute total blame to reactionary audiences. He felt that in continuing to create esoteric music for an ever-diminishing audience, composers were exercising freedom without responsibility. In his view, a composer's franchise was necessarily tempered by obligations to both performers and listeners. His solution to the dilemma of reconciling creative integrity and accountability came in the form of *Gebrauchsmusik* ("music for use"), which was directed toward a variety of performers at different levels of achievement and which was both accessible to listeners and consistent with Hindemith's own aesthetic ideals. Some of this music was created for schoolchildren to sing and play, but much of it was solo or chamber music written for neglected instruments (such as string bass or tuba) that had long been without a literature of their own. Hindemith's instrumental music was carefully constructed, with the idiosyncrasies of the instrument and technical limitations of the average-to-good performer in mind. These works were gratefully received and widely performed by their beneficiaries.

After experimenting with alternative means of pitch organization, Hindemith reached the conclusion that tonality was an inescapable fact of musical life. He saw it, however, as an elastic reality rather than a rigid natural law. Tonality in his hands would have been unrecognizable in the nineteenth century. His melodies modulate so rapidly that the listener has no opportunity to settle into a sense of key before one center shifts to another. His harmonies, which are frequently quartal, offer little reinforcement for tonal focus except at an occasional cadence, which confirms the listener's hunch that tonality has been lurking there all the while. Much of Hindemith's music is contrapuntal in texture. At first, he began with the premise that counterpoint should be purely linear, without any concern for the sounds which were produced vertically. In his later works, however, after coming to terms with the inevitability of tonality, he was much more circumspect in regard to vertical considerations.

In addition to his extensive accomplishments as a composer, Hindemith contributed to the advancement of music through his various roles of teacher, philosopher, and author. His influence on the coming generation was profound, particularly in the United States, where he worked with many gifted young musicians during his tenure at Yale University from 1940 to 1953.

NADIA BOULANGER'S STUDENTS

American composers finally plunged into the musical mainstream during the 1920s. The composers of that generation elected to further their musical education not in Germany, but in Paris, where most of them placed their talents in the hands of the redoubtable Nadia Boulanger. Not a composer herself, Boulanger was not dedicated to perpetuating any specific style of music. All her students were free to choose their own modes of expression, but she was uncompromising in her demand that each must develop solid craftsmanship. When they emerged from the crucible of her tutelage, they were well disciplined, but they were not molded in any consistent pattern. Their styles were diverse but, for the most part, conservative in regard to departures from tonal traditions. These composers were proudly and self-consciously aware of being American, and to give their music a distinctively nationalistic flavor, they often wove jazz, folk songs, cowboy ballads, black spirituals, and hymn tunes into the fabric of their compositions.

COPLAND

One prominent Boulanger protégé was Aaron Copland (b. 1900). Famous before he was out of his twenties, he went on to become an elder statesman of American music. In style his music was sometimes severe, sometimes amiable, depending on whether his concern of the moment involved abstruse theory or the rewinning of disgruntled audiences. He was at his amiable best in ballet, a medium for which he developed a strong affinity. Orchestral arrangements of his ballet music are among his most popular works, with *Appalachian Spring* the best known, closely followed by *Billy the Kid* and *Rodeo.* All three are vibrant with energy and distinctly American in character. *Rodeo,* as the title suggests, deals with cowboys; its slender plot evolves around the metamor-

A scene from Aaron Copland's *Rodeo,* in the 1960 American Ballet Theatre production.

phosis of a tomboyish cowgirl who becomes the belle of the ball. The denouement comes in the finale, "Hoedown," heard in the recorded example. The exhilarating music immediately establishes the atmosphere of a square dance. Only briefly does the pace slacken, slowing down as if out of breath, but it quickly resumes the original tempo with renewed vigor. The rowdy nature of this music is eminently suitable for portraying the rough-and-ready character of the American frontier.

Side 10 Band 3

MUSIC IN SOUTH AMERICA

VILLA-LOBOS

South America, too, was heard from in the post-Romantic period. The Brazilian Heitor Villa-Lobos (1887–1959) was the first indigenous composer to attract the Western world's attention. He was a man of many styles: his prolific output reflects variously the influence of native melodies and rhythms, the exciting new trends of the times, and the traditions of Western music in general. Many of his works erupt in primitive violence, but the *Bachianas Brasileiras,* inspired equally by the style of J. S. Bach and the folk music of Brazil, are gentler in style. The recorded example, the

Aria from *Bachianas Brasileiras No. 5,* is a lyric serenade that begins and ends with wordless vocalization, using a text only in the contrasting section. The melodic ambiance is distinctly Brazilian, but the deft evasion of cadences within sections is reminiscent of Bach.

Side 10 Band 4

TWENTIETH-CENTURY OPERA

Opera remained relatively untouched in the immediate post-Romantic era. Early in the century, few non-Romantic operas were written, fewer were staged, and only one full-length opera of that period—Debussy's *Pelléas et Mélisande*—continues in the current repertoire. Perhaps it was because the new dissonance and melodic angularity were basically instrumental in concept and were better served by pitch-secure instruments than by singers, for whom intonation is often more difficult. But whatever the reason, the insurgents were content to leave opera to the Romanticists and explore new sounds through other media. Ballet was the new focal point in musical theater; it offered dramatic scope within a nonvocal, flexible format that could cooperate with new styles, allowing imaginative experimentation in the dance as well as in the music.

Twentieth-century opera (defined stylistically rather than chronologically) did not get off the ground until the 1920s, and during the next twenty years, European operagoers were exposed to all degrees of modernity. Representing the extreme left was Alban Berg's *Wozzeck,* which is still in the repertoire; representing the far right was Prokofiev's *The Love For Three Oranges.* From the twelve-tone school came *Moses und Aron* by Schoenberg. All by himself, Hindemith covered the middle ground: his Expressionist opera, *Cardillac,* leaned to the left of center, the comic *Neues vom Tage* veered towards the right, and his masterpiece, *Mathis der Maler* was near dead center in style. Stravinsky's *Oedipus Rex* and Milhaud's *Christophe Colomb* were stylistically moderate, and both were categorized under the "opera-oratorio" heading, legitimizing nonstaged (concert) presentation.

In the United States, opera companies still lived in the Romantic era, and Verdi, Wagner, and Puccini remained on the boards while any opera that smacked of modernity went homeless. The concert performance provided a measure of solace for those who wanted to hear the new styles—and these were generally not

A scene from a Berlin Opera production of Alban Berg's *Wozzeck.*

opera buffs but adherents of the avant-garde in general. Operas by Webern, Bartók, and Schoenberg, among others, were first heard by Americans in concert performances.

American composers' contributions to modern opera should not be allowed to pass without mention. Early efforts included works by two composer-poet duos: Deems Taylor (1885–1966) and Edna St. Vincent Millay, who collaborated in *The King's Henchman,* and Virgil Thomson (b. 1896) and Gertrude Stein, who created *Four Saints in Three Acts.* George Gershwin composed his opera *Porgy and Bess* with the Met in mind, but the operatic community, then as now, refused to accept it as a legitimate opera. Despite international acclaim, *Porgy* remains a homeless waif in America—it is out of its element on Broadway, and it is still unwelcome at the Metropolitan. Except for bit parts, the cast of *Porgy* is completely black. The story centers on a crippled beggar (Porgy) and his love for Bess, whose weakness for men and "happy dust" (probably cocaine) makes the course of true love an uphill climb. Their duo-aria "Bess, You Is My Woman Now," heard in the recorded example, occurs near the end of Act I, before the onslaught of crises and calamities. It is a declaration of undying love in true operatic tradition, clothed in beautiful melody and presented with passionate conviction.

Side 10 Band 5

FILM MUSIC

The thirties also saw the emergence of a brand-new medium for interaction between music and drama. Movies were coming of age, and as they progressed beyond *The Perils of Pauline* dramatically, they began to make corresponding advances musically. Technical problems of synchronization between sound and picture had been solved, but artistic problems involving music were new territory. For a composer, the sound track offered a fresh challenge and demanded a different discipline. Unlike the continuous music and the rhythmic flexibility of opera and ballet, film music had to start and stop unobtrusively and had to be absolutely exact in timing, down to the last fraction of a second. Film music derived from and served the dramatic element—establishing and developing mood, underscoring action, and building tension. It was the first coupling of the two arts that allowed music no opportunity to relegate drama to a subordinate role.

Each week the heroine of the movie serial *The Perils of Pauline* (below) was left in some desperate danger; thus the term "cliff-hanger."

Earlier low-grade, low-budget movies had pirated shamelessly from music in the public domain, and motley bits and snatches had been pieced together, often by unimaginative hacks, to form sound tracks that were musically incongruous. When the film industry developed artistic aspirations, every aspect of film making came in for refinement, and studios began to hire real composers to provide superior music. Some, like Erich Korngold (1897–1957), created film scores of genuine musical value that are currently being rediscovered and issued as recordings. For high-budget films, producers in the United States and Europe commissioned the finest composers available—generally from the more conservative camps. Composers recruited during the late thirties and early forties included Copland *(Our Town),* Honegger *(Pygmalion),* Prokofiev *(Alexander Nevsky),* and Walton *(Henry V).*

MUSICAL HUMOR

Despite wide variety in individual styles, twentieth-century composers—with the exception of Schoenberg and his followers—shared a penchant for humor. Their approaches to playfulness were as various as their styles, extending from subtle wit to broad, belly-laugh buffoonery and including most of the shadings in between. But only rarely did anything resembling the good-natured persiflage of Classicism appear; twentieth-century sophistication and cynicism inclined more to irony, satire, sarcasm, and even burlesque. Parody figured prominently. The inclusion of familiar tunes was a common device, with the humor of the situation depending on surprise, distortion, or irreverence. Romantic clichés, appearing suddenly in infelicitous surroundings, were always good for a laugh, as were heavy-footed tonal progressions in a light, nontonal setting.

And there was a subtler kind of humor as well. A genius for constructing melodies that were inherently funny was particularly evident among the Russians, and harmonic or textural incongruities were universal witticisms. Extreme ranges were facetiously combined or alternated, and instrumental color often reinforced the comic element. Titles sometimes set the tone, giving a clue that something funny was in the offing, but the creative sense of humor of the post-Romantic composers needed no verbal crutch.

Shostakovich was particularly adept at the creation of humor, with his sense of comedy tending more toward musical pratfalls than witty epigrams. His ballet *The Age of Gold* satirizes the capitalistic system unmercifully, but the humor depends neither on visual buffoonery nor plot—it is inherent in the music itself. The Polka, the recorded example, is pure burlesque. It begins with a caterwauling clarinet, whose ascending shriek is punctuated by an inappropriate cluster, and then a xylophone takes over with an impudent and angular melody (see graph, page 26). Assorted woodwinds intervene and engage in a facetious dialogue, which is abruptly interrupted by a pedestrian tonal melody in the brasses—a complete non sequitur. Instrumentation, extremes of register, melodic shape, and improbable juxtapositions all contribute to the humor of this movement, and rhythm joins forces with these elements in the frantic dash toward the final cadence.

Side 10 Band 6

Audiences conditioned by Romanticism to approach a concert with veneration and solemnity were at first nonplussed by this kind of irreverent musical farce, but once their inhibitions were overcome, they responded with delight. The saving grace of humor reestablished a measure of communication between composers and listeners, and shared laughter helped to close the gap.

14. Music since 1945

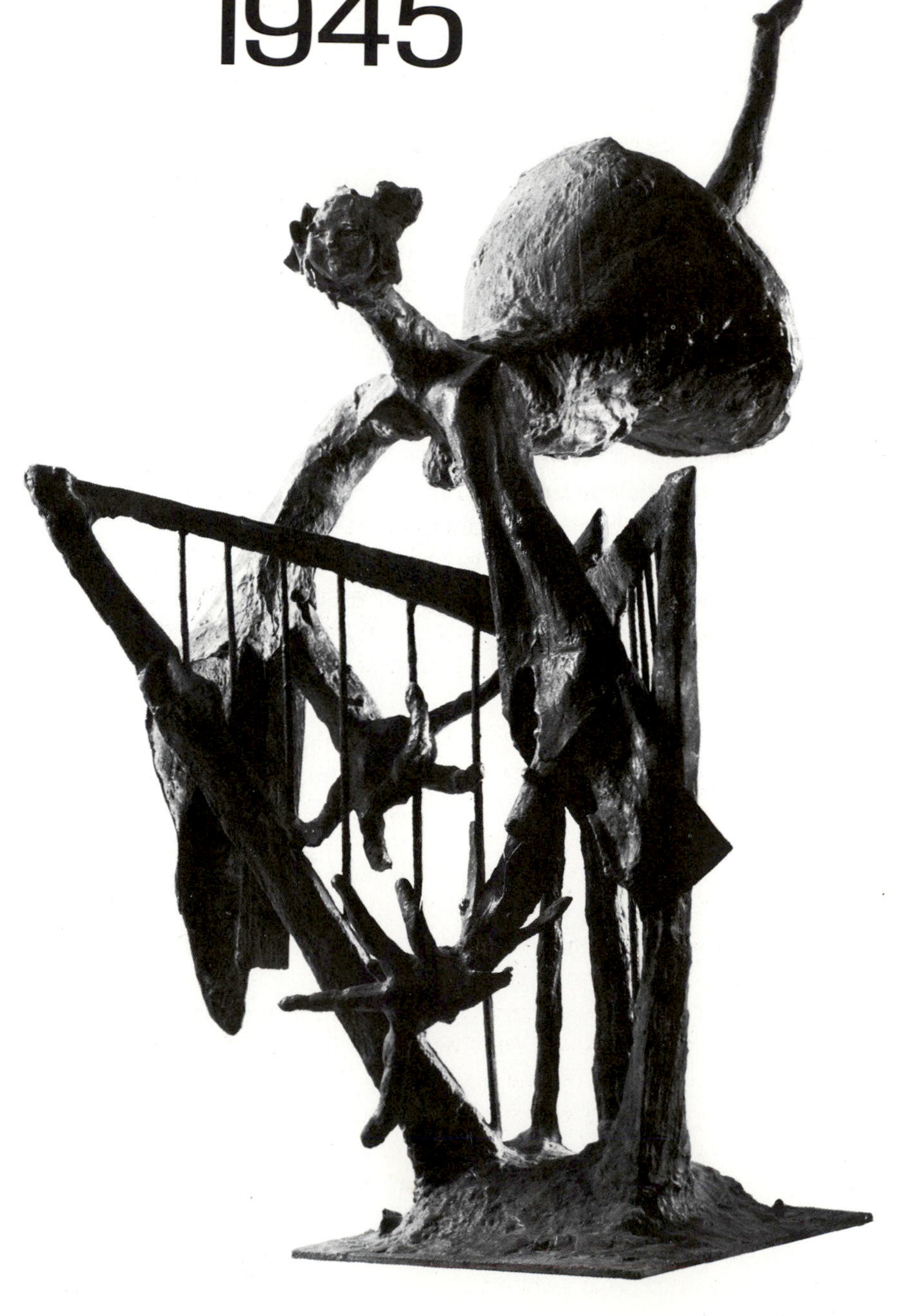

JUST PRIOR TO and during the Second World War, many European composers sought refuge in the United States. Hitler's genocidal policy made departure a necessity for Jews and—Jew or gentile—composers found the chaotic conditions of wartime Europe scarcely conducive to creative work. The roster of refugees was a distinguished one: in the forties, Stravinsky, Schoenberg, Hindemith, Bartók, Varèse, Milhaud, Ernst Křenek (b. 1900), and Swiss-born Ernest Bloch (1880–1959) were all quietly composing and teaching in various parts of the United States. The migration of musicians did not qualify as headline material during the war, so it was only after 1945 that Americans became fully aware of the presence of their illustrious guests.

POSTWAR MUSIC IN THE UNITED STATES

As it became apparent that these European composers had every intention of remaining, an even more startling realization dawned: the United States had cornered the market in composers and was now the center of creative music in the Western World. The musical meek had, in fact, inherited the earth. But ingrained humility dies hard, and deference to European countries was replaced by deference to resident European composers. Although Copland's generation was the last to regard study abroad as imperative, it would be some time yet before Americans could confidently look to native-born musicians for leadership.

Musically, things had never been better in America, but for composers, the economic state of affairs was far from euphoric. Royalties from sales and performances of their music were inadequate to sustain them; government subsidies were nonexistent, and were considered un-American when proposed; and private patronage was all but unknown. This twentieth-century American problem had its origins in nineteenth-century Europe. Romanticists, in seeking independence from the dictates of patrons, had in effect thrown music to the wolves of free enterprise. During the Romantic period, music had prospered in the arena of supply and demand, but in the twentieth century, a shrinking base of popular support for new music created a corresponding decline in financial rewards. The crisis was at hand.

The Role of the Universities

The financial solution came clad improbably in academic regalia. Universities, affluent with the burgeoning enrollments of the post-war years, were in a position to be generous, and thus a new form of patronage was born. Composers were offered posts as composers-in-residence (professorships with minimal teaching responsibilities), leaving them ample time to pursue their creative work, free of distraction and financial anxiety. This sponsorship was eminently satisfactory to everybody. It represented economic salvation for composers; their presence on campus gave prestige to the universities; and students of composition gained the invaluable opportunity of working with outstanding creative artists while earning a degree.

Serialism and Superserialism

On the face of it, university patronage was unconditional, and certainly no composers were asked to modify their aesthetic values or mode of expression. But the university, by its very nature, stresses the intellectual life above all else, and artists in its employ cannot remain insensitive to that emphasis. It was therefore inevitable that composers should tend to rely more on intellect and less on intuition.

The scholarly objectivity of Schoenberg's theory seemed respectable, and the disciplined structure of his twelve-tone technique appealed strongly to academic composers. The younger generation called it *serial construction,* because the row, or *series,* might now consist of fewer than twelve tones, but the means of manipulating it were the same. Virtually all university composers adopted this mode of composition, and its vogue became so great that even some of the older generation succumbed. The most startling conversion was probably that of Stravinsky, for he had heretofore been utterly contemptuous of anything resembling twelve-tone procedures. His capitulation capped the victory, and serialism reigned supreme. Hindemith, however, allowed the movement to go on without him; he had always been philosophically opposed to serialism, and his convictions remained unaltered by current trends. His position was not one of mere passive nonacceptance; he was vehemently opposed to the system and very articulate in his opposition:

> Let us investigate briefly some of those allegedly "modern" achievements. The best known and most frequently mentioned is the so-called twelve-tone series. The idea is to take the twelve tones of our chromatic scale, select one of its some four hundred million permutations, and use it as the basis for the harmonic (and possibly melodic) structure of a piece. This rule of construction is established arbitrarily and without reference to basic musical facts. It ignores the validity of harmonic and melodic values derived from mathematical, physical, or psychological experience; it does not take into account the differences in intervallic tensions, the physical relationship of tones, the degree of ease in vocal production, and many other facts of either natural permanence or proven usefulness. Its main "law" is supplemented by other rules of equal arbitrariness, such as: tones must not be repeated; your selected tone series may skip from one stratum of the texture to any other one; you have to use the inversion and other distortions of this series; and so on—all of which can be reduced to the general advice: avoid so far as possible anything that has been written before. . . .
>
> Of course, there are those superrefined prophets who proudly claim that they can, by the rules of this stylistic method, write pieces in C major, which seems to be a procedure as direct as leaving one's house in New England through the front door and entering the back door by a little detour via Chicago.*

Schoenberg's system had codified pitch only—rhythm, dynamics, and texture were unshackled elements that could vary freely. Later serialists (the superserialists) permitted even less subjectivity: rhythm and dynamics were also serialized, textures were uniformly sparse, and individual tones were isolated by stark contrasts in juxtaposed registers, dynamics, and attacks. Textural ideals were patterned after the terseness of Webern, whose music represented the epitome of concentration. His musical statements are so direct and concise that many of his works last less than a minute.

The new style was uncompromising in its austerity. Its melodies were militantly antilyric and discontinuous, its harmonies were thin and prickly, and its rhythms derived from such complex mathematical theory that they sounded random. It was severe music, and its ruling principle was order. Beauty, being tarred with the brush of subjectivity, was considered irrelevant, and humor was shunned as frivolous.

*Paul Hindemith, *A Composer's World* (Garden City, N.Y.: Doubleday, Anchor Books Edition, 1961), pp. 139–41.

Resistance was predictable, but insurrection within the ranks came as a shock. This time, it was the professional performers who rebelled. The refusal of soloists, chamber groups, and conductors to program this music created a crisis even more acute than the audience antagonism of the prewar decades; in effect it denied new works a hearing in the forum of the concert hall. In many instances, performers were motivated by personal distaste for the style and sound of the music. They had no "feel" for it and, therefore, no inclination to wrestle with its unusual difficulty. Moreover, a concert artist's livelihood depends on attracting an audience, and to program compositions that are likely to reduce attendance demands a rare blend of intense commitment and zeal. Some performers believed in superserialism and kept the faith, but the majority of professionals retreated toward the past, building their programs primarily from music of previous centuries. Impressionistic pieces were often the most modern music on a program, and those who performed more recent music prudently limited their selections to works by well-established composers. A few dedicated groups and soloists undertook a crusade to propagate new music, but their concerts attracted only the faithful and the curious, and it was seldom necessary to rent a large hall to accommodate the crowd.

Once again, the universities came to the rescue. Hospitality to new ideas in music was extended to include performance as well as creation, and it became a matter of pride for campus ensembles, faculty soloists and chamber groups, and student performers to present programs that admitted some music in the present tense. But this new forum for new music was not an unmixed blessing. Relinquishing the concert hall amounted to abandoning the wider audience, which was given little opportunity to become acquainted with current trends through regular subscription concerts. Further, the seasoned receptivity of the university community to abstruse ideas gave composers an illusion of acceptance that in reality did not exist beyond the campus. And the university community itself, with its tendency to equate popular appeal with inherent inferiority, actively if not consciously encouraged composers to assume an elitist stance. Thus the rift between composer and concertgoer deepened, and communication between them virtually ceased.

In Europe, music was very much a young person's game. Since most of the older, established composers were in the

United States, the younger generation, many of whom were still in their twenties, quickly became prominent. Even the "elder statesmen" were young; at the end of the Second World War, the Italian Luigi Dallapiccola (1904–1975) was forty-one, and the Frenchman Olivier Messiaen (b. 1908) was only thirty-seven. As in America, superserialism was rampant, and everybody—except such lyric diehards as Poulenc—was composing in that technique.

The paying public was not wildly enthusiastic, but by the grace of government subsidy there was ample opportunity to hear new music in its natural habitat, the concert hall. Communication flowed freely in both directions: the composer's message was getting through to anyone interested in hearing it, and European audiences, being far less inhibited than their well-mannered American counterparts, communicated their response—favorable or hostile—in no uncertain terms.

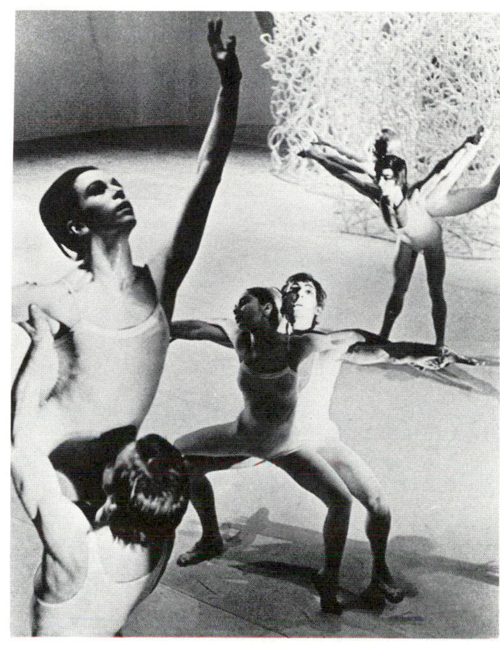

A scene from the Hamburg Ballet premiere production of *Chronochromie* (1971), a ballet by Olivier Messiaen.

THE AVANT-GARDE

Musique Concrète

Serialism's domination of postwar European music was comparatively short-lived. Before the end of the 1940s, an impressive number of composers were already looking beyond serialism. In Paris, composers were more interested in an untapped treasure of sounds that had formerly been stigmatized as "noise." These composers made no distinction between musical tone and noise. All audible phenomena were called *sounds,* and any sound was appropriate in a new technique of composition called *musique concrète* (concrete music), that was born in a Paris sound-effects studio with Pierre Schaeffer (b. 1910) officiating. This technique involved selection, recording, manipulation, mixing, and montage. Composers first assembled an inventory of recorded sounds that might include such diverse items as a bird call, the gurgle of a free-running drain, the squeal of train brakes, and a French horn sustaining a single pitch. They might leave these sounds pristine and unaltered, or they might manipulate them by rerecording at slower or faster speeds, often modifying a sound beyond recognition. (A bird call played at one-fourth the normal speed sounds two octaves lower as well as four times slower, so that it is possible to produce such an unlikely sound as a bass-baritone meadow lark singing a dirge.) Mixing was a textural process that consisted of combining the assembled sounds in layers, with dynamic levels varied to differentiate individual tone qualities or equalized to amalgamate them. Montage was the means of achieving form. It was basically a cut-and-paste operation in which layered units were ordered consecutively to produce the finished composition.

Side 11 Band 1

Prelude XI, by Ilhan Mimaroglu (b. 1926), is an example of musique concrète of the mid-sixties. The sound source is a rubber band, and the primary technology is inseparable from the tape recorder. Beginning with single sounds that relate recognizably to the generating source, the composer proceeds to modify his raw material beyond recognition. Through mixing he creates progressively more complex textures, and through montage he gives emphasis to the repetition and sequential treatment of melodic figures.

During the infancy of musique concrète, its growth was inhibited by the physical clumsiness of recording on discs. But by the early 1950s, tape recording technology had come of age, and its flexibility simplified mixing and montage and enabled composers to range beyond the confines of sound-effects libraries in assembling raw materials. Musique concrète was a new art with no precedent for guidance, so that early efforts were necessarily experimental. French composers banded together in the search for generative sound sources and effective means of organization, and the government responded by subsidizing their research. Pierre Boulez emerged as the new leader of the movement, both through his own creative work and through his endeavors to communicate the message to the musical public. The central concern of musique concrète was aural beauty—a savoring of sounds singly, in combination, and in succession. The all-encompassing scope of the movement represented the ultimate manifestation of the French passion for varied tone color.

The control panel of a synthesizer (the Arp 2500).

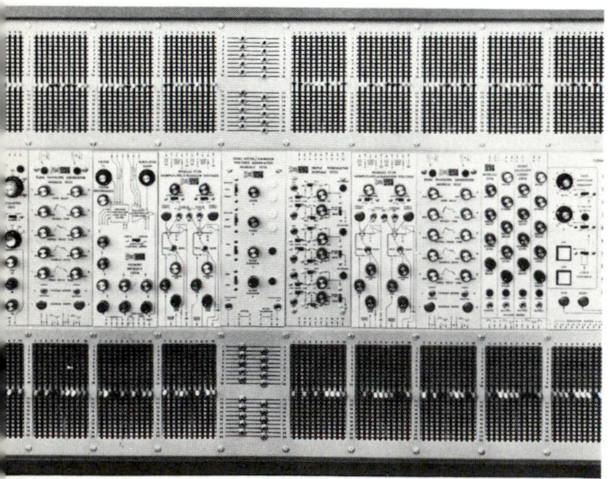

Synthesized Music

In Germany, too, composers were utilizing technology for musical purposes, but interest centered on a machine that could *create* sounds rather than on the reproduction and manipulation of an assembled sound inventory. This machine, called a *synthesizer,* was an electronic wonder that allowed a composer to shape every tone to his complete satisfaction, giving him an autonomy une-

A jazz performer at the keyboard of a synthesizer in a studio recording session.

qualed in the history of music. Dependent on no external agent other than the sound-generating machine, creation and realization of synthesized music were united in a single operation, contingent only on a steady flow of imagination and electric current. On demand, the synthesizer could produce a pure tone (without overtones) and a variety of more normal tones with some or all of the overtones included. The machine could simulate the tone quality of orchestral instruments and also create new tone colors. A characteristically electronic sound, basic in the repertoire of the synthesizer, is the so-called *white noise,* which incorporates all audible frequencies and is perceived as having no discernible pitch. In its pure state, white noise can be shaped only dynamically and in duration; but it can be manipulated by filtering and if enough pitches are filtered out, those remaining become identifiable.

Synthesized music and musique concrète utilized different raw materials, but they shared identical techniques of composition. Both existed only as recordings and both were produced by processes of layering and montage, animated by a quest for aural beauty. Neither was disadvantaged by recalcitrant performers—composers spoke directly to consumers, bypassing the performer completely, and radio rather than the concert hall was the usual agency of introduction to the public.

STOCKHAUSEN

The two types remained independent until the mid-fifties, when they were brought together. Karlheinz Stockhausen (b. 1928), for example, combined synthetic sound with boys' voices in his multisource composition *Gesang der Jünglinge* ("Song of the Youths"). This work was designed for "live" performance in the concert hall; there were no performers, of course—the music existed only on tape—but Stockhausen envisioned his music as emanating from a variety of directions, inundating the audience with a flood of sound, and he specified the location of assorted groups of loudspeakers. It was Medieval spatial deployment with a modern twist—a concept that gained increasing favor throughout the third quarter of the century.

As electronic music became more sophisticated, the emphasis shifted from sound sources to structures. Techniques of organizing and developing basic materials began to derive more and more from the idiomatic capabilities of the tape recorder rather than from the material itself. By using more than one recorder, individual units of recorded sound, called *events,* could frequently be expanded canonically. An event could be combined with itself in a simple, straightforward canon, or, with several machines playing the same event at different speeds, complex rhythmic canons could be created. All the canonic artifice of the fifteenth-century Netherlanders was brought back to life, and further canonic intricacies that mere mortals would have quailed to consider were made possible by the indomitable machines. Ostinato was another popular structural device. In tape recorder terminology it was called a *loop,* an exact term for what it was—a circular loop of tape that would repeat itself indefinitely unless interrupted by human intervention or mechanical failure.

Although most electronic music existed only on tape or disc, the possibility of live performance entered the picture with the development of the Moog synthesizer. This machine is equipped with a small keyboard that enables it to respond instantly with whatever tone quality has been prepared in advance. Since a single machine produces only one or possibly two tones at a time, a battery of synthesizers and a troop of performers are required for concert performance, to provide textural interest and contrast in tone color. More promising as a solo instrument is the recently developed *guitar synthesizer.* This guitar, with each of its six strings attached to a separate synthesizer that can be programed individually, offers an extravagant range of color combinations, all at the disposal of a single performer.

The United States was a slow starter in the electronic field. It was not until the late sixties—almost two decades after the advent of musique concrète and synthesized sound—that any sizable number of electronic studios were in operation in the United States, although there was some early isolated activity on both coasts. Iconoclastic ventures took different forms in America, and the *enfant terrible* of the American avant-garde was John Cage (b. 1912). Always a rebel, he first attracted attention with his piano music of the 1930s, in which the piano was "prepared" by the insertion of nuts, bolts, screws, and other foreign objects between the strings, to produce overtone effects along with a certain jangle. He attacked the keyboard with his fingers, his forearm, and sometimes extraneous weapons as well. In his postwar approach to the instrument Cage was gentler but no less bizarre; his piano work *4'33"*, for example, consists of four minutes and thirty-three seconds of silence, during which the performer contemplates the keyboard.

CAGE

Aleatory Music

Visual effects are characteristic of Cage's music, and theatrical elements abound in his works. In his own terminology, an "event" is more likely to represent a happening than a unit of taped sound. To add another ingredient of chaos, he espoused the principle of *indeterminacy,* in which chance is a crucial factor. In indeterminate or *aleatory* music, the composer relinquishes authority in certain elements of the process of composition—the selection and ordering of pitches, for example—and lets these elements be decided by a coin toss, a throw of the dice, or some other means. Most often aleatory music leaves the ordering of musical events to the performer so that chance enters the equation in each individual's choice of sequence. Composers are thus ironically free from any accusation of arbitrariness, although they have arbitrarily foisted on performers a number of decisions the performers may well dislike making. Americans—musicians as well as nonmusicians—tend to laugh at (possibly with) Cage. In Europe, however, he is accorded a measure of stature among composers, who have structured his theory of indeterminacy by eliminating the coin-toss element and restricting the performer's options to a few specific alternatives.

COALESCENCE IN THE NEW MUSIC

During the 1960s and 1970s, the various types of Western music began to coalesce. Experiments of the fifties were ripe for harvest, and composers were freely combining a variety of techniques and sound sources without prejudice or partisanship. Traditional instruments and voices were welcomed back as desirable media for musical expression; it was not uncommon to combine them with electronic materials in live performance. Styles differed radically, but there was an underlying unity in philosophical motivation, and that philosophy was perhaps the greatest force in shaping the music. It paralleled the prevailing cultural shift away from science and intellectual objectivity toward humanism, universality, and renewed faith in intuition and nonverbal means of communication. The relevance of this philosophy to musical considerations was summed up by Stockhausen in his "Open Letter to the Younger Generation":

> Again we are revolutionizing, but this time over the whole earth. Let us now set for ourselves the highest possible goal: becoming conscious that all mankind is at stake. . . .
>
> Let us make ourselves conscious that the human mentality, if it is not continuously fed by higher inspiration from the supramental, continuously makes different combinations of everything that is stored in it and that it can at any time assert anything arbitrary and its opposite. . . . And if we have not learned how to stop and start it, it races along without interruption. It is just a useful instrument, no more, no less: a model computer. But who needs it? And for what?
>
> The supraego is supposed to give it thought, and the supraego receives its conception from the intuitive consciousness, and the latter from the higher and highest consciousness in which the consciousness of every individual unites with supra-personal cosmic consciousness.
>
> Why do I say something like this when, after all, I am a musician and not at all a philosopher or the like? Because we musicians must live entirely on intuition. Because I have found out that everything new begins when this consciousness is reached and ever higher ascents are striven for. One is a musician, a specialist, a man with a profession only secondarily. Primarily, one is an individual spirit, which must first take up union with the universal spirit before it intends to communicate anything essential to other spirits, anything that goes beyond that which is individual and has anything to do with every other spirit.*

*Quoted in Jonathan Eisen, ed., *Twenty-Minute Fandangos and Forever Changes* (New York: Random House, Vintage Books, 1971), pp. 67–68.

New Vocabulary

Composers of the *new music*—and that is what they termed it—had broadened their base beyond the capacity of the vocabulary used traditionally to describe musical proceedings and relationships. The terms associated with a system limited to twelve pitches and metered rhythm had little descriptive relevance for an approach that often divided the octave into myriad microtones, regarded precise pitch as inconsequential, and focused on the fluidity rather than the measurability of time. New concepts were ill served by words that conjured up old expectations, and to convey new ideas more accurately, a whole new vocabulary evolved. Instead of "melody" and "accompaniment," composers spoke of *foreground* and *background,* while the term *gesture* denoted any significant linear occurrence. Vertical combinations, in which medium, register, range, and dynamics were more important than pitch, were called *sonorities*—a general term that was more inclusive and therefore more appropriate than the pitch-bound "chords." *Events* replaced "phrases," sometimes in fact as well as in phraseology, and *structures,* a word free of implications about sectional or thematic organization, was preferred to "forms." *Fabric* described the density, surface texture, and interweaving of sounds.

Composers spoke of *time* rather than "rhythm," and its flow was the important factor, not its regulation. Pulse and meter were not entirely discarded; metric rhythm was still in use, but only as one alternative among many available choices. In taped compositions, all aspects of duration and synchrony were determined in the recording studio once and for all, but in event-structured works designed for live performance, time often became a chance or aleatory element. If performers controlled the ordering of events, the flow of time entered the realm of chance; and if composers declined to specify the time of any particular event, the total duration of the composition was also left to chance. Clock time was sometimes used to indicate the duration of an event or fragment, and specific units of time (usually seconds) replaced pulse in systematizing both synchrony and the forward motion of the music. In one sense the use of clock time was a more severe regulation than meter: the rate of flow from point to point was controlled absolutely—but between points, details of rhythm were free.

Rhythmic patterns were as various as the methods of overall organization, and random rhythms were preferred to anything tinged with predictability. Interest hinged on the unexpected, and the delights of surprise far outweighed the security of the predictable in aesthetic considerations. In some compositions, the haphazard sound of rhythmic progression was a carefully wrought illusion, achieved through thoughtful planning and specific indication of exact durations; but sometimes chance really did play a genuine role in the rhythmic scheme, with the composer leaving rhythmic choices to the performer. Individual rhythmic patterns derived from widely divergent sources, including non-Western cultures (particularly Far Eastern and African), speech rhythms, and the characteristic rhythms of natural and mechanical sounds. Isorhythmic effects (page 68) occurred frequently, especially in electronic music: the simultaneous use of two loops of different lengths would produce two ostinato figures in isorhythmic relation, a technique that affected the listener's perception of structure and fabric as well as rhythm.

Traditional Sounds and New Sounds

But postwar music was not all tapes and technology. Traditional sound sources were very much in evidence, and the human voice, with all its frailty, was still appreciated as the most intimately expressive medium. Nor had old-fashioned lyric ideals completely disappeared—Poulenc was far from being the last of those who considered lyric melody indispensable in the art of song writing. Tadeusz Baird (b. 1928), for one, is a confirmed lyricist, and he has not succumbed to the attractions of the avant-garde aesthetic that his Polish compatriots so ardently embrace. He remains a conservative composer in a progressive musical society. His conservatism is exemplified in the *Four Love Sonnets* (of Shakespeare) for baritone, strings, and harpsichord. These songs are cast in an idiom that combines a suggestion of late Renaissance style with the vocabulary and emotionalism of late Romanticism. The second of these, heard in the recorded example, begins with a mildly dissonant introduction, but apart from this, it sounds as if it might have wandered into the twentieth century from some earlier epoch. Stylistic anachronisms, however, are in themselves part of twentieth-century aesthetic ideals.

BAIRD

Side 11 Band 2

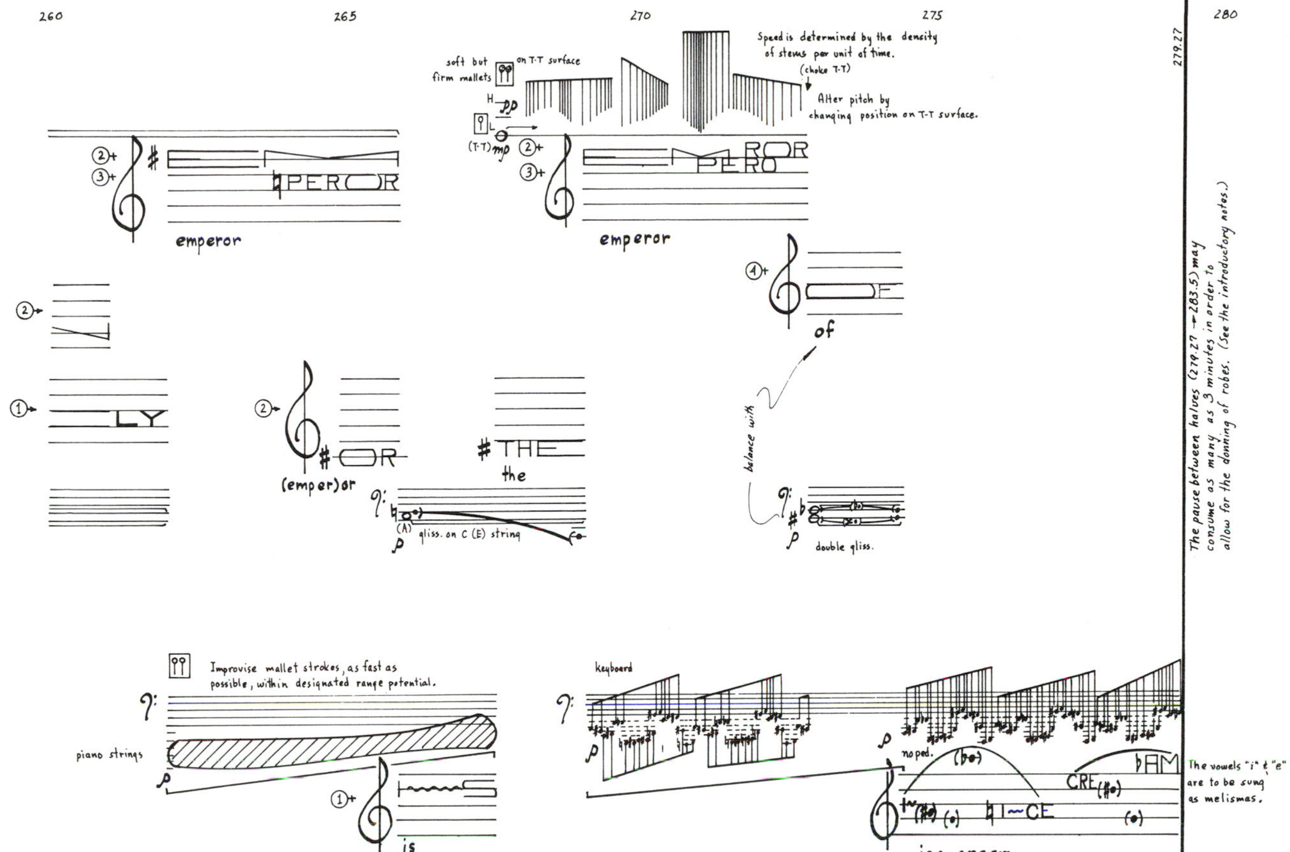

A page from the score of *The Emperor of Ice Cream* (1963) by Roger Reynolds, for eight voices, two percussionists, and string bass. (The numbers across the top mark cumulative duration in seconds.)

Far from negating the beauty of this song, they add poignancy and hints of eternal beauty to its rich fabric.

Voices, however, were no longer limited to singing. Schoenberg had opened the door to a nonlyric approach with his *sprechstimme* (roughly, "speech voice"), for which he specified that pitch was only a starting point, not to be sustained but to be left instantly in a declamatory glide. Composers of the new music went further, and sometimes used voices without any reference to pitch whatsoever. Spoken words, divorced from meaning, were employed as abstract sounds with emphasis on natural speech rhythms and the sonorous character of an individual word. (The word "scintillation," for example, is distinguished rhythmically by evenly-paced enunciation with an accent on the third syllable, and its most striking features of resonance are the sharp hiss of the initial "s," the percussive effect of the "t," the brief hum of the "l," and the softer hiss of the "sh" sound.) Nonverbal vocal noises such as wails, grunts, and snores have been used occasionally but have not thus far achieved great popularity; nonverbal use of the singing voice—treating it simply as an instrument with a special tone quality—is more typical of the new music.

PENDERECKI

Side 11 Band 3

Krzysztof Penderecki (b. 1933), an outstanding Polish composer and a leading exponent of the new music, used voices with delicacy, sympathy, and remarkable effectiveness, particulary in his choral writing. In the recorded example, the Stabat Mater from his *Passion According to St. Luke,* he combines three *a cappella* choirs; although singing predominates, the voices are occasionally called on to hiss, whisper, or mumble the text. Stylistically, this work combines elements of both past and present: it begins with plainchant (which recurs throughout the work); and it then moves on to a repeated-note theme that is developed imitatively, Bach-fashion. The cluster-dissonance that accompanies this imitation, however, is distinctly a latter-day idiom. Texture, range, and register are crucial elements in this work. It begins in a medium-low register with a static melody, and the entire first stanza is confined to men's voices singing in a severely limited range. After hovering for a time in that restricted pitch area, the sudden expansion of range in the second stanza (beginning "Qui est homo . . . ," with the entrance of soprano voices) creates a strong, dramatic effect. The Stabat Mater unfolds with little or no reference to tonality, so that the sudden appearance of a familiar major triad on the final "gloria" seems surprising but, strangely, perfectly in keeping with the essence of the work.

New sounds have also been elicited from traditional instruments, often necessitating the expansion of performing techniques. To play the new music, pianists must learn to find their way around the interior of the piano as well as the keyboard and to use other means of tone production than their fingers—for example, drum mallets on the strings. Sonorities demanded from stringed instruments frequently include nonstring sounds such as tapping the wood with fingers or bow, or bowing on the wrong side of the bridge, where pitch is completely a matter of chance. Recent writing for strings commonly calls for microtones and pitch slides in which precision is irrelevant, and in orchestral works, players within a string section, rather than playing the same line, are more likely to be called on for diverse, individual efforts. Brasses are asked to blat and woodwinds to bleat, and both are required to produce the highest note possible, whatever it might be. Brass players thump on mouthpieces with their palms, and wind players have learned to produce two or more tones at once; thus modifying the concept of "single-line" instruments. Percussionists, previously condemned to long periods of inactivity during which they had nothing to do but count the measures leading up to that one cymbal crash, are perhaps the most enthusiastic performers of new music. At last they have been elevated from second-class citizenship to full participation in the orchestral community. A wide variety of percussion instruments, almost always including chimes, is standard in new orchestral works, and the degree of activity in a percussion section often approaches that of a three-ring circus. Beyond orchestral music, percussionists are now also blessed with a developing ensemble and solo literature, admitting them to the formerly exclusive fields of chamber music and recital performance.

During the 1950s, the avant-garde focus had been on expanding admissible sound sources. The result was that once every audible phenomenon was legitimate, it was no longer possible for any composer to be "original" by using "forbidden" sounds. Thus, having no external restrictions to rebel against, the younger generation was obliged to look inward, relying on inner resources rather than extraneous gimmickry for its creative ventures. Indiscriminate lack of restriction invites chaos, and it is fortunate for the new music that the postexperimental generation seems inclined to concern itself more with what is desirable than with what is possible, and to bend its talents towards imaginative selectivity, artistic combination, and coherent organization.

Audience response to the new music is difficult to assess. Because only a few prominent performers and ensembles perform recent works, the literature remains largely unknown to the vast majority of music lovers, who constitute an untapped pool of potential converts. One might be tempted to predicate a growing audience on the basis of large attendance at and enthusiastic reception of concerts of new music at American universities, but how this music will fare in an open marketplace, characterized by expensive tickets and an exacting audience, is anybody's guess.

CONTEMPORARY OPERA

Of all audiences, operagoers are perhaps the most unalterably addicted to melody. They can at times be persuaded to forego spectacle or accept a travesty of tragedy, but to their ears, lyricism is nonnegotiable. New melodic styles introduced in the thirties met with strong resistance initially, being damned in aggregate as nonmelodic; but by the late forties, audiences were

The "floating crap game" scene from the original production of Frank Loesser's *Guys and Dolls* (1950).

becoming more selective in their damnation. The decades immediately following the Second World War were a time of expansion of operatic repertoire and styles. By the mid-fifties, operatic repertoire had been enriched by new works from Prokofiev, Thomson, Stravinsky, Hindemith, Copland, Walton, Milhaud, and Poulenc, and these operas found far wider, more receptive audiences than had those of the thirties. Representing the younger generation were the British Benjamin Britten (b. 1913) and the Italian-American Gian-Carlo Menotti (b. 1911), both conservatives who achieved popular success early in their careers and have continued to make opera a focal point of composition.

During the late fifties and throughout the sixties, the avant-garde was much more in evidence in operatic endeavors. The Swedish composer Karl-Birger Blomdahl (1916–1968) approached the composition of opera armed with manipulated tapes that incorporated both musique concrète and synthesized sound. Luigi Nono (b. 1924), an Italian with an atypical concept of melody, wrote a protest opera, *Intolleranza,* in which he decried cruelty while using voices mercilessly. And Penderecki, who first explored the techniques of new music through writing for orchestra and multiple choirs, broadened the scope of the idiom to include opera with the composition of *The Devils of Loudun.*

Resistance to new styles is strong throughout the Western world. Contemporary opera is currently engaged in a fierce struggle for existence. It is all but impossible to secure professional production of new works, and many contain musical and technical difficulties that place them beyond the reach of amateur groups.

THE AMERICAN MUSICAL

In the case of popular musical theater, however, the story is a happier one: every season sees the production of new works that join those smash hits still going strong, and the production of a work even a decade old is considered a revival. The years following the Second World War were vintage years for the American musical: it was thriving at home and popular abroad, where its stature was acknowledged by its admission as a subject for study at the graduate level in prestigious music schools. Gershwin and Kern had defined the format and brought the medium to maturity; the postwar period gave it sophistication. Some musicals dealt with American subjects in American settings: both *Annie Get Your Gun,* by Irving Berlin (b. 1888), and *Oklahoma,* by Richard Rodgers (b. 1902), focused on the West, with different degrees of wildness, while *Guys and Dolls,* by Frank Loesser (1910–1969), was set in Damon Runyon's somewhat improbable version of New York City. *Gypsy,* by Jule Styne (b. 1905), chronicled the life of a famous striptease artist, and in *The Music Man,* Meredith Willson (b. 1902) ridiculed the foibles and beamed at the essential goodness of denizens of the Corn Belt. American characters in exotic settings were featured in Berlin's *Call Me Madam* and Rodgers's *South Pacific,* and the latter, by moralizing on the evils of racial bigotry, gave the musical a social conscience. Later in the fifties, musicals went literary, led by the record-shattering *My Fair Lady,* by Frederick Loewe (b. 1904).

Productions varied in complexity of settings and elaborateness of costuming, but some element of spectacle was invariably part of the show. The dramatic element became more than simple continuity; plots were given substance, and the development and resolution of conflict gained real conviction. Dance sequences were an integral part of the production, sometimes adding sheer spectacle and sometimes furthering dramatic action. The musical numbers, while appropriate to and dramatically consistent with the plot, were primarily designed to be show-stoppers; only rarely did a song actually move the drama forward. A variety of vocal styles were used in musicals, ranging from the near bel canto of an ingenue to rhythmic speech (as in the opening scene—on a railroad train—of *The Music Man*), and in between was the adenoidal nonsinging of a lady of dubious virtue in the infamous "Adelaïde's Lament," from *Guys and Dolls*.

Julie Andrews and Rex Harrison in a scene from the original Broadway production of *My Fair Lady* (1956).

Guys and Dolls was unique in many ways, particularly in its motley assortment of ensembles, from the raucous "harmony" of a chorus of strippers to the unpretentious gospel singing of the Salvation Army, and including the contrapuntal bickering of a trio of racetrack touts, singing the "Fugue for Tin Horns" heard in the recorded example. This title is somewhat misleading; the rather clumsy melody is treated canonically instead of fugally, but the polyphonic texture is clear, and the three strands of text extolling the virtues of different horses remain fiercely independent throughout.

Side 11 Band 4

Musicals of the late sixties and early seventies hinted at a change in style; they looked much the same, but they sounded different. *Promises, Promises,* by Burt Bacharach (b. 1928), made no great departure from tradition, but its score was harmonically and rhythmically more complex than those of earlier musicals. *Hair,* by Galt MacDermot, was decidedly different; the music was in the rock idiom, which had been around for quite a while, but was new to the musical theater and represented a break with the musical past. Stephen Sondheim (b. 1930) seems to be pursuing a course of weaving music into the dramatic fabric rather than creating show-stoppers. His music is so much a part of the action that Sondheim's songs lose effectiveness when isolated. In the course of the action, particularly in *Follies,* character development or revelation is accomplished musically with impressive power, but a song which carried impact in the theater might well have little meaning for one who had never seen the show.

JAZZ

Swing

After having taken the world by storm in the 1920s, "hot" jazz experienced a couple of relatively dormant decades. Following the crash of 1929, America's mood was considerably less ebullient and seemed to require the reassuring sweetness and light of *swing* rather than the aggressive agitation of jazz. Dance styles in the swing era were less frenetic, and the preferred sound was that of a big band that provided smooth, less obtrusive music. Small ensembles were out, and with them went Dixieland, leaving jazz musicians the problem of reconciling the inherent conflict between the improvisatory nature of jazz and the unwieldy size of

Glenn Miller (foreground), one of the best-known big-band conductors, with his group at the Paramount Theater in New York around 1939.

a big band. Any solution had to be a compromise between structure and freedom. The proportions of these two components varied widely, but most bands resorted to written notation in some degree.

Black bands kept structure to an irreducible minimum, opting for as much improvisation as possible, and the great bands of the time were as distinctly individual as their leaders. Louis Armstrong (1900–1971), having cut his teeth on Dixieland, retained some of that heterophonic style in his big band. Duke Ellington (1899–1974), who had had only moderate success with small groups, found his natural expression in big-band sound and made the transition with elegance and authority. Count Basie (b. 1904) was a big-band man from the beginning, and he represented the avant-garde of swing with his driving rhythms and multilinear emphases.

White bands went the commercial route, playing "sweet swing"—a style that had little relationship to jazz by any definition but that yielded great financial rewards. A few, such as Benny Goodman (b. 1904), played jazz-based swing, but many bands limited themselves to saccharine musical inanities.

Swing was characterized by a full, rich sound. Emphasis was on one melody, smooth harmony, blend, and rhythmic togetherness. Teamwork was essential to the style, and hours of rehearsal were required to acquire precision in complex arrangements. It was a great sound, and everybody loved it—except the performers. Dedicated jazzmen were frustrated by the loss of individual identity, bored with endless rehearsals, and irritated by the tight rein that checked improvisational flights of fancy. Many had become disenchanted with the sound itself: they found the harmonies too bland, the focus on one melody dull, and the lack of rhythmic independence intolerable. A revolution was brewing throughout the forties, and the second half of that decade witnessed the end of swing and the triumph of *bop.*

Bop

Bop was performers' music—the groups were smaller than the swing bands, and each player had an individual identity. Rhythmic independence of lines was complete, often resulting in polyrhythmic textures; harmonies were sophisticated and dissonant, and every line hinted at the melody without stating it outright. It was exciting music, both to listeners and performers, but it did not lend itself to dancing—bop was music to listen to, and it was decisive in moving jazz out of the dance hall.

The jazz community was not unanimous in embracing bop—Louis Armstrong, for one, would have none of it, and he pulled no punches in denouncing the "boppers." The harmonic innovations of Dizzy Gillespie and the fragmented melodies of Charlie Parker must have seemed a totally different language to Armstrong, but it seems probable that Armstrong objected not so much to the leaders of bop as to their bumbling followers. In fact, the death of bop was hastened by the hordes of young performers who leaped into the fray with too little technique, too little understanding of musical subtleties, and too little knowledge of jazz. They imitated what they heard in the music of their idols, but their hearing was less than perfect, and they put so much emphasis on fragmentation, rhythmic freedom, and "weird" harmonies that the whole sound came unglued.

Cool Jazz

Inept interpreters were not solely responsible for the short life of bop. Its fast, frenetic violence was bound to incite a reaction, and in the early fifties, the course of jazz made a virtual about-face. The new style was reserved, given more to understatement than to extravagance, and, because emotion was kept under wraps, it was known as *cool* jazz. It was basically a simpler style than bop; its harmonic language was rich and varied, but rhythmic schemes were less complex, and melodies were more introverted. Miles Davis (b. 1926), whose name is most closely associated with cool jazz, was never completely at ease with bop, and the new sound

Louis ("Satchmo") Armstrong.

resulted from his search for a more congenial mode of expression. But for him it was only the beginning: for more than two decades, he has been a dynamic pacesetter in changing styles of jazz, and to the younger generation, he is a real and present influence, not a historic monument.

Mainstream Jazz

Cool jazz enjoyed but a brief vogue. In playing down both emotion and virtuosity, the movement had departed from the essence of jazz, lost vitality, and become effete. Reaction took many forms, and by the mid-fifties, jazz was developing in such a variety of directions that any generalization concerning style was impossible. Some artists saw salvation in a return to the roots of jazz—not a nostalgic return to Dixieland, but reentry into the mainstream through the basic materials of blues and gospel, treated with honest emotion. Fundamentalists took a simple, unsophisticated approach to their music, and the assorted styles that resulted have been variously labeled "soul," "gospel," and so on. But no matter what label is attached, the music is openly emotional, and dividing lines are often blurred by overlapping styles. A more sophisticated element in the mainstream movement stressed virtuosity and sought to develop instrumental jazz along traditional—but modern—"hot" lines. Melodic improvisation in long, sweeping lines regained favor, rhythmic innovation was very much alive, and harmonic schemes ranged from the complex vocabulary of European music to the simplicity and freshness of modal patterns.

COLTRANE

Side 11 Band 5

Outstanding among mainstream artists of the 1960s was John Coltrane (1927–1967). The recorded example, his "Alabama," descends from the blues, but transcends the older style in its moving expression of sorrow. It is an improvisation that takes shape in ABA form. The piece begins with a modal melody, played in the low, dark register of the saxophone, over a piano ostinato that persists until a cadence ends the section. The B section is more active and less mournful: drums have a prominent part, the piano is in constant motion, and the saxophone moves to a higher, less somber register. With the return of A, the saxophone resumes its original melody in the same dark register, but the piano ostinato is replaced by free-wheeling drums and pizzicato bass. In "Alabama" Coltrane's virtuosity found expression in tonal control and nuance rather than in technical fireworks; his musical honesty and artistry are evident from first note to last.

Paralleling the mainstream movement in time, but not in emphasis, was a group dedicated to elevating the stature of jazz by investing it with significant form. This group was made up of conservatory-trained jazzmen who felt that the strength of jazz was in its style and that its weakness lay in its lack of organization. By bringing to jazz some of the organizational techniques that had proved successful in concert music, this group hoped to strengthen jazz by reinforcing structure. Dave Brubeck (b. 1920) and his quartet were pioneers in popularizing this intellectual approach to jazz. Their music was primarily improvised, and the style was eclectic: textures were polyphonic, thematic material was developed along Classical lines, and the harmonic idiom was that of the twentieth century. John Lewis (b. 1920) and his Modern Jazz Quartet, disbanded in the early 1970s, leaned more strongly toward Baroque principles of linear organization with particular emphasis on fugue. Early performances were tightly structured, relying heavily on written notation, but as the group matured they developed an ability to achieve comparable structure through collective contrapuntal improvisation. Other proponents of the intellectual approach have entered the so-called third stream. This group looked not backward but sideways for techniques of organization, attempting to incorporate current concert music trends into jazz. Concert music, too, has tentatively entered the third stream, and mutual borrowing has blurred the line that once clearly divided the two types of music.

The Jazz Avant-Garde

And then there was the avant-garde, which persevered in its mission of pushing back frontiers, despite the objections of both listeners and fellow musicians. The man at the forefront of innovation in jazz was Ornette Coleman (b. 1930). Coleman is a musical iconoclast; in his quest for freedom, no element of traditional jazz is sacred—not even the beat. To escape the tyranny of tonality, he turned to neomodality, polytonality, atonality, and even microtones. He deemphasized harmony and brought texture and tone color to the fore, thereby increasing the latitude for melodic improvisation. His rhythmic sacrilege took the form of tempo changes, irregular meter, and, occasionally, no discernible beat whatever. All of this sounds like a blueprint for chaos, but it has not turned out that way. Coleman's best works reveal an intuitive logic and genuine musical substance. Somehow the feel of jazz is still there, and his imagination and originality are beyond dispute. He was the first jazz musician to receive a Guggenheim Fellowship—a well-deserved tribute both to the man and to jazz as an art form.

COLEMAN

"What Reason Could I Give," the recorded example, from the album *Science Fiction,* is less radical than some of Coleman's purely instrumental works, but it illustrates several of his departures from tradition. The slightly-out-of-tune sound is no accident: the Coleman style deliberately "bends" pitches to heighten emotional intensity. And the lack of precision in ensemble attacks is evidence of the totality of his commitment to rhythmic freedom and the individual identity of players. There is no attempt to balance different registers; the trumpets and saxophones are clustered in a medium-high register, and although the vocalist is singing in a rather low range, the impression is one of emphasis on high tessitura, with a great open space between the melody instruments and the bass. Vocal and instrumental colors are paramount, and the way in which those colors alternately blend and contrast with one another is part of the fascination of this piece.

Side 12 Band 1

Ornette Coleman.

Focus on tone color was by no means unique to Coleman; it was one feature common to all factions of the avant-garde. Electronic instruments, ranging from synthesizers to the tone-modifying fuzz-wah, began to appear with increasing frequency. Usually they were combined with acoustic (standard) instruments, but some recent recordings have featured works using electronic sounds only.

Current developments in jazz lean toward mainstream styles, avant-garde experiments, or some combination of the two. Emotionalism is back in favor, and the intellectual camp is finding few adherents among the younger generation. Improvisation figures prominently in all styles, and the term *free jazz* describes all predominantly improvised music, regardless of style. Individual musicians cross freely from one style to another, and stylistic classification applies only to the music, not the men. The music of Archie Shepp (b. 1937), for example, runs the gamut from a simple gospel hymn to unfettered improvisation. The Art Ensemble of Chicago, which was awarded a grant from the National Endowment for the Arts, has an equally wide stylistic range but leans more strongly in the avant-garde direction. Jazz audiences, by and large, are a conservative lot, and many gifted avant-garde composers have yet to win a following sufficient to enable them to make music a livelihood as well as a profession. For these composers, there is no benevolent university to act as buffer between them and a reluctant public; they must establish communication or perish. Those whose innovations spring from a sincere commitment to the expression of emotion will probably find a following; the public has an ear for honesty in jazz and is quick to reject music that smacks of hypocrisy or affectation. Bunk Johnson (1879–1949) spoke for all time when he said, "Playing jazz is like talking from your heart. You don't lie."*

IDEALS OF THE NEW MUSIC

Since the end of the big-band era, jazz has been moving closer to chamber music—in intimacy of expression and interaction among performers as well as in ensemble size. In fact, a resurgence of chamber music ideals can be found in nearly every facet

*Quoted in the booklet accompanying the set of recordings *The Smithsonian Collection of Classic Jazz,* Smithsonian Institution, 1973.

of contemporary composition. Composers of electronic music, after two decades of an "anything goes" approach, have recently revealed a tendency toward restraint, choosing their forces more selectively to approximate the sound of a small ensemble. Some electronic music evinces strong solidarity with ideals of jazz, as well. *Evolutions 2,* by Henk Badings (b. 1907), is synthesized, but the style is closely related to jazz, and the sound has more kinship with a small ensemble than with an orchestra.

Side 12 Band 2

Works combining tape with live performance are predominantly chamber music in type; coordinating the two is somewhat unwieldy and is best entrusted to a small number of performers. Many works feature a single soloist and tape; sometimes the tape provides contrasting tone colors, and sometimes it duplicates the soloist's instrumental color. And if the tape has been recorded by the soloist, performance of ensemble music by one individual ceases to be a contradiction in terms. In the recorded example, *Fantasy in Space* by Otto Luening (b. 1900), a live flute is combined with recorded flute tone that has been altered through reverberation and other forms of manipulation. The effect is one of an unreal flute ensemble which is all the more fascinating for being incredible.

Side 12 Band 3

Unalloyed concert music also seems to be gravitating toward chamber-type ensembles, although traditional groups, such as the string quartet, are comparatively rare. Diversity rather than homogeneity of tone color is preferred, resulting in ensembles that juxtapose distinctive colors in any number of unprecedented combinations. *Ancient Voices of Children,* by George Crumb (b. 1929), brings together a typically motley crew of performers: mezzo-soprano, boy soprano, oboe, harmonica, mandolin, harp, electric piano, toy piano, musical saw, and percussion. The percussion section includes both standard instruments such as gong and drums, and exotic ones such as Tibetan prayer stones and Japanese temple bells. Each of the songs and dances that make up this work uses a different combination of instruments. Each ensemble is small, and at no time are all assembled resources used simultaneously. The third movement, heard in the recorded example, features mezzo-soprano, drums, and oboe, with lesser contributions from other performers. The movement opens with the mezzo-soprano (whose part includes tongue trills, laughs, and sprechstimme) singing into an amplified piano that echoes her vocalise in ghostly tones. Then the drum enters with a bolero

CRUMB

Side 12 Band 4

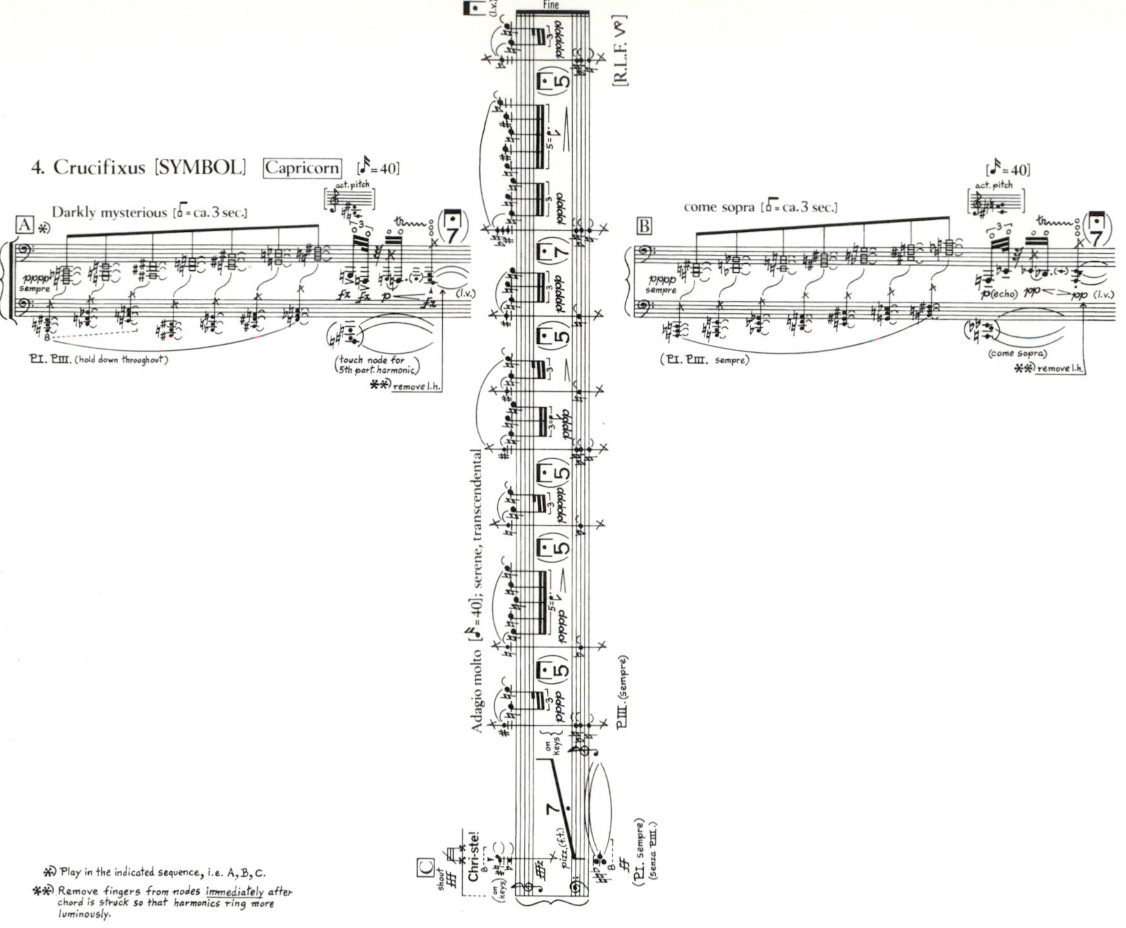

"Crucifixus" from *Makrokosmos I* (1973), by George Crumb.

rhythm that continues as an ostinato until the final cadence (and fade). The oboe's role is secondary; voice and drums dominate the movement, but the oboe's dialogue with the mezzo-soprano contributes significantly to the emotional impact of the movement.

Chamber music is a congenial medium for the new music. It offers both scope for imagination and intimacy for the communication of musical ideas and emotion. It is consistent with the ideals of the new music, which prizes subtlety and contrast in tone color, and it is also consistent with the prevailing humanistic philosophy, which values all individuality, musical as well as social. In style, the new music seems to have amalgamated features from every historical period: the heterogeneous tone colors of the Medieval era, Renaissance individuality, Classical textural variety, and Romantic emotional openness. And it appears to be a winning combination—performers are beginning to return to the fold, and audiences are responding to the emotional honesty of this music. Without undue temerity, it would seem possible, on this evidence, to postulate a brightening future for the new music.

COMPARATIVE STYLE CHARACTERISTICS

	MIDDLE AND LATE ROMANTIC PERIOD	IMPRESSIONISM	EARLY 20TH CENTURY	SINCE 1945
TEXTURE	consistent in density, tending toward thickness and solidity	varying in density evanescent rather than solid	both thick (barbarism) and thin (Neo-Classicism)	very thin textures—often isolated single tones in succession full texture in large ensembles
CADENCES	sectional cadences—clear-cut and definitive internal cadences—less decisive and somewhat unpredictable	cadences clear but not decisive; created rhythmically more than harmonically some final cadences akin to the "fade"	cadences frequently created by a consonance following a passage of unrelieved dissonance usually marked by a long note sometimes overlapping phrases minimizing cadential effect	usually marked by a long note in event-structured works silence is often used to signal the end of an event sometimes a "fade" replaces the final cadence
POLYPHONY	occasionally used, but only within a harmonic context both combined melodies and imitative techniques	seldom used individual lines blurred rather than distinct	often purely linear, creating unresolved dissonance as independent lines progress both imitative techniques and combined melodies	often related to serial technique militantly independent lines independence intensified by wide separation in range and register accomplished through layering in electronic music
HARMONY	tonal intensely chromatic harmony complex modulations, frequently to remote keys frequent use of tonally ambiguous passages	tertian harmony used nonfunctionally tonal center obscure some use of modes a little use of quartal harmony	tertian harmony used nonfunctionally quartal harmony new use of old modes (neomodality) simultaneous use of two or more keys (polytonality) no key at all (atonality)	atonality "sonorities" replace chords microtonal clusters pitches often approximate rather than precise

COMPARATIVE STYLE CHARACTERISTICS (CONTINUED)

	MIDDLE AND LATE ROMANTIC PERIOD	IMPRESSIONISM	EARLY 20TH CENTURY	SINCE 1945
RHYTHM	primarily consistent meter; occasional meter change within a section tempo changes from section to section elasticity of tempo within a section subdivisions variable, including uncommon ones (fives, sevens) subdivisions combined	primarily consistent meter, but some meter change within a section tempo changes from section to section elasticity of tempo within a section subdivisions variable, including uncommon ones (fives, sevens)	changing meter combined meters no meter tempo changes from section to section some rubato subdivisions variable subdivisions combined	no stable pulse no meter; flow of time replaces regulation of rhythm random rhythms duration, both of details and of entire compositions often indeterminate
DYNAMICS	shaded very wide range	shaded wide range, with the soft end of the scale predominating	often brutal; very loud level sustained for a prolonged period often restrained, scaled toward the lower half of the dynamic range both shaded and terraced dynamics wide range	dynamic extremes juxtaposed (a very loud tone followed by a very soft tone) dynamic range expanded through amplification extremely wide range
ARTICULATION	primarily legato	detached for delicacy superlegato for richness or indistinctness	often percussive frequently detached some legato	new techniques of attack: explosive, breathy, etc.
VOCAL FORMS	solo song oratorio	solo song	solo song chamber ensembles using or featuring a vocalist	speaking as well as singing voice frequently used, both solo and in chorus voice used as an instrument in chamber ensembles large choral forms

	MIDDLE AND LATE ROMANTIC PERIOD	IMPRESSIONISM	EARLY 20TH CENTURY	SINCE 1945
INSTRUMENTAL FORMS	short piano piece symphony symphonic (tone) poem concerto sonata	short piano piece symphonic (tone) poem concerto	short piano piece symphony concerto sonata string quartet chamber works (no standard ensemble) orchestral suite	orchestral works (no standard form) chamber works (no standard ensemble) forms derived from tape technique works for percussion ensemble
INSTRUMENTAL TONE COLOR	rich, dark color; sometimes brilliant blend and contrast	subtlety in tone colors, singly and combined blur as well as blend delicacy rather than richness of tone	harsh, strident tone contrasted with muted, delicate tone sometimes blend, sometimes contrast in ensembles new tone colors from strings	contrast between instruments blend within an orchestral section (i.e., violins) new tone colors from old instruments new tone colors from new instruments new tone colors through tape manipulation
ORCHESTRA	very large (80–110) strings additions to woodwinds: piccolo, English horn, bass clarinet, contra-bassoon addition to brasses: tuba percussion section greatly enlarged	large (80–90) strings addition to woodwinds: saxophone brasses harp prominent percussion section small	very large (80–110) and very small (15–25), both sizes including a comparatively large percussion section	large (80–90)—frequently including a large percussion section with exotic as well as standard instruments
MUSICAL THEATER	opera, music drama operetta ballet	opera ballet	opera ballet (and modern dance) musical comedy film operetta	opera musical comedy film mixed-media works (including music, live and taped, film, drama, and dance)

Illustration credits continued

116. Organ in calligraphic setting, The Bettmann Archive
144. *Woman at the Piano,* c. 1917, by Elie Nadelman. Wood, stained and painted, 35⅛" high. Collection, The Museum of Modern Art, New York. The Philip L. Goodwin Collection
160. German woodcarving of a violinist, 18th century. By permission of The Victoria and Albert Museum, London
182. Scene from the ballet *Les Noces,* by Igor Stravinsky. Photo by Inter Nationes/Enkelmann, German Information Center
198. Steinway piano interior, from the Paris Exposition, 1867. Photo by Kalmbach
226. Mechanical trumpet player, Deutsches Museum, Munich
246. *Man with Mandolin,* 1917, by Jacques Lipchitz. Stone, approx. 29¾" high. Yale University Art Gallery, Collection Societé Anonyme
274. *Harp Player II,* 1960, bronze, by Bernard Reder. Collection of Whitney Museum of American Art
Text Illustrations: p. 4 (bottom) From "The Bowed String and the Player" by John C. Schelleng. *The Journal of the Acoustical Society of America,* pp. 27, 35, vol. 53, 1953
5 (top) Gary S. Thorpe/*Scientific American,* Feb. 1974, pp. 110–11. (bottom) From *The Songs of Insects* by George W. Pierce, © 1948, Harvard University Press, p. 142
6. From *The Band Director's Guide* by Kenneth L. Neidig. Prentice-Hall, 1964, p. 293
9. The New York Public Library, Branch Libraries, Picture Collection
13. Musée Unterlinden, Colmar
16 (top) © Robert M. Lightfoot III. (bottom) The New York Public Library, Branch Libraries, Picture Collection
21. Prints Division, The New York Public Library
29. Picturepoint Ltd., London
30. Prints Division, The New York Public Library
34. Ghana Information Services
37. A. Benoit, Paris
38. René Burri/Magnum
42. From *Psychology: Its Principles and Meanings* by Lyle E. Bourne Jr. and Bruce R. Ekstrand, © 1973 The Dryden Press, fig. 3-13, p. 71
43. Max-Yves Brandily, Paris
44. Gisèle Freund/Magnum
47. Vincent/AAA Photo, Paris
48. R. Catti
52. From *Psalter of Queen Isabella,* English, 1303–1308. Cod. gall. 16, f. 17v, Bayerische Staatsbibliotheque, Munich
53. The Philadelphia Museum of Art
59. The Bettmann Archive
60. From *Roman de Fauvel,* French, 14th-century MS. fr. 146, fol. 34R, Bibliothèque Nationale
61. Alinari/Scala
62. From *The Book of Chess of Alfonso the Wise,* 13th-century MS., j. T. 6. fol. 9R, Library of El Escorial Monastery
64. The Bettmann Archive
65. By permission of the Master and Fellows of Trinity College, Cambridge
66. Musée Condé
72. Edwin Smith
76. The Trustees of The British Museum
79. Österreichische Nationalbibliothek, Vienna
80. From *Historia Plantarum* by Conrad Gesner, vol. 1, plate 25, Urs Graf-Verlag Dietikon/Switzerland, 1972
81. From *Codex Atlanticus,* by permission of Johnson Reprint Corporation, New York and Giunti-Barbera, Florence
82. Alinari/Scala
83. Kunsthistorisches Museum, Vienna
84. Anders/Staatliche Museen Preussischer Kulturbesitz Kupferstichkabinett
85, 89. The Metropolitan Museum of Art
93. Photo Nuovo Poligrafico Alterocca, Terni, Italy
100. National Museum, Prague
101. Art Reference Bureau
102. Reproduced by permission of The Huntington Library, San Marino, California
103. Lee Boltin
104. Alinari/Scala
105. (top) Werner Bischof/Magnum. (bottom) Guilford Courthouse, National Military Park, Guilford, N.C.
106, 108, 109, 112, 113. (top) Reproduced by permission of Harcourt Brace Jovanovich, Inc. from *Music: A Design For Listening,* third edition, by Homer Ulrich. © 1957, 1962, 1970 by Harcourt Brace Jovanovich, Inc.
107. Stadtmuseum, Munich
110. (top) *The Village Festival,* by Hans Sebald Beham. Courtesy Museum of Fine Arts, Boston, Gift of William Norton Bullard. (bottom) © Begouen Collection, Photo by J. Vertut/S.P.A.D.E.M.
111. Musée de l'Homme, Paris
113. (bottom) Archives Photographiques
114. Edo, Tosa School, Tosa Mitsunori, Courtesy The Smithsonian Institution, Freer Gallery of Art, Washington, D.C.
119. Simoner/Austrian National Tourist Office
125, 126. Bibliothèque Nationale
129. Haarlem Tourist Office, Holland
132. Bibliothèque-Musée de l'Opéra, Paris
133. Bibliothèque Nationale
134. The John Omwake Playing Card Collection, on indefinite loan to the Cincinnati Art Museum from The United States Playing Card Company
135. Austrian National Tourist Office
146. Rhoda Nathans
147. (top) Dick Frontain. (bottom) Mariedi Anders Artists Management, Inc.
148. Hugh Tracey, International Library of African Music
149. B. Anderson/Monkmeyer Press Photo Agency
150. Collection of the Corcoran Gallery of Art, Washington, D.C.
153. Robert Alan Gold/Juilliard School of Music
155. The Bettmann Archive
158. Christian Steiner/New York Philharmonic
162. Hirmer Fotoarchiv
164. Bibliothèque Nationale
169. H. Roger-Viollet
173. By permission of The Victoria and Albert Museum, London
176, 179. Austrian National Tourist Office
180. From *You've Had It, Charlie Brown,* by Charles M. Schulz, Holt, Rinehart and Winston, Inc., 1969
184. Trustees of The British Museum
185. Collection, Musuem of Modern Art, New York, Gift of the Artist
186. Greek National Tourist Office
187. Louis Faurer/Time-Life Picture Agency © Time Inc.
188. British Tourist Authority
189. The Lynn Farnol Group, Inc.
190. Martha Swope
191. The Metropolitan Museum of Art, Joseph Pulitzer Bequest, 1955
195. French Cultural Services
196. British Tourist Authority
200. Österreichische Nationalbibliothek, Vienna
201. © Beth Bergman
205. The Byron Collection, Museum of the City of New York
208. Bibliothèque Nationale
212. Dr. Harald Busch
215. Fred Fehl
219. French Government Tourist Office
221. John Blomfield
229. Wide World Photos
233. Collection of Jack Bradley
234. Wide World Photos
235. Wide World Photos
240, 242. Courtesy RCA Records
249. Hubert Josse/Bibliothèque de l'Arsenal
253. Van der Becke and R. Bernard/German Information Center
259. Collection of Jack Bradley
260. The Bettmann Archive/S.P.A.D.E.M.
261. Culver Pictures
262. The Lynn Farnol Group, Inc.
263. Ronald Feldman Fine Arts Inc.
268. Fred Fehl
270. German Information Center
271. The Museum of Modern Art/Film Stills Archive
279. German Information Center
280, 281. Arp Instruments, Inc.
287. *The Emperor of Ice Cream,* by Roger Reynolds, copyright © 1963 by C. F. Peters Corporation, New York
290. Eileen Darby/Graphic House
291. Fred Fehl
293. The Duncan Schiedt Collection
295. Jack Bradley
298. Don Schlitten
300. "Crucifixus" from *Makrokosmos, vol. I,* by George Crumb, copyright © 1974 by C. F. Peters Corporation, New York

Index

Page numbers in italics refer to illustrations.

A 6
B 7
C 8
D 9
E 0
F 1
G 2
H 3
I 4
J 5